DICTIONARY OF
CELTIC MYTHOLOGY

DICTIONARY
OF
CELTIC MYTHOLOGY

Peter Berresford Ellis

CONSTABLE · LONDON

First published in Great Britain 1992
by Constable and Company Limited
3 The Lanchesters, 162 Fulham Palace Road
London W6 9ER
Copyright © 1992 Peter Berresford Ellis
ISBN 0 09 471390 1
Printed in the United States of America

A CIP catalogue record for this book
is available from the British Library

do mo chara
Muiris Mac Cana
astralaí agus staraí

Preface

Following the publication of my *A Dictionary of Irish Mythology* (1987) there was a considerable expression of interest on both sides of the Atlantic and many readers were curious to place the Irish myths in their wider Celtic context. My publishers therefore suggested that I produce a further volume, *A Dictionary of Celtic Mythology*, to accommodate this heightened interest in the subject.

The present volume is not designed to be an extension of *A Dictionary of Irish Mythology*. It is a self-contained volume. Naturally, it contains repetition with respect to many of the Irish entries; this is, of course, inevitable as Irish mythology constitutes the largest surviving section of Celtic mythology. However, *A Dictionary of Irish Mythology*, by virtue of its scope, carries a more detailed account of the Irish myths while this volume concentrates on the general sweep of Celtic mythology and also makes comparisons between the various branches of the Celtic myths.

I have produced a composite alphabetical dictionary and made no effort to split the work into subsections dealing with the separate cultures: Irish, Welsh, and so on. However, the individual Celtic culture is clearly identified in each entry, and in the case of entries deriving from the two major Celtic cultures, abbreviations are given for identification: [I] = Irish and [W] = Welsh.

As with *A Dictionary of Irish Mythology*, I should also point out that a major problem has been that of obtaining a consistency in the spelling of names. For the general reader this involves not simply the natural orthographical changes of a language over the centuries but also the numerous Anglicised distortions. Should Aranrhod be Arianrhod or Cúchulainn be Cú Chulaind? Should Cei be Kai or Kay? I have attempted to choose the most popular form in the native language, but where the choice has been a difficult one I have resorted to cross-references.

However, I make no apologies for stressing that this work is not all-embracing. It would need several volumes and a team of scholars working for many years to compile such a work. This should be looked upon merely as an introduction to the treasure house of Celtic mythology. This work is essentially for the lay reader; a guide for enthusiasts by which they may pick their way through the fascinating labyrinth of one of the world's oldest written mythologies. As with *A Dictionary of Irish Mythology,* this is simply a who's who and what's what of the epic sagas and tales; an accessible, easy-to-read handbook, giving an immediate reference to the gods and goddesses, the heroes and heroines, the magical weapons, fabulous beasts, and Otherworld entities that populate the myths of this rich European culture.

Peter Berresford Ellis
Lios na nAislingí
September 1991

Introduction

The Celtic languages contain one of Europe's oldest and most vibrant mythologies. By virtue of the fact that they were written down only early in the Christian period, the Celtic languages and therefore Celtic mythology are predated by Greek and Latin. But the mythology is a development from a far earlier oral tradition. Contained in many of the stories are voices from the dawn of European civilisation, for the Celts were one of the great founding peoples of Europe. It is generally thought they commenced their spread across Europe from their original homeland around the headwaters of the Rhine, Rhône, and Danube rivers, which still bear their original Celtic names, at the start of the first millennium B.C. By the third century B.C. the Celts were settled from the central plain of Turkey in the east through the Balkans, Hungary, Czechoslovakia, Austria, Switzerland, and northern Italy to France, Belgium, Spain, and Britain and Ireland. They were the first Transalpine European civilisation to emerge into recorded history.

Their political influence and geographical power started to decline in the first century B.C., primarily in the face of the advance of the ruthless military empire of Rome. Conquest and assimilation into the *pax Romana* were the order of the day. Area by area, the Celts were either pushed back, annihilated, or assimilated. The only Celtic area that escaped Roman conquest was Ireland and, to a lesser extent, northern Britain. It has been argued, therefore, that the early Irish legends and tales are a true "window on the Iron Age," uninfluenced by contact with Rome. But due to the fact that the myths were not committed to writing until the early Christian era, when Christianity and its attendant Latin culture had been imported from Rome, the argument is a moot one. Analysis shows that many Christian scribes tended to bowdlerise the pagan vibrancy of the myths and give them a Christian veneer.

Following hard on the heels of the Roman conquest came the rise of the Germanic conquerors, the Franks pushing into Gaul to create France and the Anglo-Saxons carving out England in a formerly Celtic Britain.

Today, when we speak of the Celts, we refer to only six peoples who have survived into modern times: the Irish, Manx, and Scots, who constitute the Goidelic- (or Gaelic-) speaking branch; and the Welsh, Cornish, and Bretons, who represent the Brythonic-speaking branch. The definition of Celtic, even among the ancient Greeks and Romans, was a linguistic one. Professor Eoin MacNeill summed up the definition in succinct terms in *Phrases of Irish History* (1919): "The term Celtic is indicative of language, not of race." A Celtic people are a people who speak, or were known to have spoken within modern historical times, a Celtic language.

Sadly, of the 16.5 million people who live in the Celtic countries today, only 2.5 million speak a Celtic language. It has been estimated that perhaps a further one million speakers of a Celtic language may be found among emigrants, some particularly concentrated in the Welsh-speaking area of Patagonia, Argentina, and the Scots Gaelic speakers of Cape Breton Island, Nova Scotia, Canada. Therefore, we may well be standing at the deathbed of Celtic civilisations, for if the same political and economic forces continue into the twenty-first century, Celtic-speaking communities may well not survive into the twenty-second century.

For centuries the Celtic languages, and their attendant cultures, suffered at the hands of their conquerors. It was state policy, enacted by law, to attempt the eradication of these languages and supplant them with English and French. This policy of cultural genocide has today largely succeeded. Only Irish is an official state language, being the first official language of the 26-county Irish state. Irish has no recognition in the six partitioned counties. Welsh achieved a status within Wales only with the enactment of the Welsh Language Act in 1969. And while the Manx government unanimously agreed, on July 10, 1985, that "the preservation and promotion" of the Manx language was official policy, the last native speaker, Ned Maddrell, had died on December 27, 1974; since then the language has passed into the hands of enthusiasts and revivalists. Scots Gaelic and Breton still suffer debilities by lack of recognition and promotion by the state. The Cornish language, the last native speakers of which died out in the eighteenth and nineteenth centuries and which has been the subject of a revivalist movement since the beginning of this century, is ignored by the authorities and treated as something of a music hall joke outside of Cornwall.

Of these six Celtic communities, only two now have their own governments. In Ireland, the Irish Republic comprises (*de facto*) 26 out of the 32 counties on the island, having achieved self-government in 1921. The Manx also have their own government and represent a Crown dependency constitutionally outside the United Kingdom territory. The people of the six Celtic communities are the modern-day heirs of the unique and fascinating Celtic civilisation.

If, however, it is not the destiny of Celtic civilisation to survive, the Celts will have left behind them evidence of three millennia of a cultural continuum and a contribution to European cultural heritage in art, literature, and philosophy that is second to none. Our knowledge of what we will term "Celtic mythology" stems from two basic traditions, those recorded in Ireland and in Wales in the early Christian period.

It is from the Irish tradition that we have our oldest mythological tales and sagas, for Irish is Europe's third-oldest literary language, predated only by Greek and Latin. Dr. Georges Dottin has argued that "it is probable that the most ancient pieces of the epic literature of Ireland were written before the middle of the seventh century; but how long previously they had been preserved by oral tradition—this is a point difficult to estimate." We have a record of the numerous *Tech Screpta,* or great libraries, of Ireland during the period of the so-called "Dark Ages," which was, of course, a "Golden Age" of Celtic learning, a time when Ireland was famous for her colleges and centres of learning throughout Europe—when even English kings were sent to Ireland for an education. However, the Viking raids from the end of the eighth century saw entire libraries looted or destroyed.

Therefore, the oldest surviving complete manuscript books that provide the sources for Irish mythology date from the twelfth century. *Leabhar na hUidre,* known as *The Book of the Dun Cow,* the *Leabhar Laignech,* or *Book of Leinster,* and a book known by its Bodleian Library reference—Rawlinson Manuscript B 502—constitute the earliest rich source texts. The *Leabhar na hUidre* was compiled under the supervision of Mael Muire Mac Céilchair, who was killed by marauders at the monastery of Clonmacnoise in A.D. 1106. The *Leabhar*

Laignech was originally called *Leabhar na Nuachongbála,* after Noughaval in Co. Leix, and was compiled by Aed Mac Crimthainn, head of the monastery at Tír-dá-ghlas (Terryglass in Co. Tipperary). It was compiled around A.D. 1150. The Rawlinson Manuscript appears to have been compiled about the same time at Clonmacnoise.

Professor Kuno Meyer, in his introduction to *Liadain and Curithir; A Love Story* (1900) listed 400 sagas and tales in manuscript. He added the figure of a further 100 that had been brought to light since he had compiled his list and mentioned an estimated additional 50 to 100 tales that could lie in libraries still undiscovered. He believed, therefore, that there were some 500 to 600 tales, of which only 150 had been translated and annotated when he was writing. Eleanor Hull, in the introduction to her work *The Cuchullin Saga in Irish Literature* (1898), made a similar estimation. It is surprising that the bulk of these manuscripts still remain unedited and untranslated.

Old Irish was the standard literary language throughout the Gaelic-speaking world until the late medieval period. The spoken language of the Manx and Scots had begun to diverge from the standard about the sixth or seventh century. There is evidence that shows that bards and storytellers wandered freely from one country to another plying their craft. We have an account of the chief bard of Ireland, Seanchán Torpéist (ca. A.D. 570–647), arriving on the Isle of Man with 50 of his followers and entering into a literary contest there. So the legends and tales of Ireland were a common heritage in Scotland and Man.

It was not until the sixteenth century in Scotland that a distinctive Scottish Gaelic literature (as opposed to the Common Gaelic of Old Irish) began to emerge. At this time the Reformation had caused the learned intercourse between Ireland and Scotland to diminish and, left to its own resources, a Scottish Gaelic tradition rose. The *Book of the Dean of Lismore,* a miscellany compiled in 1516 by the Dean of Lismore (Argyll), was a compilation of poems and sagas, including many about the Fianna of Fionn Mac Cumhail. Yet, curiously, though the book was written in Gaelic, it used an English phonetical form of orthography, the writers showing complete disregard for the Irish standard orthography. The main wealth of the mythological tradition among the Celts of Scotland lay in a continued oral tradition that was not copied down until the eighteenth and nineteenth centuries.

Manx, the third Gaelic language, does not appear in identifiable written form until A.D. 1610. Around 1770, however, John Kelly copied down a piece of oral folklore entitled "Manannán Beg, Mac y Leirr, ny slane coontey yeh Ellan Vannin" (Little Manannán, Son of Leirr, or an account of the Isle of Man). Kelly copied two versions of this ballad [Manx Museum Mss. No. 519 and No. 5072; see also William Cubbon, "Our Literary Treasures," *Isle of Man History and Antiquarian Society Proceedings,* Vol. IV]. It would appear that the original composition had been made during the time of Thomas III of Man (1504–1521), for it describes his landing on the island in 1507. The Manx expert J. J. Kneen has confirmed this by recognising four-teen examples of obsolete grammar showing a time far earlier than the eighteenth century for its composition. The ballad is a unique contri-bution to the literature concerning Manannán, the ocean god. Not long after this time, the Rev. Philip Moore copied down from oral tradition another ballad, "Fin as Oshin," a copy of which, dated 1789, is now in the British Museum. The ballad is a Manx interpretation of an episode from the story of Fionn Mac Cumhail and his son Ossian.

The Brythonic branch of the Celtic languages began to diverge into Welsh, Cornish, and Breton in the fifth and sixth centuries A.D., and it is in Welsh that our main early Brythonic mythological sagas have survived. However, the Welsh material is nowhere near as extensive or old as the Irish tales and sagas. While Welsh was certainly flourishing as a literary language by the eighth century, apart from fragmentary remains the oldest book wholly in Welsh is the *Black Book of Car-marthen,* dated to the twelfth century. As to the mythological tales, they are preserved in two Welsh sources: *The White Book of Rhydderch* (1300–1325) and the *Red Book of Hergest* (1375–1425). The stories in these two books constitute what is called in Welsh the *Mabinogi,* or in English, *The Four Branches of the Mabinogion.* There is evidence that at least three tales originated far earlier than the surviving written forms. "Culwch and Olwen," for example, reflects a period two centu-ries earlier in custom, style, and vocabulary.

Like Irish, Welsh produced a greater wealth of manuscript archive during the latter medieval period.

Although Cornish had produced a written form by the tenth cen-tury, nothing survives in Cornish that is reflective of the myths and legends of the *Mabinogi.* We could argue that we have a fragment of a

Cornish version in the poem translated by John of Cornwall into Latin hexameters during the twelfth century and entitled "The Prophecy of Merlin." John claims he is merely translating from an earlier Cornish manuscript, and to help us he puts glosses of Cornish words in the margins. These forms certainly put the manuscripts back to the tenth century. The oldest surviving copy of this manuscript is dated October 8, 1474, and is in the Vatican Library. While the Cornish scholar Henry Jenner accepted this manuscript as genuine in 1903, he was referring to it as "a medieval fake" in 1913 ["The Tristan Romance and Its Cornish Provenance," *Journal of the Royal Institute of Cornwall,* Vol. XVIII]. However, he does not declare his reasons for changing his mind, and so far there is no good explanation for believing it was a correct decision.

It must be remembered that the oral tradition of storytelling was as strong among the Brythonic Celts as it was among the Goidelic Celts. Like the Irish, Manx, and Scots, who had their *seanchaidhe,* or oral storyteller, the Brythonic Celts had their *cyfarwydd.* There was a constant intercourse of missionaries and teachers between Wales, Cornwall, and Brittany from the fifth century even into Tudor times. And while there was no literature in Breton before the fifteenth century, it does not mean there was none in oral form. The Breton *lais,* the stories of Arthur and of Tristan, shared with their cousins in Wales and Cornwall, were seized upon by Chrétien de Troyes (fl. 1160–1190), who wrote some of the earliest Arthurian romances; by Beroul, who wrote the oldest extant Tristan poem; and by Marie de France (ca. 1200), who admitted that she was adapting the poetic saga of the Breton bards.

However, the oldest text in Breton dates from the year 1450 and is *Dialog etre Arzur Roe d'an Bretounet ha Guynglaff* (The Dialogue of Arthur, King of the Bretons, and Guynglaff). Guynglaff or Gwnec'hlan was a druid and seer and the work is of literary curiosity, being a uniquely Breton contribution to the sagas. By the end of the fifteenth century, Breton literature started in earnest with *Buhez santaz Nonn hag he map Deuy* (The Life of St. Nonn, Son of Devy), a long hagiographic poem, setting a tradition for such works that continued up to the French Revolution. But there is nothing else that enriches our knowledge of the mythology shared with the other Celts outside of oral tradition. It was not until 1839 that Théodore Hersart de la Villemarqué published *Barzaz Breiz: Chants populaires de la Bretagne,* which was an anthology of Breton folksongs and oral survivals that dated back to the origins of Brittany.

It is interesting that from the historical and mythological traditions of the Brythonic Celts—the Welsh, Cornish, and Bretons—two of the world's most famous romances have been derived. The first is the saga of Arthur, who was in reality a British Celtic chieftain of the fifth or sixth century, fighting against the Anglo-Saxon invasion of Britain. A great Celtic hero, whose first surviving reference is in the poem *Y Gododdin* (written at the end of the sixth century by Aneurin), Arthur's story took on glosses from various storytellers, showing many parallels to the Irish hero Fionn Mac Cumhail and his warriors of the Fianna, until Geoffrey of Monmouth made the story available outside the Celtic world in his twelfth century Latin work *Historia Regum Britanniae.* Chrétien de Troyes and Marie de France, from Breton sources, added to the legend. Then English, French, and German poets added their own versions until the legend of Arthur took on a momentum almost unrelated to its Celtic origins.

The second famous romance is that of Tristan and Iseult. From a sixth century memorial stone at Castle Dore, near Fowey, in Cornwall, we know that a Drustanus (philologically identified as Tristan) was buried there and he was the son (not the nephew) of Mark of Cornwall. The scholar Joseph Bédier, in *Le Roman de Tristan par Thomas* (Paris, 1902, 1905), argued that all the known Tristan stories could be traced back to five primary versions and these five primary versions were themselves derivatives of a single poem. The earliest form was written by Beroul and, it was argued, by Thomas of Brittany. Professor Joseph Loth, in *Contributions à l'étude des Romans de la Table Ronde* (Paris, 1912), goes further and suggests that there was a Celtic original written in Cornwall by a man who knew the country very well at the time and that this version was probably written, therefore, by a Cornishman prior to the eleventh century. The text was then taken to Brittany and there translated into French, perhaps by Thomas of Brittany.

It is not the purpose of this work to deal in depth with these two Celtic tales, which have become part of world mythology and romantic saga, the inspiration of an entire literature, of drama, films, operas, tone poems, and symphonies. Only where these two romances touch the roots of their Celtic originals are they dealt with. For those interested in pursuing the development of what is now called the

"Arthurian Saga," a good composite study is found in the unfortunately misnamed *Mythology of the British Isles,* by Geoffrey Ashe
(1990), although this work, which subsumes things Celtic to an
Anglo-Saxon tradition, is of only marginal interest to the student of
Celtic mythology.

Alas, the Celts of the European mainland left no extensive written
literature, and the few literary remains that we have help us very little
in making any useful comparison to the insular Celtic mythology. The
Celtic gods of Gaul are seen only through what Tacitus called the
interpretatio Romana. In *The Celtic Gauls: Gods, Rites and Sanctuaries*
(1988), Jean Louis Brunaux argues that there existed two groups of
deities in the Gaulish Celtic pantheon: the first could be interpreted
from Indo-European cognates while the second went back to what he
called Neolithic origins. But lack of documentary evidence for the
functions can only make for guesswork. Once more, we have a tendency to try to find cognates among the insular Celts. J. A.
MacCulloch, in *The Religion of the Ancient Celts* (1911), first attempted to make a comparative table of such deities.

Our knowledge of mythological tradition in Gaulish is therefore
fragmentary and basically confined to names of deities that sometimes
seem cognate with those in Irish and Welsh tradition. However,
according to Professor Proinsias Mac Cana (*Celtic Mythology,* 1970):

> What we know of the mythology of the continental Celts
> hardly suggests a sustained correspondence with that of
> Ireland and Wales, and this cannot be due entirely to the
> unequal documentation. Even among the insular Celts
> the differences are, at first glance, much more evident
> than the underlying similarities.

Yet I would argue that the reverse is true; that similarities are more
evident than the differences.

For example, the heroic saga of Fionn Mac Cumhail in Irish tradition has a significant parallel in the British Celtic tales of Arthur and
his warriors. The similarity of the stories of the birth of Fionn and
Arthur and the infidelity of the hero's wife with his nephew are other
points of resemblance. The parallel between Amairgen and Taliesin
has also been remarked on. Kuno Meyer and Alfred Nutt, in *The
Voyage of Bran* (1895), point out that "of all the products of Welsh

romance the *Hanes Taliesin* is the one that testifies most strongly to the community of mythic tradition between the race to which it is due and the Goidels of Ireland."

J. F. Campbell, in his *Popular Tales of the West Highlands* (1860–1862) commented that when he read the Welsh tale "Culhwch and Olwen," "it was like a confused dream made up of fragments from all that I had read and collected during the last two years." He goes on to say that "It is impossible to read the text of the *Mabinogion* . . . without seeing the strong resemblance these traditions bear to modern Gaelic popular tales."

Celtic mythology relies predominantly, as I have shown, on the Irish and Welsh traditions in whose early literary forms the myths were first recorded. These, of course, represent the Goidelic and Brythonic linguistic groups. The similarity between these two has been explained by some observers as a kinship derived from a common Celtic heritage. This community of mythic tradition may well be ascribed to a common Celtic root but, I would venture, *only partially*. There is indeed proof that fundamental resemblances in Irish and Welsh tales not only go back to the common Celtic ancestry of these two peoples but also, and more significantly, to the close and continuous intercourse between Ireland and Wales during the period when the oral traditions were being set down as literature. Indeed, this factor seems to have been overlooked by many analysts.

In a panegyric addressed to Constantius Chlorus in A.D. 256, it is recorded that the Irish were making common cause with the British Celts against the Roman administration in Britain. During the next several centuries we find the Irish frequently raiding Britain, with some settling down, such as the tribe of the Dési from Bregia (Co. Meath), who found a new home in Dyfed about the third century A.D. The *Expulsion of the Dési* tells how the High King, Cormac Mac Art, expelled the tribe, whose chieftain was Eochaidh Allmuir. From Eochaidh, an Irish scribe traces a lineage to one Teudor Mac Regin, who was ruling in Dyfed at the time the tale was written. This lineage has been confirmed in a Welsh source contained in an eleventh century manuscript [Harl. 3859, British Museum] showing that Hywel Dda actually descended from the expelled Irish chieftain.

And, of course, this was the period of the *perigrinatio pro Christo*, in which Irish missionaries and British missionaries frequently travelled to and fro, sometimes to study, sometimes to preach and establish church foundations. From both Irish and Welsh sources we hear of Irish settlements in Britain, one of the most famous being the establishment in Dál Riada in Scotland on Airer Ghàidheal (Argyll—the seaboard of the Gael). But other settlements in Wales and in Cornwall were quickly absorbed into the Brythonic-speaking orbit.

During the period of the sixth and seventh centuries the intercourse between Ireland and Wales was at its closest and most continuous. This was the period of ecclesiastical intercourse, the heady days of the Celtic Church. And from the period of the fifth to seventh centuries we find the presence of Ogham inscriptions in Britain, with the majority mainly in Wales. Of these inscriptions in Ogham, the major portion are bilingual with Latin. The immediate conjecture one makes from this is that the Irish engravers of these inscriptions added the Latin to make the inscription intelligible to the ecclesiastics of the British Celts.

From both Irish and Welsh sources we find many examples of intermarriage; we find political asylum being given to Irish refugees. Lughaidh Mac Con is said to have sought refuge in Britain, recruiting an army there before returning to fight the battle of Magh Muccruimhe. Aed Guaire fled to Britain from the wrath of Diarmuid Mac Cearbhaill. Fogartach Ua Cearnaigh lived in exile in Britain for a while but returned to become High King (A.D. 715—723), according to the *Annals of Ulster*.

More importantly, we find from the ninth century *Life of St. Winnwaloe,* written by the Breton Wrdistan, that many Britons, escaping from the Anglo-Saxon invasions, not only went to Brittany but "abandoned their native land to seek refuge, some among the Irish." The Britons settled in Ireland in large numbers and had quite an impact there. We learn from the *Annals of Ulster* that in A.D. 682 the Britons fought the Irish at the battle of Rathmore in Moylinny. The *Annals of Tighernach* record a battle in A.D. 702 at Magh Cuilinn between the Britons and the Ulstermen. The *Annals of Ulster* tell us that Ceallach's Britons fought in the battle of Selg, near Glendalough, Co. Wicklow, about A.D. 708, Ceallach apparently having recruited a mercenary force of British Celts. In A.D. 797 the Britons joined forces with the Ulster tribes at Magh Muirtheimne (Louth).

There are many such examples from Irish sources showing that significant groups, perhaps entire clans, of British Celts settled as refugees in Ireland—fleeing from both Anglo-Saxons and from the

Danes (Vikings). Within a few generations these groups were totally absorbed into the Irish nation. Even to the middle of the twelfth century the Welsh, fighting with varying degrees of success against the English incursions, looked upon Ireland as a refuge and a supplier of aid against the enemy.

This period of intercourse afforded ample opportunities for literary borrowings, facilitated by the common Celtic ancestry with a similarity of language structure, idiom, traditions, law, and philosophy. During this period of the fifth to ninth centuries, the Irish and Welsh monasteries were the repositories of learning. For the Celts, unlike the rest of Europe or, indeed, their Anglo-Saxon neighbours, this period was a "Golden Age of Learning" and not the "Dark Ages." In both Ireland and Wales, monks were the scribes who set down the earliest texts, transcribing them into fabulous illuminated manuscripts. It is impossible not to believe that there was an interchange of manuscripts between the two peoples—the Irish and Welsh.

Indeed, in the *Leabhar Laignech* (The Book of Leinster), it is recorded that Guaire Aidne, a king of Connacht (A.D. 617–622), it is wanted to hear the *Táin Bó Cuailgne* recited. Seanchán Torpéist, the chief bard of Ireland, assembled all the storytellers of Ireland but it was discovered that none of them knew the saga in oral form in its entirety. Seanchán Torpéist then asked which of his pupils would be willing to go to Brittany to learn the *Táin* for a "wise man had taken [it] to the east in exchange of the *Cuilmenn*." The *Cuilmenn* was the Irish name given to the *Origines* or *Etymologiae* of Isidorus of Seville (ca. A.D. 560–636), an encyclopaedia of arts and science. Dr. Heinrich Zimmer argues that this "wise man" was St. Gildas, who had visited Ireland about A.D. 565. Gildas founded the monastery at Rhuys in Brittany. However, the date of Gildas' visit would make it unlikely he had a copy of the *Origines* at that time. But dating at this period is never an exact science.

The *Historia Brittonum* of Nennius was known in Ireland, and actually the Irish version has been preserved in five Irish manuscript books. The primary Irish translation is ascribed to Gilla Coemgin around 1071. We hear that the Welsh monk and scholar Sulien, who had studied in Ireland about 1059–1072, returned to Wales with many Irish manuscripts.

To sum up, I would hypothesise that the marked similarity between Irish and Welsh stories lies in the fact of the close literary connections between Ireland and Wales during the period that the two literatures were being originated. The idea was first fully argued by Cecile O'Rahilly in her *Ireland and Wales: Their Historical and Literary Relations* (1924).

As the political fortunes of the Celtic peoples declined and, one by one, the surviving nations were conquered and incorporated into alien cultural traditions, the continuity of their mythological traditions was almost destroyed. In this respect Ireland suffered more than Wales, for its native intelligentsia was systematically eradicated through the seventh century conquests, with the learned classes of society especially being singled out and killed or sent into exile. Books in Irish during the seventeenth and eighteenth centuries were printed in Antwerp, Brussels, Paris, and Louvain and had to be smuggled into the country. The attempts to eradicate the Irish language and culture that followed did not, however, entirely destroy the mythic traditions that, for the majority, turned into an oral folklore tradition once more. In Wales, the experience was slightly different. The laws attempting to "utterly extirp" the Welsh language and culture did not destroy the native intelligentsia nor drive them into exile. Printing in the language became a native occupation and the literary as well as the oral traditions continued to flourish.

Many still worked in the native Celtic languages, developing the mythological themes. Micheál Coimín (1688–1760) was producing works such as *Laoi Oisín ar Thír na nOig* (Lay of Oisín in the Land of Youth). But while some worked with the native languages, others began collecting the oral traditions and translating them into English and, in the case of the Breton traditions, into French.

The "cultural bomb" that sparked a new interest in Celtic mythology and, as a by-product, instigated the European "Romantic Movement" in literature was the work of a Scotsman, James Mac-Pherson of Kingussie (1736–1796), who published *Fragments of Ancient Poetry Collected in the Highlands* (1760), *Fingal* (1762), and *Temora* (1763), all of which, he claimed, were translations from ancient Scottish Gaelic manuscripts. They became known collectively as *Ossian* (Oisín being the son of Fionn Mac Cumhail).

Dr. Samuel Johnson denounced MacPherson's works as forgeries, causing a bitter controversy. Whether the works were merely highly subjective translations of oral Celtic traditions in Scotland rather than translations from manuscript sources, they cannot be called "forgeries," for they are reflective of the oral legends that had been passed down. *Ossian* had a profound effect on European literature, influencing writers as diverse as William Blake (himself the son of Irish immigrants from Rathmines, Dublin), J. W. Goethe, and Lord Byron. The influence extended even to political figures such as Napoleon Bonaparte and Marshal Bernadotte, afterwards King Charles XIV of Sweden, who had married Desirée Clary, daughter of Joseph Cleary, a Dublin merchant who had opened a branch of the family business in Marseilles. Their son Oscar, named after the grandson of Fionn Mac Cumhail, became Oscar I of Sweden.

Ossian now became "literary parent" to such works as Joseph Walker's *Historical Memoirs of the Irish Bards* (1786), *Reliques of Irish Poetry* by Charlotte Brooke (1789), and *Irish Ministrelsy* by James Hardiman (1831); in Wales, *Specimens of the Poetry of the Ancient Welsh Bards* by J. Evans (1764) and his *Musical and Poetical Relics of the Welsh Bards* (1784); and, in Brittany, *Barzaz Breiz: Chants populaires de la Bretagne* by de la Villemarqué (1839).

These works awoke a new interest in the legends of the Celtic peoples. There was an enthusiasm generated by collectors of folktales. Even the Brothers Grimm became fascinated by Celtic legends. In Ireland, William Carleton (1794–1869) produced *Traits and Stories of the Irish Peasantry* (1830) and *Tales of Ireland* (1834). T. Crofton Croker (1798–1854) published *The Fairy Legends and Traditions of the South of Ireland* (1825) and *Legends of the Lakes* (1829). In Scotland J. F. Campbell produced *Popular Tales of the West Highlands* (1860–1862). Cornish folklore and legends were collected in Robert Hunt's *Popular Romances of the West of England* (1865). In Wales, Lady Charlotte Guest translated *The Mabinogion* from *Llyfr Coch ó Hergest* (the Red Book of Hergest), which was published in three volumes in 1849.

Such works heralded the start of a period that was to become known as "The Celtic Renaissance." The interest prompted the holder of the chair of poetry at Oxford University, Matthew Arnold (1822–1888), to give four lectures, subsequently published in *Cornhill Magazine*. The articles were then reprinted in book form in 1867 as *On the Study of Celtic Literature*. Arnold argued for the establishment of a chair of Celtic studies at Oxford. The last thing he wanted to do, he said, was keep the Celtic languages alive. The sooner the Celts fused into "one homogeneous English speaking whole," the better. He ignored the Bretons but presumably felt they should become French. However, Arnold recognised the wealth of the Celtic cultural achievements and felt they should be studied as an academic subject. The result of his plea was that the first chair of Celtic studies was established at Jesus College, Oxford, within a few years, with John Rhys becoming its first incumbent. By the 1880s there were also chairs of Celtic studies at Edinburgh, at Trinity College in Dublin, and at the University Colleges of Cork and Belfast. A new wave of study at scholarly level began and the ancient texts were identified and examined.

During the last two decades, there has been an extraordinary interest in Celtic culture and history. Departments of Celtic Studies have been opened at universities from as far afield as Nagoya, Japan; Sydney, Moscow, Oslo, Ottawa, and so forth around the world. Even UNESCO established a "Project for the Study and Promotion of Celtic Cultures" in 1984. And of all the subjects encompassed by Celtic studies, it is Celtic mythology that has achieved a great popularity, not only among university students but with a wider general public in many countries.

During the current century there have been countless popular retellings of the myths, while modern fantasy writers have seized upon characters or particular tales to create a new literature.

In Celtic mythology one enters into a fascinating world of fantasy that is remote from the world of Greek and Latin myth, and yet one is aware that the Celtic stories seem to share a curious Mediterranean warmth rather than fall under the brooding bleakness that permeates Nordic and Germanic myth. The English poet Laurie Lee once remarked that the Celts were Mediterraneans sheltering in the northern rain. It is difficult at times to realise that we are considering a northwest European culture. A happy spirit pervades even the tragedies. There is an eternal spirit of optimism. Death is never the conqueror and we are reminded that the Celts were one of the first cultures to evolve a sophisticated doctrine of the immortality of the soul. The druids taught that death is only a changing of place and that life goes on with all its forms and goods in the Otherworld. When a soul dies in this world, it is reborn in the Otherworld and when a soul dies in the Otherworld, it is reborn in this. Thus birth was greeted with mourning and death with exaltation by the ancient Celts, customs that the Greeks and Latins remarked on with some surprise.

Both the deities and human heroes and heroines are no mere physical beauties with empty heads. Their intellectual attributes are equal to their physical capabilities. And they are totally human in that they are subject to all the natural virtues and vices. No sin is exempt from practice by the gods or the humans. Their world, both this one and the Otherworld, is one of rural happiness, a world in which they indulge in all the pleasures of life in an idealised form: love of nature, art, poetry, games, feasting, and heroic combat. Celtic mythology is essentially a heroic one, although the Irish stories belong to a more ancient Heroic Age, while the Welsh stories have more the gloss of a medieval courtly quality.

Celtic mythology is one of the bright gems of European and, I would venture, world culture. It is both unique and dynamic, a mythology that ought to be as well known and valued as that of ancient Greece and Rome. Professor Kenneth Jackson, in *A Celtic Miscellany* (1951), pointed out that the uniqueness of Celtic myth lies in the fact that the Celts "are inclined to desert the natural and possible for the impossible and supernatural, chiefly in the form of fantastic exaggeration. One should not misunderstand this, however; it was not done in all seriousness, but for its own sake, for the fun of the thing."

Above all, as we tackle the Celtic myths, we should never forget that quality of mischievous fun that runs throughout them. They are meant to be enjoyed as well as learnt from.

A

Abarta. [I] "The performer of feats." A mischievous member of the Tuatha Dé Danaan who sought to become the servant of Fionn Mac Cumhail. He was also known as Giolla Deacair ("The Hard Servant"). He captured some of the Fianna and took them to the Otherworld. Fionn chased after him with Faruach, who could make a ship by magic, and Foltor, the best tracker in Ireland, and managed to rescue them.

Aberffraw. [W] The ancient royal seat of the kings of Gwynedd on Ynys Mon (Anglesey) and site of Branwen's marriage feast.

Abred. [W] A synonym for Annwn, the innermost circle from which all life sprang.

Accasbel. [I] A follower of Partholón who built the first tavern in Ireland.

Achren. [W] A synonym for the Otherworld.

Adhnuall. [I] A hound belonging to Fionn Mac Cumhail that was stolen by Arthur, son of the king of Britain. The Fianna chased him and recovered the hound. Later, after a battle in Leinster, Adhnuall strayed and circled Ireland three times until he returned to the battlefield. Reaching a hill where three of the Fianna were buried, he gave three howls and died.

Adna. [I] Chief poet of Ireland during the early days of Conchobhar Mac Nessa and a champion of the Red Branch. He was father of the poet Neide. The name is also given to an explorer sent by Ninus, King of Assyria, to report on conditions in Ireland.

Aedan. [I] The warrior who slew Mael Fhothartaig, son of Ronán, king of Leinster. The deed was done on the order of Ronán himself, for he was jealous of his own son. Aedan was slain in turn by the sons of Mael Fhothartaig.

Aedh. [I] There are many who bear this name in the Irish sagas. Among them is the father of Macha Mong Ruadh. He was king of

Ireland in the fourth century B.C., ruling alternatively with his brothers Dithorba and Cimbaeth. Another was a son of Fionn Mac Cumhail. Then there was a king of Oriel (Airgialla) who carried a shield called Dubhghiolla (Black Servant) on whose rim Badb, one of the goddesses of war, perched in the form of a crow. Aedh was said to be the original name of Goll Mac Morna, the leader of the Fianna who slew Fionn's father. Another prominent Aedh was the dwarf of Fergus Mac Léide of Ulster, who accompanied the poet Eisirt to the kingdom of the Faylinn, a land of little people ruled by Iubdan.

Another Aedh was son of the god Bodb Dearg. Yet another was son of Ainmire who became High King and made war on the wily Brandubh, king of Leinster. This Aedh was defeated and perished at Brandubh's hands because he lost a magic cowl that protected him from being wounded or slain in battle. In another version he is slain by Ron Cerr, a spy of Brandubh, while a Christian addition has the cowl given him by St. Colmcille.

Aedh is one of the four children of Lir, the ocean god, who was changed into a swan by his stepmother, Aoife. Another was a son of Miodchaoin. He and his two brothers, Corca and Conn, were slain by the three sons of Tuireann. Yet another was a giant, sometimes given as Aeda. He was a young man, smooth-featured and of surpassing beauty, who bore a red shield and a huge spear. He slew Bebhionn, daughter of Treon of the Land of Maidens, because she refused to wed him. Bebhionn was a beautiful giantess who sought aid from Fionn Mac Cumhail and his Fianna because she had become betrothed to Aedh against her will. After she was slain, the Fianna chased him, but when they reached the sea they found Aedh in a great war galley that was waiting for him and he escaped.

Finally we have Aedh Dubh. He slew the High King Diarmuid Mac Cearbal in the house of Banbán in accordance with a prophecy given by the druid Bec Mac Dé.

Aeí, Plain of. [I] The place of the bull strife at the end of the Táin saga. This was where Donn, the Brown Bull of Cuailgne, and Finnbhenach, the White Horned Bull of Connacht, had their last great battle. They fought for three days and nights before the White Horned Bull was slain, but the Brown Bull was mortally wounded.

Áes. [I] Sometimes Oes. People or folk. *Áes sidhe,* "the people of the hills," or *áes dana,* a learned class that included poets, judges, doctors of medicine, metalworkers, and woodworkers.

Aethlem. [W] One of two hunting dogs in the saga of Culhwch and Olwen that can only be held by Cyledyr. The other is Aned.

Afagddu. [W] "Utter darkness." The most ill-favoured man in the world. Son of Tegid Foel of Penllyn and Ceridwen. To compensate for his ill looks his mother boils a cauldron of inspiration and science so that her son will become learned and know the mysteries of the world. The kettle has to be boiled for a year and a day. Ceridwen puts Gwion Bach in charge of stirring it while Morda, a blind man, is to supply the firewood. Things go wrong and Afagddu is denied this gift. See **Gwion Bach.** Afagddu has a brother, Morfan, who is a warrior with Arthur and who is so ugly that when he fought at the battle of Camluan no man would engage in combat with him, fearing he was a devil.

Afallon. [W] See **Avalon.**

Age, Feast of. [I] Fleadh Áise. One of the annual festivals of the Tuatha Dé Danaan held at each of their palaces in rotation.

Agnoman. [I] Father of Nemed who led his people from Scythia to Ireland but who had to fight with the Fomorii.

Agrona. British goddess of slaughter, found in the river named Aeron (Wales), cognate with the Mórrígán. There is a "Washer at the Ford" legend surviving here that tends to confirm the idea that the two goddesses of death and battle may be cognate.

Aí. [I] Sometimes given as Aoi Mac Ollamain. The poet of the Tuatha Dé Danaan. When his mother was pregnant the house was rocked by a great wind and a druid foretold that he would have wonderful powers. The king ordered the child to be slain but his father, Olloman, saved him and he fulfilled the prophecy.

Aibell. [I] Sometimes Aiobhell. She ruled a *sídhe* in north Munster but little is known of her before she was relegated in popular folklore to the status of a "fairy." She became the guardian spirit of the Dál gCais, the Dalcassians or Ó Bríen clan. Her dwelling was at Craig Liath, the grey rock, near Killaloe. Her name means "beautiful." She possessed a magic harp, but those who heard its music did not live long afterwards.

Aichleach. [I] He slew Fionn Mac Cumhail during a rebellion of the Fianna. See **Uigreann.**

Aidín. [I] A foreigner who became the wife of Oscar. Hearing of his death at the battle of Gabhra, she died of grief and was buried by Oisín, Oscar's father, on Ben Edar (Howth) where an Ogham stone was set up in her memory.

Aige. [I] A daughter of Broccaid Mac Brice. Because of the envy of a druidess, she was turned into a fawn and slain by the warriors of Meilge, the High King. See **Meilge.**

Ailbe. [I] A daughter of Cormac Mac Art who answered a set of riddles put to her by Fionn Mac Cumhail, won his love, and was invited to live with him. The name also occurs as that of the hound of Mac Da Thó.

Aileach. [I] A major fortress in Ulster whose ruins still stand five miles northwest of Derry in Co. Donegal. It was said to be built by the Tuatha Dé Danaan, and it was here that Mac Cuill, Mac Cécht, and Mac Gréine and their wives, the goddesses Banba, Fótla, and Éire, decided to divide Ireland between them. It was also the royal residence of the kings of Ulster and later the kings of Ireland until the fourth century A.D. It became the seat of the Ó Néill kings until the early twelfth century, when it was destroyed by Murchertagh, of Munster.

Ailill. [I] A common name in Irish myth, in which there are about eight prominent Ailills. It was the name of a king of Leinster who was poisoned by Cobthach, king of Bregia, and whose son was made to eat his flesh. The son was struck dumb and became known as Móen (dumb).

Perhaps the most famous of the Ailills was Ailill Mac Máta, king of Connacht and husband of Medb. He features prominently in the *Táin Bó Cuailgne* saga. He was eventually slain by Conall Cearnach in revenge for the death of Fergus Mac Roth. Ailill is also the name given to the brother of the High King of Ireland, Eochaid. This Ailill fell in love with his brother's wife, Étain. But Étain did not reciprocate his love and arranged for Ailill to fall into an enchanted sleep from which he awoke cured of his love.

Ailill Agach, "Edge of Battle," was the father of the famous Mael Dúin whose death started him on his fabulous voyage. Then there was Ailill of Aran, who offered his three daughters in marriage to the ocean god Lir. Another was Ailill Dubh-dédach, who, rather like Achilles in Greek mythology, could be harmed by no weapon and yet had a weak spot and so was slain by Art during his quest for the beautiful Delbchaem. Ailill Olom of Munster raped the love goddess Áine, who had her revenge and slew him. Finally, there was the Ulster king Ailill, who was father of Étain Echraide.

Áille. [I] Wife of Meargach of the Green Spears, who was slain by Oscar at the battle of Cnoc-an-Air. In revenge Áille had her druid, Fer Gruadh, drug and capture Fionn Mac Cumhail, Oscar's grandfather. The Fianna pursued Fer Gruadh, but the druid placed them all under his control until Conan tricked him into releasing them. Oscar killed him and Áille committed suicide.

Aillén. [I] Son of Midhna. A malevolent Otherworld creature that came out of the cave of Cruach each year at the feast of Samhain and burned down the royal residence at Tara after lulling the defenders asleep with enchanted music. Fionn Mac Cumhail was able to resist the music by pressing his spear to his forehead. Fionn then drove off the beast and beheaded it. In one of the several variants, Amairgen is given as the slayer of the beast.

Aillinn. [I] Also Ailinn. The daughter of Laoghaire Mac Fergus Fairge (in another version, the daughter of Eoghan Mac Daithi). The granddaughter of the king of Leinster who falls in love with Baile, son of Buain and heir to the kingdom of Ulster. Ulster and Leinster were deadly enemies, and here we have a "Romeo and Juliet"tragedy. Aillinn and Baile arranged to meet on a shore near Dun Dealgan (Dundalk). Baile reached the appointed place first. A stranger approached and told him that Aillinn had died when she was prevented from coming to the meeting place. Baile dies from a broken heart. The stranger then appears to Aillinn and tells her of Baile's own death. She dies of grief. We are not told who the malevolent stranger is apart from the fact that he is one of the gods. Baile is buried at Traigh mBaile (Baile's Strand) and a yew tree grows from his grave; from Aillinn's grave grows an apple tree. The poets of Ulster and Leinster cut branches from the trees and carved the story of the tragedy in Ogham on the wands made from the branches. According to the end of the story, 200 years later, when Art the Lonely was High King, the Ogham wands were gathered from Ulster and Leinster and taken to the Tech Screpta, or library, at Tara. As the wands were put into the library they sprang together and could not be separated.

Aimend. [I] A sun goddess who was daughter of the king of Corco Loigde.

Áine. [I] Goddess of love and fertility. She was the daughter of Eogabail, foster son of the sea god Manannán Mac Lir. She has also been identified with Anu, mother of the gods as well as the Mórrígán, goddess of battles. These identifications seem suspect. Áine was continually conspiring with mortals in passionate affairs. One tale has her being raped by Ailill Olom. There are many later tales of Áine, and even during the last century the love goddess was worshipped on Midsummer Eve [D. Fitzgerald, "Popular Tales of Ireland," *Revue Celtique,* vol. IV].

Ainlé. [I] Sometimes Ainnle. Son of Usna and one of the two brothers of Naoise who followed him into exile and was eventually slain at the Red Branch Hostel.

Airgtheach. [I] The White House, one of the islands of earthly paradise seen during the Voyage of Bran.

Alaw. [W] Ynys Mon. Where Branwen dies.

Alba. Sometimes Albu or Albain. Scotland. The modern Scottish Gaelic name for Scotland is still Alba. The name came into general use when Coinneach Mac Alpín became High King of the united kingdoms of Dál Riada and the Tuatha Cruithin in A.D. 844. Later after the victory of Carham, it included the Strathclyde kingdom and Cumbria.

Albion. An ancient Celtic name for Britain, referred to by Greek geographers. It was ousted by the Celtic "Britannia." The Romans thought Albion was connected with *albus,* Latin for "white"and referring to the cliffs of Dover. More likely it comes from the same root as the Celtic for "heights" or "high hills," which is found in the Alps, Albania, and so on. According to Geoffrey of Monmouth, claiming a Celtic tradition, Albion was a giant, begotten by a sea god, who ruled on the island, while Holinshed, in his *Chronicle,* makes Albina into a princess who arrived on the island with a band of 50 women banished for killing their husbands.

Ale of Goibhniu. [I] Whoever drank it gained immortality.

Alisanos. Gaulish god of stones.

Allen, Hill of. [I] Anglicised from the dative form Almain of the name Almu. Nuada, chief druid of Cahir Mór, built the fortress there, "its ramparts enclosing many white-walled dwellings and a great hall towering high in its midst." Fionn Mac Cumhail, a descendant of

Cahir Mór, made it his fortress. The story of "Cath Almaine," the battle of Allen, which is not to be confused with a historic battle in A.D. 722, was when the hero Fergal Mac Máile Dúin fought with the warriors of Leinster. He was slain and his head cut off. The head being where the soul reposes, it was treated well and set up on a pike while Badb, one of the triune goddesses of death and battle, hovered above it in the form of a crow. That evening the head of Donn Bó, who had also been slain and decapitated, began to sing a song of praise for Fergal. Donn Bó had been famed for his song in life.

Amaethon. [W] See **Amathaon.**

Amairgen. [I] Son of Milesius, a warrior and poet who compares closely to Taliesin in Welsh myth. It is Amairgen who pronounced the first judgment in Ireland and decided that Eremon should be the first Milesian king of the country. Three poems are accredited to Amairgen. The first is his famous and extraordinary incantation to Ireland given in the *Leabhar Gabhála* (Book of Invasions), in which he subsumes everything into his own being. The philosophical outlook of this poem parallels the Hindu concepts in the *Bhagavadgita.* More importantly, there is a parallel in the Welsh tradition in Taliesin's song at Arthur's court.

A second Amairgen appears in Irish myth in the person of the father of Conall Cearnach and foster father to the poet Athairne. He also is a poet, and during Bricriu's Feast he boasts of his valour, wisdom, fortune, and eloquence.

Amathaon. [W] The son of Don. He appears in the story about the tasks of Culhwch—some 40 tasks that have to be accomplished in order to win the hand of Olwen. In one case a great hill has to be ploughed, sown, and reaped all in a single day. Only Amathaon is capable of this task, but he refuses. He seems to be a god of agriculture but appears fighting against Bran in the battle of Achren.

Amr. [W] Son of Arthur by whom he was slain and buried.

Andoid. [I] One of four people who survived the Deluge outside Noah's Ark, the story obviously entering Irish myth with the coming of Christianity.

Aned. [W] One of two hunting dogs that can only be held by Cyledyr in the story of Culhwch and Olwen; the other is Aethlem.

Angus. [I] See **Aonghus.**

Animal Cults. Animals as gods, malevolent beings, and companions appear in profusion in Celtic mythology. In fact, they play as important a part in the myths as do the human characters.

The divine bull and magical cows are an important motif, and perhaps the *Táin Bó Cuailgne* is the most famous demonstration of this. Trigaranus, the three-horned bull of Gaul, is also found in Britain. We have the survival of the Gaulish name Donnotauros, "Brown, of Kingly Bull." Boann is one of several goddesses connected with cattle; her name seems to signify "she of the white cattle." The story of the cow of Buchat Buasach has an Otherworld bull owned by the Mórrígán attempting to make off with it.

Well known are stories of boars and magical pigs. The boar is the Celtic cult animal *par excellence*. The meat of the boar was a sacred dish served during the feasts of the gods in the Otherworld. Celtic myths are littered with destructive pigs and boars. Most famous in the Welsh sagas is the hunt for the great boar Twrch Trwyth, which features in the story of "Culhwch and Olwen." The parallel in Irish myth seems to be Torc Triath, the king of boars, who was one of the possessions of the goddess Brigid. Supernatural pigs also emerge from the Cave of Cruachan, the entrance to the Otherworld. The Gaulish "Mercury" appears with the epithet *Moccus* (Welsh *moch,* Irish *muc,* meaning "pigs").

Cats also appear, although they don't often play a prominent role. In Irish myth, one cat is guardian to an Otherworld treasure and is able to change itself into a ball of fire.

Horses play their part. Horses of fantastic colours appear from the Otherworld. The wife of the Irish god Midir, Étain Echraide, is by her very name connected with horses. Some scholars have suggested her equivalent to be Rhiannon in Welsh saga. Epona, the Divine Horse, was a Gaulish divinity and won special favour among the cavalry of the Roman army, being the only Celtic goddess known to have been worshipped in Rome.

Stags, deer, and fawns also have magical qualities. They often are gods and goddesses who have been shape-changed, such as Oisín's mother, Sadb. We have the Irish goddess Flidhais, who ruled over the beasts of the forest and whose cattle were the wild deer. Stags sometimes appear with three antlers to indicate their supernatural qualities. Indeed, horned animals usually have three horns—the mystical Celtic trinity.

The bear is also a significant animal and the name Art (bear) occurs in many Irish proper names. In Gaul there was Dea Artio, as well as a Dea Arduinna, shown seated on a wild bore, and an Artaios, claimed as a "Mercury" equivalent. Math is another form of bear, as in Mac Mathghamhna (son of the bear).

Fish, particularly salmon, are also mystical and repositories of wisdom and knowledge. Fionn Mac Cumhail eats of the Salmon of Knowledge and obtains wisdom.

Dogs, particularly hunting hounds, also feature as animals to be treated with respect, and shape-changing into dogs or hounds features in the sagas. Fion Mac Cumhail's sister is so changed and gives birth to two hounds that always accompany Fionn.

Finally, magic or divine birds are also a popular Celtic motif. Characteristic is the shape-change into swans, the wondrous birds of the Otherworld assigned to Rhiannon and who correspond, it would seem, to the birds accompanying a Gaulish goddess of surviving carvings. It is, of course, the crow or raven that symbolises the triune goddess of death and battles.

Anind. [I] A son of Nemed. Loch Ennell, Co. Westmeath, is said to have burst from his grave when it was being dug. He is associated with Dún na Sciath (Fort of Shields), a stone circular fort still standing on the west bank of the loch.

Anluan. [I] Son of Maga, a Connacht warrior who was slain by Conall Cearnach. Anluan was the brother of Cet. They went to battle against Ulster in the service of Ailill and Medb at the head of three thousand warriors. During the challenging for the hero's portion in the story of Mac Da Thó's boar, Conall, challenging Cet, produced the severed head of Anluan and threw it at him.

Annales Cambriae. Annals of Wales. Latin text of the tenth century that refers to Arthur. It mentions that Arthur wore a cross on his shield at the battle of Mount Badon where he defeated the Anglo-Saxons, and refers to the battle of Camluan, where Arthur fell with Medraut (Mordred) in A.D. 537.

Annwfn. [W] See **Annwn.**

Annwn. [W] A traditional name of the Cymric Otherworld. It is also referred to as Caer Feddwid, "Court of Intoxication," where sparkling wine is the normal beverage. It is also Caer Siddi, a land where a fountain flows with sweet wine and where age and sickness are unknown. Among its treasures is a magic cauldron, featured in

"The Spoils of Annwn" (*Preiddeu Annwn*), which has become the
basis for the Christian Arthurian legend of the Holy Grail. In this
version, Arthur and his warriors make a disastrous expedition to
Annwn to carry off the magic cauldron, a chief symbol of kingship
and authority in the ancient Celtic world. But of the three shiploads
of warriors who set out, only Arthur and seven men return.

Gwydion also led a magical host against the dark gods of Annwn,
helped by his son Lleu and his brother Amathaon. They fought the
battle of Godeu, or the Trees. His enemies are Arawn, king of
Annwn, who is aided, strangely, by Bran, ruler of the Island of the
Mighty. The aim of the war is to secure for the human world the
dog, deer, and lapwing. The quasi-mythical bard Taliesin says:

"I have been in the battle of Godeu, with Lleu and Gwydion,
"They changed the forms of the elementary trees and sedges."

Answerer, The. [I] See **Freagarthach.**

Anu. [I] The mother goddess. Sometimes given as Ana and also occurs
as Búanann, "the lasting one," mother of all heros. It is generally
accepted that she is one and the same deity as Dana or Danu. Hence
the gods are the Tuatha Dé Danaan, children of Dana. The mountains called "The Paps of Anu" in Co. Kerry are named for her.

Aobh. [I] Sometimes Aebh. The eldest daughter of Ailill of Aran and
foster child to the Bodb Dearg. Her sisters were Aoife and Arbha.
She was chosen to be the wife of the ocean god Lir and had four
children by him. The first were the twins Fionnuala and Aedh; the
second were the twins Fiachra and Conn. But she died in childbirth. See **Aoife.**

Aoife. [I] There are three prominent characters who bear this name.
The first Aoife, the daughter of Árd-Greimne and sister of
Scáthach, was a warrior princess of the Land of Shadows. Her sister
Scáthach went to war with her but tried to leave Cúchulainn, who
was her pupil at the martial arts academy she ran, behind. However,
Cúchulainn followed Scáthach to the Land of Shadows. Aoife challenged him to single combat. By a ruse Cúchulainn won the contest
and spared her on condition she make peace with Scáthach. Aoife
then fell in love with Cúchulainn and became his mistress. When
he left he gave her a gold ring. She told him that she would bear his

child. Years later a young warrior named Conlaí arrived in Ulster. Cúchulainn challenged and slew him, not knowing, until the boy was dying, that he was his own son by Aoife.

The second Aoife is the second daughter of Ailill of Aran. She was foster daughter of the Bodb Dearg. On the death of her elder sister, Aobh, she married the ocean god Lir and became stepmother to her sister's four children. She was jealous of them and ordered her attendants to slay them. When they refused she used magic to change them into swans. The children of Lir, in swan shape, had to spend a total of 900 years on various waters. According to the enchantment, when a southern princess married a northern prince, they would be released from the spell. When the Bodb Dearg found out what Aoife had done, he changed her into a demon of the air and no more was heard of her. See also **Lir.**

The third Aoife was the lover of Ilbrec, son of Manannán Mac Lir. She was changed into a crane and while in this form was killed. Her skin was used to make the Treasure Bag of the Fianna, sometimes called "The Crane Bag." See **Treasure Bag of the Fianna.**

Aoi Mac Ollamain. [I] See **Aí.**

Aonbharr. [I] A magical horse that could travel on land and sea.

Aoncos. [I] An Otherworld island that was supported on a single pillar of silver rising out of the sea. It was seen by Mael Dúin on his fabulous voyage.

Aonghus. [I] Of the six prominent characters in Irish myth who bear the name Aonghus, it is the love god, Aonghus Óg, who first comes to mind. He was son of the Dagda and Boann and his palace was Brugh na Boinne at New Grange by the River Boyne. He was of beautiful appearance, and four birds, representing his kisses, always hovered around his head. In the story "The Dream of Aonghus," Aonghus Óg saw a beautiful maiden in a dream and fell sick for the love of her. He asked his mother for help, and she enlisted the help of the Bodb Dearg, her brother. The girl was identified as Cáer Ibormeith, daughter of Ethal Anubhail of the Dé Danaan of Connacht. Aonghus Óg asked Ailill and Medb, rulers of Connacht, to persuade Ethal Anubhail to give him his daughter. But Ethal Anubhail said it was not in his power to do this because Cáer lived in the shape of a swan and on the Feast of Samhain would be found with 150 other swans swimming on Loch Bel Dragon (Lake of the

Dragon's Mouth). If Aonghus Óg could identify her, it would be up to Cáer to decide if she wanted to go with him. Aonghus Óg identified Cáer; they went to his palace by the Boyne and lived together. Aonghus Óg was also foster father to Diarmuid Ua Duibhne (Of the Love Spot) and tried to save him and his lover Gráinne from the vengeance of Fionn Mac Cumhail by the use of magical devices. When Diarmuid was slain by a magic boar (actually the son of Aonghus Óg's steward, Roc, by Diarmuid's own mother), it was Aonghus Óg who placed his body on a gilded bier and transported it to his palace, where he was able to breathe a soul into it whenever he wanted a conversation with Diarmuid.

The second Aonghus, Aonghus of the Terrible Spear, was a chieftain of the Dési who killed Cellach, son of the High King Cormac Mac Art, with a spear and knocked out the eye of Cormac with its butt. This is the incident that results in "The Expulsion of the Dési."

Among the other characters bearing the name Aonghus are Aonghus Bolg, an ancestor of the Firbolg, also regarded as an ancestor of the Dési; a son of the Bodb Dearg; Aonghus Mac Aedh Abrat, brother of the goddess Fand, who sang to Cúchulainn on his sickbed and cured him from his sickness; and, lastly, Aonghus Mac Lámh Gabuid, a warrior who challenged Cet of Connacht during the bragging contest in the tale of Mac Da Thó's boar. He is described as tall and fair-haired. Cet cut off his father's hand and this is why Aonghus challenged him.

Arannan. [I] A son of Milesius born in Spain. He climbed to the top of the mast of his ship as the Milesians were invading Ireland, fell into the sea, and was drowned.

Aranrhod. [W] Also given as Arianrod. Daughter of Don and sister of Gwydion. Math, son of Mathonwy, who always had to sleep with his feet resting in a maiden's lap, "unless the turmoil of war prevent him." Gilfaethwy had abducted his foot holder, Goewin, and married her, so Math was looking for a new maiden to fulfil this role. Gwydion suggested his sister. She is brought before Math and asked to step over his magic wand as a test of her virginity. As she does so, two boy children drop from her womb. Gwydion manages to pick up one child and conceal it in a chest. The other, however, is a yellow-haired boy who immediately leaps into the sea and takes on its nature, being known thenceforth as Dylan Eil Ton—Dylan, Son of the Wave. The other child, concealed by Gwydion and who seems to be his own child, is named Lleu Llaw Gyffes.

Arawn. [W] King of Annwn. Pwyll of Dyfed is hunting in Glyn Cuch when he sees a strange pack of hounds bringing down a stag. He drives them off and sets his own hounds onto the stag. A strange hunter appears and rebukes him for his discourtesy. He is Arawn, king of Annwn—the Otherworld. To redeem his friendship, Pwyll has to agree to swap forms with him for a year and then slay Arawn's enemy, Hafgan. He can only strike Hafgan once, for a second blow would restore his strength. Additionally, he must not make love to Arawn's queen during the year he shares her bed in the guise of Arawn. Pywll accomplishes his tasks and returns to Dyfed, hailed not only as lord of Dyfed but "head"of Annwn.

Arbeth. [W] Sometimes given as Narbeth. Chief court of Pwyll, lord of Dyfed, where Pwyll holds a great feast and *gorsedd* on his return from Annwn. The *gorsedd* mound at Arbeth is the centre of the mysterious adventures of both Pwyll and Pryderi. Whoever sat there would see wonders or, alternatively, suffer wounds and blows. It was here that Pwyll first saw his future bride, Rhiannon; here that Pryderi sat when an enchantment fell on Dyfed; and here that Manawydan was about to execute a thieving mouse, which turned out to be the wife of the magician Llwyd, who had enchanted the land. Llwyd, in return for his wife's freedom, was forced to disenchant the land.

Arca Dubh. [I] He slew Cumal, father of Fionn Mac Cumhail, chief of the Fianna. In other versions of the tale the killer is named as Goll Mac Morna, who became the new leader of the Fianna. There are two versions featuring Arca Dubh. One is that Cumal could only be slain by his own sword while lying with his wife, and this was done by Arca Dubh, who was his servant. The other is that Arca Dubh was hiding in the grass by a river and threw his spear at Cumal while he was swimming.

Ardan. [I] A son of Usna and one of Naoise's brothers who followed him into Alba and was killed at the Red Branch Hostel. See **Naoise.**

Arddu, Black Stone of. [W] On the Llanberis side of Snowdonia. There is a belief that whosoever spent a night under the haunted stone emerged in the morning either an inspired bard or insane.

Ard-Greimne. [I] The name means "High Power." He is lord of Lethra and father of two famous female warriors—Scáthach and Aoife.

Ard Macha. [I] (Armagh.) Capital of Ulster, founded in 370 B.C. by
Macha Mong Ruadh. The story is interwoven with another Macha
who is goddess of battles. Armagh (The Height of Macha) was a
short distance from Emain Macha, which throughout the Ulster
Cycle is the seat of the kings. See **Emain Macha.** St. Patrick
founded his religious centre there, and it is now the seat of the
primacy of the Catholic Church in Ireland. *The Book of Armagh,*
completed by Derfdonnach at Armagh in A.D. 807, is now in
Trinity College, Dublin.

Ard Rí. [I] Old spelling Ard Rígh, "the High King." According to the
ancient bardic king lists, Slaigne the Firbolg was the first High King
of Ireland, and from his accession until A.D. 1 there were 107 High
Kings: 9 Firbolg, 9 Dé Danaan, and 89 Milesians. From A.D. 1 until
the last High King of Ireland, Ruaraidh Ó Conchobhar (A.D. 1161–
1198), there were 81 High Kings listed. Ruaraidh Ó Conchobhar
signed the Treaty of Windsor in October A.D. 1175, accepting
Henry II of the Angevin Empire as suzerain of Ireland. There is
evidence that a High King system also existed in Alba, with
Coinneach Mac Alpín recognised as the first High King of Alba in
A.D. 844. With the overthrow of MacBeth (A.D. 1040–1057) by
Callum a' chinn mhòr (Malcolm Canmore), the structure of the
monarchy changed. Malcolm was the first to use the non-Celtic
theory of kingship and claim kingship "by hereditary right." He had
been brought up in England under a different system. In Celtic
society, kings were elected to office by their chieftains and clan
assemblies. There is a good argument for the existence of the High
Kingship as an institution elsewhere in the Celtic world, for the
Celtic tribal and provincial systems of government produced petty
kingdoms over which "High Kings" ruled. Vortigern, the king of
Britain at the time of the first Anglo-Saxon invasions, bears a name
that actually means "High King" or "overlord."

Argadnel. [I] "Silver Cloud." One of the islands of earthly paradise
seen during Bran's fabulous voyage.

Argetlámh. [I] See **Nuada.**

Arianrod. [W] See **Aranrhod.**

Art. [I] High King of Ireland. Son of Conn of the Hundred Battles.
Known as Art Aenfer (Solitary). According to the king lists he
ruled at Tara from A.D. 220 to 250. He wins the love of Delbchaem

(Fair Shape), and his son by another maiden becomes the famous Cormac Mac Art, patron of Fionn Mac Cumhail and the Fianna. In one tale Conn has taken the goddess Bécuma Cneisgel as his concubine. She had been expelled from the Otherworld, and because of her the country grew infertile and miserable. She was also jealous of Art and, while playing fidchell with him, contrived to force him into a journey involving terrible dangers. Art succeeds in his journey, returns with Delbchaem, and is able to banish Bécuma. Art eventually perishes at the battle of Moy Muchruinne. On his way there he passes the night at the house of Olc Acha, a smith. There he sleeps with the smith's daughter, Achtan, and gives her his sword, golden ring, and ceremonial clothing for safekeeping so that her child would claim the inheritance. The child is Cormac Mac Art.

Artaius. A Gaulish god whom the Romans identified as Mercury and who seems to be a pastoral deity.

Artepomaros. Gaulish, an epithet for Caesar's identification of the Gaulish "Apollo." It means "he who possesses a great horse." An epithet for Belenus.

Arthur. Perhaps the most famous of Celtic mythological figures. Arthur was undoubtedly a historical person, living during the late fifth and early sixth centuries A.D. But by medieval times he and his warriors had become firmly embedded in mythology, and they share many of the themes associated with Fionn Mac Cumhail and his Fianna. The first literary reference to Arthur comes in a poem by Aneirin, written in the late sixth century A.D. In *Y Gododdin,* Aneirin writes of an attempt by 300 picked warriors led by Mynyddawn Mwynfawr, chieftain of the tribe whose capital was at Dineiddyn (Edinburgh), who set out to recapture Catraeth (Catterick) from the Saxons.

References to the historical Arthur can be found in Gildas (A.D. 500–570), the British Celtic monk who wrote *De Excidio et Conquesta Britanniae* (Concerning the Ruin and Conquest of Britain); Nennius (ca. A.D. 800), another Celtic historian, in his *Historia Brittonum,* credits Arthur with twelve major victories over the invading Anglo-Saxons; the *Annales Cambriae* (ca. A.D. 955), a Latin history of the rise of Cymru (Wales), records Arthur's victory at Mount Badon and that Arthur and Medraut (Mordred) fell at the battle of Camluan in the year A.D. 537.

The Celts tended to make their heroes into gods and their gods into heroes, and over the next few centuries following the death of the historical Arthur, the Celts embellished his story with earlier mythological themes, giving him a special circle of warriors (who later became Knights of the Round Table but were closer to the Fianna of Fionn Mac Cumhail). In medieval times, Christian themes also began to replace the intrinsically Celtic elements—the search for the magic cauldron of plenty from the Otherworld became a search for the Christian Holy Grail. Some elements retain their pure Celtic form—Caladcholg, the magic sword of Fergus Mac Roth, became by means of a Latin corruption of the name "Excalibur," Arthur's sword.

By the time Geoffrey of Monmouth (ca. A.D. 1100–1155) produced his *Historia Regnum Britanniae (History of the Kings of Britain),* the character of Arthur had developed into its popularly accepted form. Geoffrey was considered to be the creator of the heroic image of Arthur. Yet Geoffrey claimed that he had done no more than translate his *Historia* from "a very ancient book in the British language." While the claim is generally regarded as spurious, it is not without credibility (see **Historia Regnum Britanniae**).

When the Arthurian legends were given permanent form in Malory's *Morte d'Arthur* (ca. 1496), Arthur had been transformed from a Celtic chieftain fighting against the English conquest of Britain to an English medieval king cloaked in romantic knightly chivalry.

Arthurian Saga. A great body of literature has grown up around the personality of Arthur, the great bulk of it having very little to do with the tale's Celtic provenance. For a discussion of the historical references, see **Arthur.** In terms of Celtic mythology, Arthur occurs as a character both in Welsh and Irish mythology, with references in the folktales and legends of the other Celtic peoples. Cornwall, for example, while only having a slight claim to producing any early Arthurian literature in its language (see **Cornish**), claims to have been Arthur's home territory.

In Welsh mythology, the story of "Culhwch and Olwen" is perhaps the earliest known full-fledged Arthurian tale in a Celtic language. This is in the "Independent Native Tales" of the *Mabinogion,* and although it dates to the early eleventh century, it reflects language and customs from a far earlier date. There are also three late Arthurian tales in the *Mabinogion:* "The Lady of the Fountain," "Peredur, Son of Eefrawg," and "Geraint, Son of Erbin." Arthur also appears in "The Spoils of Annwn," which is a tenth century poem and clearly a prototype for the "Holy Grail" quest.

Interestingly, because of the similarities of Arthur and his "knights" to Fionn Mac Cumhail and the Fianna, Arthur appears in Irish myth as the son of the king of Britain and steals the hounds of Fionn, Bran, and Sceolan. The Fianna pursue Arthur to Britain and recover the hounds and Arthur swears fealty to Fionn. However, in medieval times, Arthurian tales became highly popular in Irish literature and the use of Arthurian characters in Irish narratives and tales was a frequent device. In *Eachtra an Mhadra Mhaoil* (Adventures of the Crop-Eared Dog), Sir Gawain (in Irish, Sir Bhalbhuaidh) helps the dog, in reality the son of the king of India, recover his human shape. This is an Arthurian story composed in Ireland in the fifteenth century. Another Irish addition to the saga, dated from the fifteenth century, is entitled *Céilidhe Iosgaide Léithe* (Visit of the Grey-Hammed Lady). There are references to the story from other sources that suggest it was a highly popular tale of the time. As well as numerous "home grown" Arthurian tales in Ireland, there were direct translations such as the fifteenth century *Lorgaireacht an tSoidhigh Naomhtha* (Quest for the Holy Grail), edited by S. Falconer, 1953.

There are are least 25 identified Arthurian tales in Irish from the medieval period. However, the Arthurian saga, while popular, never assumed the importance in Irish literature as did the Fenian sagas, the tales of Fionn Mac Cumhail and his Fianna, in which many of the motifs of the Arthurian cycle are preserved in forms closer to the original Celtic.

Arthur has become popular in world literature but not through Celtic eyes. From Geoffrey of Monmouth's *Historia,* whether based on a translation from a Celtic language or not, the Norman poet Wace conceived and wrote his *Roman de Brut,* in which a more medieval and knightly setting was introduced and in which the "Round Table" appears for the first time. Then innovations to the story and its collation into a new narrative form were produced by the French poet Chrétien de Troyes (fl. A.D. 1160–1190), who added the idea of courtly love and produced the earliest literary version of the "Holy Grail" legend. Then came the English poet

Layamon (fl. A.D. 1198–1207), producing the first of the Arthurian legends to be composed in English, but who effectively mixed some native Celtic folk traditions into his saga.

In thirteenth century Germany Gottfried von Strassburg and Wolfram von Eschenbach added to the saga. In the fourteenth century, in England, two more important developments were made with *The Alliterative Morte d'Arthur* (ca. 1360) and *Sir Gawain and the Green Knight* (ca.1370). *Sir Gawain and the Green Knight* is regarded as the greatest single Arthurian legend in Middle English writing and introduces two major motifs—the "Beheading Game" and the "Temptation to Adultery." The authors of both pieces are anonymous.

However, neither was original and both were borrowed from Celtic mythology. The "Beheading Game" appears in the Red Branch Cycle with Cúchulainn, in the role of Gawain, being invited to behead Uath Mac Imoman during the "Feast of Bricriu." In another version, it is Cú Roí who invites the Ulster warriors to cut off his head on condition that he be allowed to cut their heads off at the appointed time.

The tales involving a "Temptation to Adultery" are many and popular.

In the fifteenth century, Sir Thomas Malory's *Le Morte d'Arthur* gave the ultimate shape to the saga that William Caxton chose for printing in 1485.

In modern times, from Tennyson's *Idylls of the King* through to tales by William Morris, John Masefield, Mark Twain, and T. H. White's classic *The Once and Future King* (1958), Arthurian stories have become almost countless, their appeal timeless.

It is perhaps ironic that the deeds of a remote Celtic chieftain of the sixth century, fighting to turn back the Anglo-Saxon invasion and the creation of England out of part of Celtic Britain, should have inspired stories that have featured in the literatures of many countries for at least ten decades.

Artio. Gaulish goddess, found on a bronze from Berne and probably cognate with Art (Irish for "bear"), because the goddess sits before a huge bear, offering fruit to it.

Artur. [I] A son of Nemed who led his people in battle against the Fomorii at Cramh Ros.

Astrology. As a means of divination, astrology is rarely mentioned in Celtic myth. Yet Pomponius Mela (ca. A.D. 43) referred to the high regard in which the druids were held for their "speculations by the stars." Flavius Magnus Aurelius Cassidorus (ca. A.D. 490–583), mentions a certain Celtic tribe, the Getae, as being learned in natural and moral philosophy and knowing the "course of the twelve signs of the zodiac, and of the planets passing through them and of the whole of astronomy." The Sicilian Greek, Strabo (64 B.C.–A.D. 24), spoke of a Celtic druid named Abaris in Athens discussing such matters with the Greeks. At a time when astronomy and astrology were the same science, the Celts were, according to Cicero, Caesar, Pliny, Tacitus, and other classical writers, masters of astronomy.

In Whitley Stokes' study *Three Homilies* we find contemporary reference to St. Colmcille casting a horoscope to determine the best time for his foster son to commence his education. By the tenth century A.D., the *Saltair na Rann (Psalter of Quatrains)*, composed at the end of that century, states clearly that every educated person in Ireland had to know the signs of the zodiac with their names, in order, and the correct month and day when the sun entered each sign. The *Saltair na Rann* is one of the primary indications of the widespread knowledge of astrology in Ireland at this time. Indeed, according to Cormac Mac Cuileannain (A.D. 836–908), writing in *Sanas Chormaic (Cormac's Glossary)*, it is stated that all intelligent people could estimate the hour of the night throughout the year by studying the position of the moon and stars. In Welsh tradition, in *Hanes Taliesin*, Taliesin is claimed as an astrologer, among his other talents.

Why the neglect of astrology in Celtic mythology when the evidence of its everyday use from an early period is clear? We have Cathbad casting a horoscope for Deirdre at her birth. But we find other forms of divination widely practised in Celtic society. Could astrology have been frowned on by Christianity? Certainly Fergal, from Aghaboe, Co. Laois, who became St. Virgil of Salzburg, was admonished by Pope Zacharias (A.D. 741–752) at the behest of St. Boniface for his "cosmographical speculations." But Christianity tended to embrace astrology as a science until the seventeenth century ("The Age of Reason"). One of the most famous of Irish medical manuscript books is the *Book of the O'Lees* (now in the Royal Irish Academy), written in 1443, partly in Irish and partly in Latin. It is a complete system of medicine. The pages are curiously ruled and divided so that the writing forms patterns resembling the astrological zodiacal figures.

Astonishingly, there has been little historical study in this fascinating area of Irish and, indeed, Celtic culture. The first serious study was the paper "Astrology in Ancient Ireland," given by Muiris Mac Cana (Maurice McCann), a historian of astrology, to the Irish Astrological Association in Dublin, May 27, 1991. His paper was published in the association's journal, *Aspect* (1992) and in the astrology journal, *Cao Times* (New York).

Athairne the Importunate. [I] A druid and poet who is described as an overbearing satirist from Bed Edar (Howth). He was foster father of the poet Amairgen (not the Milesian). Under the laws of hospitality no gift demanded by a poet could be refused. He demanded the eye of the one-eyed King Luain of Connacht. But when he demanded Búan, the wife of Mesgora Mac Da Thó, and was refused, he went to Conchobhar Mac Nessa of Ulster and demanded that Ulster make war on Leinster for its affront to the laws of hospitality. In the war Mac Da Thó is killed.

Áth Liag Fionn. [I] The ford into which Fionn Mac Cumhail threw a flat stone attached to a golden chain that had magical properties. A prophecy said the stone would be found on a Sunday morning that would mark exactly seven years before the world came to an end.

Áth Nurchair. [I] The ford of the Sling Cast in Westmeath. This is where Cet waited in ambush in order to hurl his "brain ball" at Conchobhar Mac Nessa. The slingshot lodged in Conchobhar's forehead. Fingen, his physician, said if the ball was extracted Conchobhar would die. Seven years later Conchobhar fell into a rage, the ball burst in his head, and he died.

Avagddu. [W] See **Afagddu.**

Avalon. [W] Annwn, the Otherworld or "Land of the Dead," "Land of Eternal Youth," "The Summer Land," and so on.

Avon Dia. [I] Abhainn Dea, a stretch of river that held back its waves for fear of the mighty duel in the river ford (Ath Ferdia, now Ardee, the ford of Ferdia) between the champions Cúchulainn and Ferdia.

B

Bach Bychan. [W] "Little Little-one." Trystan's servant.

Badb. [I] A goddess of death and battles who is regarded as a triune deity: Badb, Nemain, and Macha meeting under the name the Mórrígán. Badb's name signifies a crow or raven, which is a constant Celtic symbol of the war goddess. She was married to Net, who appears as an even more shadowy war god. In an account of the historical battle of Clontarf, A.D. 1014, it is said that Badb appeared shrieking over the heads of the warriors during the battle.

Badon. Battle of Mount Badon, dated by the *Annales Cambriae* to A.D. 516–518. The site of Arthur's twelfth great victory over the Anglo-Saxons in which 960 Saxon chieftains are said to have died. In the famous tale of the *Mabinogion*, Rhonabwy dreams of Arthur and his men gathered on the battlefield. Arthur's victory at Badon gave the Celts several decades of peace before the Anglo-Saxons pressed on with their conquest.

Balor of the Evil Eye. [I] A god of death and the most formidable of the Fomorii. His father was Buarainech. He had one eye, whose gaze was so malevolent that it destroyed whoever gazed upon it. The eyelid had to be levered up by servants. This is a fairly close description of Yspaddaden, the giant father of Olwen, with the exception that when his eyelid was levered up the eye did not destroy those on whom it gazed. As it was prophesied that Balor would be slain by his own grandson, he locked his only daughter, Ethlinn, in a crystal tower on Tory Island. Yspaddaden was not willing that his daughter should be married, either. In the case of Ethlinn, Cian, with the help of a druidess, Birog, managed to enter her tower and sleep with her; their child grew up to become Lugh Lámhfada, who fulfilled the prophecy by slaying Balor at the Second Battle of Magh Tuireadh, taking out the giant's eye with a slingshot.

Ban. [W] King of Benoic. A foreign monarch who becomes an ally of Arthur. His brother is made into Bors of Gaul in *Le Morte d'Arthur*.

Banba. [I] A triune goddess with Banba, Fótla, and Éire representing the sovranty and spirit of Ireland. She was the wife of Mac Cuill, son of Ogma. Her name has been used over the centuries as one of the symbols for "Mother Ireland."

Bard. A class of poets known throughout the ancient Celtic world. Bards, poets, and minstrels held a high position in Celtic society and were closely associated with the druids. Diodorus Siculus observed: "They have also lyric poets whom they call bards. They sing to the accompaniment of instruments resembling lyres, sometimes a eulogy and sometimes a satire." The bards were a highly trained and professional group—the repositories of Celtic history, legend, and folklore as well as poetry. They were under the patronage of chieftains and kings. Marcus Porcius Cato (234–149 B.C.) remarks on the sophistication of Celtic eloquence and rhetoric. Poseidonius (ca. 135–50 B.C.), quoted by Athenaeus (ca. A.D. 200), records an incident that might well have come straight out of the Celtic mythological tales. A feast was given in Gaul by a chieftain named Louernios, whose name means "fox."

> A Celtic poet who arrived too late met Louernios and composed a song magnifying his greatness and lamenting his own late arrival. Louernios was very pleased and asked for a bag of gold and threw it to the poet, who ran beside his chariot. The poet picked it up and sang another song saying that the very tracks of Louernios' chariot on the earth gave gold and largesse to mankind.

But the bards were also powerful and in one myth, a satire composed by the bard Fafne, caused blotches to appear on the face of Meilge, the king. See also **Filidh**. Bardic schools flourished in historical Ireland and were finally suppressed in the seventeenth century.

Bardsey. [W] Bardsey Island—Ynys Enlli in Welsh—lies off the extreme western end of the Lleyn Peninsula, in Gwynedd. It is the island where Merlin, with nine attendants and the thirteen treasures of Britain, eventually goes and is held in a magical sleep for all time. See **Myrddin**. The island later became known as the "holy island of saints," for here the Celtic saint Dyfrig (Dubricius), a major church leader of the second half of the fifth century, spent his last days, dying there on November 14, A.D. 612. His relics were removed from the island and placed in Llandaff in A.D. 1120. An interesting point is that medieval legends name Dyfrig as the archbishop who crowned Arthur as king.

Bean Sídhe. [I] Popularly known in English as "banshee." Literally, "woman of the hills," or, in modern usage, "women of the fairies." After the gods went underground and were transformed, in popular mind, to fairies, the banshee became a female fairy attached to a particular family; she warned of approaching death by giving an eerie wail.

Bebhionn. [I] A beautiful giantess, daughter of Treon of the Land of Maidens, who was promised to Aedh against her will and sought help from Fionn Mac Cumhail and the Fianna. Aedh slew her.

Bebo. [I] Wife of Iubdan of the Faylinn, or Little People. She had an affair with the king of Ulster.

Bécuma. [I] She dwelt in the Land of Promise and had an affair with Gaiar, son of Manannán Mac Lir. Because of this she was banished to the human world, where she persuaded Conn of the Hundred Battles to take her as his wife. She grew jealous of his son Art and tried to get him banished.

Bedwini. [W] Arthur's bishop, mentioned in the "Dream of Rhonabwy."

Bedwyr. [W] A warrior of Arthur's court who accompanies Culhwch in his search for Olwen and wounds the giant Ysbaddaden. He appears in the later forms of the Arthurian tales as Sir Bedivere.

Bel. See **Belenus.**

Belenus. Gaulish god cognate with Bel, Belinos, Beli, and Bíle in Ireland and Britain. Caesar compared Belenus to Apollo and treated him as a solar god, dispenser of light, and a healer. The find at Trunholm shows him conveying a solar disc on his horse-drawn chariot. Numerous sanctuaries and places were named after him, and his image appeared on many Gaulish coins.

There are many places in Europe named after Belenus. In London we have the survival of Belinos' or Bíle's Gate, which has come down to us as the famous Billingsgate. His name is also to be found in personal names such as that of one of the most notable Celtic kings of Britain before the Roman invasion—Cunobelinus—Cuno (Hound of) Belinos. Shakespeare has given him greater fame as Cymbeline. See also **Beltaine.**

Beli. [W] Husband of Don, he is god of death, and a later form of
Belenus (above). He corresponds to Bíle of Ireland. He is also father
of Lludd and Llefelys. Often called Beli Mawr, he is claimed as an
ancestor deity from whom several royal lines of Wales claimed
descent.

Beltaine. A feast known in the Gaelic world (Ireland, Man, and
Scotland). It is translated as "fires of Bel." One of the four major
Celtic festivals falling on May Eve and May 1, it was also known as
Cetshamhain. It was customary to observe the festival by lighting
bonfires, hence Bel-tinne, fires of Bel. This was the time when the
Celts offered praise to Bel, Belenus, or Bíle, who was not only a god
of death but of life as well, for he is sometimes represented as a solar
deity and he was regarded as having gained victory over the powers
of darkness by bringing the people within sight of another harvest.
On that day the fires of the household would be extinguished. At a
given time the druids would rekindle the fires from torches lit by
"the sacred fires of Bel," the rays of the sun, and the new flames
symbolised a fresh start for everyone. Numbers of cattle from each
herd would be driven in ancient circles as a symbol of this purifi-
cation. The festival was widely known, even surviving until recently
in southern France. In Cornwall the May Bonfires are still lit. Until
the nineteenth century the Scottish Law Term starting in May was
known as the Beltane Term. Significant events in Celtic myth
happen at Beltaine. It was then that Parthólon came to Ireland. This
pre-Christian ceremony was claimed for Christianity and merged
with the feast day of St. John the Baptist.

Bendigeid Vran. [W] See **Bran the Blessed.**

Bíle. [I] God of death who is cognate with Bel and Belenus. In some
texts he is known as "Father of Gods and Men" and husband to
Dana. In other texts he appears as the father of Milesius and
significantly came from "Spain," a synonym for the Otherworld.
Among his duties was to gather the souls and accompany them to
the Otherworld.

Blathnát. [I] The name is cognate with the Welsh Blodeuwedd but
their traditions are separate. Sometimes given as Blanid, she is
daughter of Mend, king of Inis Fer Falga. Cú Roí, the king of
Munster, carries her off to his fortress, which is constructed so that
no one can find the entrance. Cúchulainn attempts to rescue her,
and she helps him by emptying milk into a stream that runs

through the fort. He is able to gain access and slays Cú Roí. Among the prisoners, however, is Fer Cherdne, Cú Roí's bard. As the victorious procession winds its way along some cliffs, Fer Cherdne, in revenge for his master's death, grabs Blathnát by the waist and jumps over the cliffs with her, killing them both.

Bleheris. [W] A Welsh bard whose name is identical with Bledhericus, mentioned by Giraldus Cambrensis, and whom Bréris, quoted by Thomas of Brittany, gives as an authority on the Tristan story. Nothing seems to have survived of his writings.

Blodeuwedd. [W] "Flower-aspect," a beautiful maiden conjured out of the flowers of oak, broom, and meadowsweet by Gwydion and Math to be the bride of Lleu Llaw Gyffes. She is unfaithful and attempts to kill Lleu in favour of her lover Gronw Pebyr, but Lleu kills him and she is turned into an owl, outcast among even the birds. There seems a similarity here to the Irish Blathnát (Little Flower).

Boann. [I] The water goddess and wife of Nechtan, another water god. Her name means "she of the white cattle." Nechtan kept a sacred well, Segais' Well, which was the source of the inspiration of knowledge (see **Nuts of Knowledge**). Only four persons were allowed to go there. Boann refused to accept this geis, or taboo, and walked contemptuously around the well in a left-hand circle, whereupon the waters of the well rose up and drowned her. Its course formed the river named after her—the modern Boyne. In another version, however, she escaped while the waters formed the river.

In another tale, as wife of Elcmar, the Dagda wants to sleep with her and sends her husband on an errand. While he is away, the Dagda has his affair with Boann and she bears him a son. But the Dagda has caused the nine months to seem like one day to Elcmar so that he returns home, thinking a day has passed. The son of Boann and the Dagda is the love god Aonghus Óg. Some Christian scribes confused matters by trying to make Boann into the wife of the Dagda in accordance with Christian morality.

Bodb Dearg, The. Bodb the Red, son of the Dagda, who succeeded him as ruler of the gods. He dwelt at Loch Dearg on the Shannon. He helped Boann identify the girl in Aonghus Óg's dream as Cáer. He had a daughter named Sadb who, through her affair with Fionn Mac Cumhail, became mother of Oisín.

Bóramha. [I] "Cattle counting." A tribute exacted from the people of Leinster by the High King Tuathal Teachtmhair as recompense for the actions of Eochaidh, king of Leinster, who insulted Tuathal's daughters Fithir and Dairne and caused their deaths. Eochaidh was killed by Tuathal, and Leinster agreed to the tribute. It was seldom paid, however, although the title of Brían Bóramha (Brian Boru) (A.D. 941–1014) would indicate that he had successfully imposed the tribute on Leinster during his reign.

Borvo. Also Bormo, Bormanus. Gaulish deity associated with thermal waters. The name seems to denote seething or turbulent waters. The name survives in several place-names, such as Bournbonne-les-Bains. He is represented with a female companion, Damona, "Divine Cow." Bors, which could be a variation of this name, is represented in Arthurian legend as a king of Gaul and brother of Ban of Benoic. Professor John Rhys argues that Bors was a synonym for Myrddin (Merlin).

Bran. [I] The Bran fleetingly referred to in the *Book of Leinster* as a son of Lir and brother of Manannán, and a god of the Otherworld, is doubtless cognate with Bran the son of Llyr in Welsh myth. But the more famous Bran of Irish myth is the son of Febal who set out on the famous "voyage tale," which has been dated to the eighth century A.D. The story, however, is essentially pre-Christian in character. Bran has a vision of a beautiful woman who causes him to set out with his three foster brothers and twenty-seven warriors on a voyage to find the country from which the woman came. After numerous adventures, in which he meets the sea god Manannán Mac Lir, and lands on numerous mystical islands, Bran eventually comes to Tír na mBan, the Land of Women. Here Bran and his men stay. The men grow restless and long to return to Ireland. But they are warned that if they set foot on Ireland they will age suddenly for they have been away many centuries. They set sail, in spite of the warnings. As they near the shore, one of the crew leaps ashore and before their eyes he ages and turns to dust. Bran writes his story on Ogham wands and throws them ashore before turning his ship back into the unknown.

Bran the Blessed. [W] Son of Llyr. Ruler of the Island of the Mighty (Britain), brother of Manawydan and of Branwen. Their story features in the second branch of the *Mabinogi*. They have two half brothers—Efnisien, who creates hostility, and Nisien, the peacemaker. When Bran's sister, Branwen, marries Matholwch, the Irish king, Efnisien, who has not been consulted, mutilates Matholwch's horse. In compensation, Bran gives Matholwch a magic cauldron brought from Ireland that can resuscitate slain men, although the process leaves them bereft of speech.

When Bran hears that Matholwch, though forced by his people, is punishing Branwen for Efnisien's insult, he leaves seven of his chieftains to rule Britain and takes an army to invade Ireland. Matholwch offers his submission to Bran "lest the country be spoiled." However, as peace is being discussed, Efnisien insults the Irish and casts Gwern, son of Matholwch and Branwen, into a fire. In the terrible battle that follows between Matholwch and Bran, Bran is mortally wounded by a poison arrow in the foot. He tells his companions to cut off his head and take it back to Britain. And Efnisien sacrifices his own life in order to destroy the magic cauldron that keeps giving life to the slain Irish warriors. In the end, only five pregnant women are left alive to repopulate Ireland, and only seven Britons survive to return to their own land. They are Pryderi, Manawydan, Taliesin, Gluneu son of Taran, Ynawc, Grudye, son of Muryel, and Heilyn, son of Gwynn Hen. Bran's head is taken back for burial in a strange voyage that takes many years, during which the head of Bran remains alive, talking and eating, once more reinforcing the Celtic concept of the soul dwelling in the head.

Meanwhile, Branwen dies of a broken heart, having returned to Anglesey, where she is buried by the banks of the Alaw.

There are some affinities in this tale to the second battle of Mag Tuired in Irish myth [see *Branwen, Daughter of Llyr,* Proinsias Mac Cana, University of Wales Press, 1958].

Brandubh. [I] A board game played by the heroes and gods. The name signifies "black raven." It seems similar to fidchell. There have been several archaeological finds of board games in Celtic graves. Such a game was found in a grave in Welwyn Garden City, England, and a wooden board with sockets for pegs was found in Ballinderry, Co. Westmeath. There was also a person named Brandubh, a king of

Leinster who coveted the wife of Mongán, the son of Manannán Mac Lir, who was his good friend. Mongán had to use his magic powers to get his wife back.

Branwen. [W] Daughter of Llyr, sister of Bran and Manawydan. She marries the Irish king Matholwch and bears him a son, Gwern. However, her half brother, Efnisien, had insulted Matholwch, and Matholwch is forced by his people to make her suffer for the outrage. She is forced to do menial tasks in the kitchens for three years. She rears a starling and teaches it to speak, conveying to her brother Bran, ruler of the Island of the Mighty, news of her unhappiness. Bran invades Ireland. As Matholwch is about to make peace, Efnisien intervenes again and this time kills her son, Gwern, by casting the boy into a fire. In the ensuing battle Matholwch, Bran, and everyone except five pregnant Irish women and seven British warriors are killed. Branwen is a figure of dignity and restraint throughout the tale. Now, as she sees the devastation wreaked in her name, she dies of a broken heart. She is buried on the banks of the Alaw, which was thereafter called Ynys Branwen.

Breasal. [I] The High King of the World, who lived in the west. His country was called Hy-Breasal or Hy-Brasil, which became the legendary Atlantis, only visible to human eyes once every seven years. The name of Hy-Brasil appeared in records as a real place. A. Dalorto (ca. A.D. 1325), a Genoese cartographer, believed it to be southwest of Ireland. When explorers came to South America they thought they had found the legendary country and thus gave the name Brazil to the land they had discovered.

Bregon. [I] A son of Milesius, sometimes recorded as father of Bíle and Ith. However, Bíle also appears as the father of Milesius, and as the husband of the mother goddess Dana.

Brehon Laws. [I] The oldest surviving codified law system in Europe. The ancient laws of Ireland, named from *breitheamh*, a judge. The laws are sophisticated and complex, the result of many centuries of practice and oral tradition. They were thought to have been codified first in the fifth century under the instigation of St. Patrick. It has been said that the Irish law tracts are probably the most important documents of their kind in the whole of western Europe by reason of their extent, their antiquity, and the tradition they preserve. Their roots are in ancient Indo-European custom and not in Roman Law. Of the surviving tracts the *Senchus Mór* deals with civil law, while the *Book of Acaill* deals with criminal law. Both of these are to be found in the *Book of the Dun Cow*, which is one of the most complete copies of the tracts that survives. The language of Irish law, *Bérla Féini* as it is called, is ancient. In spite of English attempts to destroy this law system, it persisted for centuries, with many English colonists turning to it for judgments. Even through the seventeenth century the laws were still in use in parts of Ireland. They were finally suppressed during the Penal Law period.

Comparisons with the codified Welsh Law system, the Laws of Hywl Dda, are fascinating as they show a commonality of social perceptions.

The most detailed account of the Brehon Law system is given in the six volumes of *Ancient Laws of Ireland,* Dublin, 1865–1901.

Breizh. See **Brittany** and **Breton.**

Brendan. [I] The historical Christian saint appears here because of his fabulous voyage, *Navigatio Sancti Brendani* (The Voyage of Brendan), which became one of the most popular stories during the Middle Ages and was translated into many European languages. The tale seems to have been based on the earlier "Voyage of Mael Dúin." Like Mael Dúin, Brendan discovers an island populated by spirits in the form of birds, finds a crystal column in the sea, sails a translucent sea, and comes upon an island of giant smiths. One point of difference is that Brendan lands on an island that turns out to be Jasconius, a giant whale, and finds himself becalmed in the Sargasso Sea.

Bres. [I] There are three characters named Bres: a Dé Danaan who was killed in the first battle of Magh Tuireadh; a son of the Fomorii Balor, mentioned in the story of the children of Tuireann; and, more well known, the son of Elatha, the Fomorii king, who marries Brigid, the goddess of fertility, who becomes ruler of the Dé Danaan when Nuada loses his hand. Bres was handsome but a tyrant, and when he is displayed as ruler, he seeks the aid of the Fomorii and sets in motion the events leading to the second battle of Magh Tuireadh. He is captured and his life is spared by the Dé Danaan on condition that he advise them about agriculture, and, for a while, he appears as an agricultural divinity.

Breton. (Brezhonek) The language of Brittany, which diverged from a common British Celtic (Brythonic) in the fifth century A.D. It is estimated that there are currently 800,000 speakers of the language in Brittany, forming the largest group of native speakers of a Celtic language [*Le Monde de l'Education,* September 1976]. Little survives in Breton in terms of mythological tales compared with the corpus of Irish and Welsh manuscripts. Like Cornish, Breton has its series of medieval miracle plays such as *Burzu bras Jean* (1530) and *Buhez santes Barba* (1557). Also, it produced saints' lives such as *Buez Santes Nonn hag he map Deuy* (The Life of St. Nonn, Son of Devy) as well as religious poetical works such as *Tremenvan an itron gwerches Maria* (The Passing of the Virgin Mary), *Pemzec levenez Maria* (The Fifteen Joys of Maria) and *Buhez Mabden* (Life of Man). *Mellezour an Mary* (The Mirror of Death), composed in 1519 and printed in 1575, remains another classic of Breton literature. Father Jehan Lagadeux's *Catholicon,* dated 1465 but first printed in 1499 at Trégueir, was the first Breton, Latin, and French dictionary of the language. However, to the fifteenth century belongs the classic *Dialog etre Arzu Roe d'an Bretounet ha Guynglaff* (The Dialogue of Arthur, King of the Bretons, and Gwenc'hlan).

Breton Lai (or Breton Lay). A rhymed story that became popular in England during the fourteenth century. The Breton *lais* usually dealt with Celtic themes and often drew on material from the Arthurian cycles. It is felt that this type of tale was transmitted into England via French translation rather than directly from Breton forms. Marie de France (ca. A.D. 1200) was famous for her Breton *lais,* versified narratives full of Celtic myth and atmosphere, often using Arthurian legend. She seems to have spent most of her life at the English court. Of the fifteen *lais* that are extant, *Sir Launfel* is the best known. Launfel is a knight at Arthur's court who falls in love with a fairy. Guinevere accuses Launfel of insulting her and Arthur swears to have him executed, but the beautiful fairy carries Launfel off to Avalon. This became a popular tale in a fourteenth century version and was used in *The Vision of Sir Launfel* by James Russell Lowell (1848). Other Breton *lais* that survive are *Sir Orfeo* and Chaucer's *The Franklin's Tale.*

Brían. [I] The eldest son of Tuireann by the goddess Brigid. With his brothers Iuchar and Iucharba he slew Cian, Lugh Lámhfada's father. As compensation Lugh demands that the three brothers must fulfil eight tasks. They set out to do so in a voyage tale that has been deemed the Irish equivalent of "Jason and the Golden Fleece." In all the adventures Brían plays a leading role. But in fulfilling the tasks, the brothers, returning to Ireland, meet their doom.

Briareus. [W] He stands guard over the sleeping Myrddin on Bardsey Island.

Bricriu. [I] Known as Bricriu Nemthenga—of the Poisoned Tongue, he was an Ulster champion known for his bitter tongue and desire to cause trouble. In many ways he is the Irish equivalent of the Welsh Efnisien. He caused strife between Cúchulainn and the other Red Branch warriors. In the famous tale "Fled Bricriu," eight warriors had to guard him from his angry companions. He is also the creator of trouble in the "Tale of Mac Da Thó's Boar." However, when he is asked to judge the contest between the Brown Bull of Cuailgne and the White Horned Bull of Connacht on the Plain of Aeí, he is trampled to death by the fighting bulls.

Brigantia. "The High One," tutelary goddess of the Brigantes of Britain and cognate with the goddess Brigid, regarded as one of the principal Celtic goddesses. Her name also survives in the river and place-name Brent in England and in the Braint in Ynys Mon in Wales. She might be the source of Caesar's Celtic "Minerva," and she may well have been the model for Britannia.

Brigid. [I] A triune goddess who appears as a goddess of healing, a goddess of smiths, and, more popularly, a goddess of fertility and poetry. Seemingly cognate with Brigantia in Britain, she is the daughter of the Dagda. For a while she was the wife of Bres, the half Fomorii ruler of the Dé Danaan. She had three sons by Tuireann. In many tales she appears to be the counterpart of Dana, mother of the gods. The festival of Imbolg (February 1) was sacred to her as this was the fertility festival, marking the coming into milk of the ewes.

A Christian saint, known as "Mary of the Gaels," not only takes Brigid's name but many of her traditions. St. Brigid was born in Faughart in A.D. 450 and died in Kildare in A.D. 523. As an Irish saint she is second only to St. Patrick. Numerous written accounts of her life began to circulate and her cult became widespread after her death, doubtless helped by the confusing of the tradition of the goddess with her. Many ceremonies and stories associated with the goddess were ascribed to the Christian saint; not the least is the fact that February 1 is now her feast day. R. A. S. Mac Alistair put forward the theory that St. Brigid was a priestess of the goddess who converted to Christianity. In most accounts of her life, her father is cited as a druid called Dubhthach.

Britain. The island of Britain was Celtic when it became known to the Mediterranean world in the fifth century B.C. Many archaeologists claim Celtic settlement in Britain as dating back to the Urnfield civilisation of the Bronze Age (ca. 1200–750 B.C.), which is often called "Proto-Celtic." It has been argued that the first Celtic language spoken in Britain was Goidelic, regarded as the older form of Celtic. A speculated language shift took place around the sixth century B.C. It has been suggested that Albion was an early Celtic name for Britain, soon ousted by Britannia. In Old Irish, Albain was used as the name for the whole island before being confined to northern Britain (Scotland), where, in modern Gaelic, Alba is the name for Scotland and Albannaich the name for a Scotsman.

In spite of Caesar's military expeditions in 55 B.C. and 54 B.C., Britain retained its independence to become a respected trading country. During the period of Cunobelinos ("Hound of Bel," who was to become Shakespeare's Cymbeline—A.D. 10–40), Britain was exporting wheat, cattle, gold, silver, iron, leather goods, hides, and hunting dogs to Europe. In fact Strabo argued that trade with Britain was producing more revenue for Rome than would accrue if the island were to be conquered by Rome and the treasury had to pay for a standing army and civil service to run the country. However, in A.D. 43 Rome did invade. It took forty years to create a fairly peaceful province in southern Britain. Northern Britain was a failure so far as military conquest went and the Romans contented themselves with walls (Hadrian and Antoninus) in attempts to hem in the Celtic tribes of the north.

When Rome finally pulled out of Britain in A.D. 410, a Celtic Britain emerged again. This would be comparable to India emerging again after nearly two centuries of English rule. While educated people spoke Latin as well as British Celtic, the vast majority of people were still Celtic-speaking.

Britain was now suffering attack from the Saxons, Angles, and Jutes from the Jutland peninsula. Domestic problems, however, caused a ruler, known to us as Vortigern (overlord or High King), to invite some Jutish mercenaries to help him. These mercenaries eventually turned on Vortigern and established their own kingdom in Kent, the former land of the Cantii. Within a few years, groups of Angles and Saxons were landing on the southern and eastern coasts. The Britons, the indigenous Celtic population, were pushed slowly westward or simply annihilated. There is no evidence that the Celts were assimilated or intermarried to any extent with the invaders. Works that present the British Celtic view include *De Excidio et Conquestu Britanniae* (The Ruin of Britain) by Gildas (ca. A.D. 500–570), Nennius' *Historia Britonum* (ca. A.D. 800), and *Life of Winwaloe,* about the sixth century abbot also known as Guénolé and Gunwalloe, by Wrdistan, who lived during the ninth century. Gildas is an especially contemporary source arguing the wholesale slaughter of the Celts in southeastern Britain and the mass migration of survivors to Brittany, Spain, and into the western areas of Britain. There is also evidence of the migration of British Celts into Ireland.

Dr. Mario Pei, in his study of Anglo-Saxon prior to the Norman Conquest, points out that any widespread intermarriage would have resulted in numerous loan words from Celtic into Anglo-Saxon. Such emphatically is not the case and leads him to believe that British Celts and invading Anglo-Saxons had little social intercourse [see *The Story of the English Language,* Mario Pei, George Allen & Unwin, London, 1968].

It was during this period, the early sixth century, that we hear of a Celtic chieftain named Arthur fighting the invading Anglo-Saxons and winning twelve major battles against them, halting their advance across Britain. The *Annales Cambriae* records the death of Arthur and Modred at the battle of Camluan (Camlann) in A.D. 537–539. Around this historical personage, the Celts began to build, with typical richness, allegory and legend. These legends were transported to other European cultures in the medieval period.

For five centuries the British Celts and Anglo-Saxons contested the land of Britain until the defeat of the last serious Celtic confederation at Brunanburh in A.D. 937. It was here, at a point variously placed in Northumberland, that Athelstan defeated the Celts and their Danish allies in a two-day battle recorded in Icelandic saga and the *Anglo-Saxon Chronicle.* It was in support of this confederation that the British Celtic poem *Armes Prydain Vawr* (Prophecy of Great Britain) was written in the early tenth century and found in the *Book of Taliesin.* Ironically, the "Great Britain" of the prophecy is a Celtic Britain again. Welsh, Irish, the Cymry of Cumbria, Strathclyde, and Cornwall, and the Manx as well as the Danes of Dublin will "banish the Saxon foe from the land," says the poet.

After the British Celtic defeat at Brunanburh, the term "British" tended to be dropped as the Celts accepted the new boundaries enforced on them. They were now Welsh, Cornish, Scots, and, albeit briefly, Cumbrians.

Britan. [I] A Nemedian who, having fled from Ireland after the victory of Morca and the Fomorii over his people, settled in the island of Britain and gave his name to it.

Britannia. In modern times Britannia has come to mean the personification of what is called the "British Empire," which, in reality, has its foundations firmly in England. There is discussion whether it should be more realistically referred to as the "English Empire," for the Celtic populations of those nations that shared the island of Britain with the English were the first to be conquered and colonised by them. Having retained their national identity and continued to seek self-government from England into modern times, it can be argued that these nations were simply part of the English Empire and were never part of the imperial ethic except in a subservient role, usually as Anglicised functionaries of the empire, which was clearly English in culture and administration and in the economic exploitation of the empire.

It could well be that the British (the original Celtic inhabitants of Britain, before the coming of the Anglo-Saxons) thought of Britain as being personified by a goddess figure, Britannia, in much the same way that Éire (Ireland) is a triune goddess with Banba and Fótla, representing the sovranty of the country. The earliest known representation of Britannia, given as a female figure sitting on a globe and leaning with one arm on a shield while grasping a spear in the other hand, occurs on a British coin issued during the Roman occupation at the time of Antoninus Pius (ca. A.D. 161). The motif did not reappear until it was placed on an English copper coin in 1665, during the reign of Charles II.

British. The Celtic inhabitants of Britain (more generally referred to as Britons) prior to the Anglo-Saxon invasions. Also their language. The term was actually used until the tenth century A.D., when the Britons lost hope of recovering the island of Britain from the invading Anglo-Saxons (the ancestors of the English). They then began to call themselves Cymry (compatriots), for Welsh and Cumbrians, Kernewek for Cornish, and Breizhek for Bretons. The British language (now referred to as Brythonic Celtic) is the ancestor tongue of Welsh, Breton, and Cornish. It was similar and mutually intelligible with Gaulish on the European mainland. Its divergence into the three languages that have survived into more recent times began during the sixth and seventh centuries. At this time the Anglo-Saxon invasion had split the British Celts into isolated pockets, hence the language separation. Cumbrian became extinct in the fourteenth century.

Brittany. In the fifth and sixth centuries A.D., refugees from Britain, escaping the invasion and westward movement of the Anglo-Saxons, fled to the Armorica peninsula and joined their Gaulish cousins. The peninsula was renamed "Little Britain." They quickly merged with these native Celts into a strong kingdom. But for the next few centuries, the Bretons had to contend with the westward expansion of the Franks, seeking to exert their dominion throughout Gaul and renaming it "land of the Franks"—France.

The Bretons held their own and on November 22, A.D. 845, the Breton King Nominoë defeated the Franks at Ballon, forcing Charles le Chauve to sign a treaty recognising Breton independence. Brittany lost its complete independence six centuries later when the armies of Francis II were defeated on July 28, 1488, at Saint Aubin-du-Cormier by the French of Charles VIII. There followed a "Union of Crowns" by the enforced marriage of Anne of Brittany with Charles VIII in 1491. After the death of Charles in 1498, Anne was forced into marriage with Louis XII.

On September 18, 1532, a Treaty of Union between France and Brittany was signed at the Chateau du Plesis-Macé, Angers. This agreed that Brittany should remain a self-governing entity within the broader French state, retaining its ancient Parliament (États). Brittany settled down to its new position with a sullen acceptance, sometimes bursting into insurrection against French centralisation. Breton sympathies were with the Americans during the American War of Independence, and many Bretons, such as Lafayette, Count Guichen, and Colonel Armand (Armand Tuffin de la Rouerie) played leading roles in the American revolutionary forces. In fact, 333 Breton officers are listed fighting for the Americans and 16 warships were fitted out in Brittany in 1778 to help them.

Many of these Bretons returned home with the new creed of republicanism and "Rights of Man" and laid the foundation in Nantes and Rennes for the wider French Revolution. However, the result of the French Revolution was the abolishment of the Breton Parliament in 1790 when "everyone in France was declared equal." The inequality of this lay in fact that the Bretons were not French. The "abolition of the Breton nation" created a reaction. On January 18, 1790, de la Houssaye, president of the Breton Parliament, protested to the National Assembly. *"Les Corps out des privileges. Les nations out des droits!"* (Parliament has privileges. Nations have rights!) There was a general uprising against the French in 1793 led by George Cadoudal and Armand de la Rouerie. French republicans found themselves fighting Breton republicans and Breton royalists (as many were pushed back into the royalist camp by the centralist attitude of the French republic). The war went on for years, mainly after 1804 as a guerrilla war or the war of the *chouans*. The return of the monarchy and the later republics did nothing to return any form of autonomy to Brittany. Brittany survived the nineteenth century as a predominantly Celtic-speaking country. In 1914 some 1.5 million of its 2.5 million population spoke Breton. In spite of the decline to 800,000 speakers today, Brittany remains essentially Celtic in attitude, and many have not lost the desire to see it self-governing once more.

Bruigh na Boinne. [I] Palace of the Boyne, identified with New Grange, which was first the fortress of Nechtan and later the home of the love god Aonghus Óg.

Brunanburh. A historical battle of A.D. 937 that is variously placed on the east coast of Britain, usually in Northumbria. It is of immense importance as the Celtic defeat that caused the Celts to accept the kingdom of England, to cease calling themselves "Britons," and to give up their dream of eventually driving the English invaders into the sea and reestablishing a Celtic Britain.

A Celtic confederation was formed to attempt to curb the aggressive expansionist policies of Athelstan of England. In the tenth century, a poem entitled *Armes Pyrdein Vawr* (The Prophecy of Great Britain) was written in support of this confederation. It survives in the *Book of Taliesin*. The poet urges the Cymry of Wales, Cumbria, and Strathclyde, the Cornish, the Scots, the Manx, and the Irish, including the Norse-Irish of Dublin, to join together.

"And this vast confederacy of peoples shall rout the Saxon foe and banish him from the land." Both Cynan and Cadwaladr are invoked to help in the struggle.

Constantine II (A.D. 900–942), High King of Alba, is mentioned as the leading force behind this alliance; Owain of Cumbria, Olaf of Dublin, Aralt of Man and the Isles, Hywel Dda of Wales, Donnchadh of Ireland, and Cynan of Cornwall must all have played their part.

The *Anglo-Saxon Chronicle* says Athelstan made his way north to face this formidable alliance. The skirmishing took several days. A defector from the Celtic alliance saved Athelstan's life by revealing the plans for a night attack on Athelstan's tent. A Saxon bishop was killed in this foray. Both Anglo-Saxon and Icelandic sources say it was fought over a two-day period. The English army suffered severely—two of Athelstan's cousins, Alfric and Athelwin, were slain. But the Celts and their allies were finally defeated. No longer would the supremacy of the isle of Britain between Celt and Saxon be in contention.

Brut y Tywysogion. [W] A thirteenth century text, "The Chronicle of the Princes" (of Wales), from A.D. 664. It ends in 1164.

Buile Suibhne. [I] "The Frenzy of Sweeney." Suibhne was a warrior of the Dál Riada who was driven insane by the injuries he sustained at the battle of Moira. He took off on a mad flight through the wild places of Ireland in search of peace of mind. The tale is a powerful image of a frenzied mind. And Suibhne returns to a oneness with nature. It became a common motif for poets to compose nature poetry in the name of Suibhne for several centuries. The Suibhne here is obviously cognate with the story of Suibhne Geilt, a king cursed by St. Ronán who assumed the characteristics of a bird, leaping from tree to tree. Suibhne Geilt (or Mad Suibhne) had his counterpart in the Welsh Myrddin Wyllt.

Bull. The bull is a symbol of strength and virility and also wealth in many cultures. This is also so in the Celtic cultures and especially in Irish myth, where the epic of the *Táin Bó Cuailgne,* the war fought over the Brown Bull of Cuailgne, is one of the most famous and prominent expressions of this. The *Book of the Dun Cow* describes a *tabhfheis,* or bull feast, in ancient Ireland associated with the election of a High King. A druid would eat the flesh of a bull and drink its blood. He was then put to sleep by four other druids, and the person that he dreamed about would be the future High King. If he lied about his vision, then the gods would destroy him. In respect of the Brown Bull of Cuailgne of the *Táin*, it is interesting to note the existence of a Gaulish name, Donnotauros, "Brown or Kingly Bull." The cult of the bull was widespread in the Celtic world, and images of Tarvos Trigaranus, the three-horned bull, are found both in Gaul and Britain.

Bwbachod. Welsh household sprites, like brownies or pixies. In modern Welsh a *bwbach* is a bogey or scarecrow.

Bwlch. [W] One of Arthur's three warriors who possess the brightest and sharpest weapons in Britain. The others are Cyfwlch and Syfwlch.

C

Cacmwri. [W] A servant of Arthur who helps track down the magical boar Twrch Trwyd.

Cadw. [W] Cadw of Pictland is the only man who is allowed to shave Yspaddaden the Giant.

Cadwaladr. [W] King of Gwynedd and son of Cadwallon who came to be regarded as the promised deliverer of the British Celts. He would, like his father, return and lead them to victory over the Anglo-Saxons. He is invoked in the poem *Armes Prydein Vawr*. See **Brunanburh.**

Cadwallon. [W] Seventh century king of Gwynedd who managed to reunite the Celts of Wales and Cumbria for a short period. He is regarded as a hero who would one day return and lead the Celts to victory.

Cae Hir. [W] Lover of Golwg Hafddydd, Essylt's maid, and companion of Trystan.

Caer Feddwid. [W] Synonym for the Otherworld.

Cáer Ibormeith. [I] The daughter of Ethal Anubail of the *sídhe* of Uaman in Connacht. The love god Aonghus Óg dreamed of her and, having had his dream interpreted, set out to find and woo her.

Caer Siddi. [W] Synonym for the Otherworld.

Caer Wydyr. [W] Fortress of Glass. Cymric synonym for the Otherworld.

Cailleach Beara. [I] Often referred to as the Old Woman, or Hag of Beara. She originally appeared as a triune goddess with Cailleach Bolus and Cailleach Corca Duibhne. She was said to have also been known as Cailleach Buí, wife of Lugh, the god of arts and crafts. The *Book of Lecan* mentions that she had seven youthful periods, married seven husbands, and had fifty foster children who founded many tribes and nations. Beara is a peninsula on the Cork-Kerry border.

Cáilte. [I] Sometimes Caoilte, the thin man. A warrior of the Fianna and their foremost poet. He killed the god Lir in battle during the war between the gods.

Cairbre. [I] There are many Cairbres in Irish myth, ranging from the son of the god of eloquence and literature, Ogma, to the son of Cormac Mac Art who destroys the Fianna. Another Cairbre is Cairbre Caitcheann, or Cathead, so called because he has the ears of a cat. He was a usurper who ruled during a revolt against the Milesians.

Cairell. [I] A son of Fionn Mac Cumhail killed by Goll Mac Morna.

Caladfwch. [W] See **Caliburn.**

Calan Gaef. [W] October 31/November 1. Equivalent of Samhain.

Calatin. [I] A druid sent by Medb to cast spells on Cúchulainn to incapacitate him during the *Táin* war. The Clan Calatin were obviously Fomorii, and it is recorded that there were twenty-seven sons and a grandson who studied in Alba for seventeen years. All members of the clan had a hand or foot missing, which is a typical Fomorii motif. Cúchulainn slew all the male members of the clan. The women also tried to entice him to fight them—they had the advantage of being able to change their shapes.

Caliburn. [W] The magic sword of Arthur, from the Welsh *Caladfwlch,* mentioned by Geoffrey of Monmouth. This seems to be cognate with *Cladcholg,* "hard dinter," the sword of Fergus. The famous Excalibur is but a Latin corruption of these names.

Camluan. Sometimes Camlann. The *Annales Cambriae* record that in A.D. 537–539 there occurred "The battle of Camluan in which Arthur and Modred were slain: and there was death in Britain and Ireland."

Camulos. British Celtic war god. Colchester in England was called Camulodunum, "the dun or fort of Camulos." It is thought that the name was probably the basis for Arthur's mythical capital, Camelot.

Canhastyr. [W] "Of the Hundred Hands." One of Arthur's warriors who asked to accompany Culhwch in his quest for Olwen.

Cano. [I] Son of Gartnán, king of Alba, who was in exile in Ireland. Cred, a chieftain's daughter, fell in love with him, but he refused to make love to her because it would breach the laws of hospitality. He did, however, love her and gave her a stone that he said contained his life. After his return to Alba he made an assignation with Cred, but this was frustrated by Cred's jealous stepson, Colcu.

Cred, waiting at Loch Cred, became so anguished when Cano did not turn up that she dropped the stone, which fragmented, and Cano died three days later.

Caradawc. [W] Son of Bran who ruled Britain with six chieftains in his father's absence in Ireland. When news of Bran's death came, his six companions were killed by Caswallon, son of Beli, who threw the "Veil of Illusion" on Caradawc and caused his death as well.

Castle of Wonders. [W] A great castle where Peredur, in the later guise of Perceval, finds the Grail.

Caswallon. [W] Son of Beli. While Bran the Blessed is fighting Matholwch in Ireland, Caswallon leads an insurrection in the Island of the Mighty (Britain) and, on the news of Bran's death in Ireland, becomes its ruler.

Cat. A mystical animal in Celtic myth, especially in the Irish tales. There are eight words for "cat" in Irish, one of which, *puss,* has been borrowed into English as a pet-name for a cat. Cats permeate the myths. One, for example, Irusan of Knowth, would often make off with people. Monstrous cats dwell in caves, while Lughtigern (mouse lord) is a heroic animal.

Cathbad. [I] The personal druid of Conchobhar Mac Nessa and, in some versions, his father. He married Maga, widow of Ross the Red, and his children were Dechtiré, mother of Cúchulainn, Elbha, the mother of Naoise, and Findchaem, mother of Conall of the Victories. He features in most of the Red Branch sagas.

Cath Godeu. [W] Battle of the Trees. See **Archen.**

Cathubodba. A broken inscription in Gaul, ". . . *athubodba"* would seem to be Cathubodba. This may well be the Gaulish equivalent of Badb Catha, "war fury," and therefore a goddess of war.

Cauldron, Magic. This is an essential theme in Celtic mythology. The quest for a magic cauldron is a popular motif in both major branches of the myths. The Dagda, father of the gods, had a magic cauldron from Murias, and no one parted from it hungry. Cúchulainn and Cú Roí stole from a mysterious castle a magic cauldron that produced gold and silver. Midir the Proud owned another magic cauldron. The parallels in Welsh myths involve the quest for a cauldron in "The Spoils of Annwn," which is regarded as the prototype for the "Holy Grail" stories. There is also the "Cauldron of Rebirth," which is a magic cauldron given to Bran the Blessed and which he then gives to Matholwch. A slain warrior cast into it will come out alive but bereft of the power of speech. Cauldrons, perhaps as the instrument in which food was cooked, had a special place in ancient Celtic society. The surviving cauldrons from the period vary in size and material, often being made from bronze, copper, or silver and always richly decorated. The most magnificent example is the Gundestrup Cauldron, dated to the first century B.C., and now in the National Museum, Copenhagen.

Caves. Caves play a prominent part in Celtic mythology as places of natural and religious significance. They provide entrances to the Otherworld, like the Cave of Cruachan. A cave on an island in Loch Derg is known as "St. Patrick's Purgatory" and is regarded as the mouth of Hell. A medieval tale about the adventures of a knight named Eoghan in this cave was one of the most widely known "vision" tales prior to Dante. In Ireland, the storytellers had a group of tales classified as "Caves," but sadly, hardly any of the tales that occur in this list have survived.

Cei. [W] The churlish steward to Arthur. In the later versions of the Arthurian tales, he becomes Sir Kay. He accompanies Culhwch on his quest for Olwen and later refused Peredur entrance to Arthur's court, believing him to be a rustic.

Céile Dé. An early Christian order meaning "servants of God" and sometimes known as the Culdees. Recorded as being founded by St. Mael Ruain of Tallaght (d. A.D. 792), they were a loose-knit order with no central authority. They appeared in Ireland and in Scotland, where the last known reference to them was in the fourteenth century. It is thought that it was these distinctly Celtic monks who were responsible for setting down the bulk of Irish myths in written form.

Celemon. [W] Daughter of Cei.

Celt. The Celtic peoples were one of the great founding civilisations of Europe. They were the first European people north of the Alps to emerge into recorded history. The term is linguistic and not racial. In modern times the Celts are divided between the Goidelic (Q) Celts—the Irish, Manx, and Scots—and the Brythonic (P) Celts—the Welsh, Cornish, and Bretons. Gaulish, identified as a P Celtic language, died out around the fourth or fifth century A.D. Today only sixteen million people live in a Celtic country, and of these only 2.5 million speak a Celtic language, as do, possibly, a further one million outside the Celtic areas.

Though writing was known to them, and used on funeral stones and pottery prior to the first century B.C., it was not until the Christian era that the change in religious perceptions allowed the Celts to shake off the old druidic prohibition against committing their store of knowledge to written form. It is from the sixth century A.D. that an extensive written testimony in the Celtic languages survives, including one of Europe's oldest and most vibrant mythologies, which until the Christian period had been handed down in oral tradition.

First recorded by the Greeks as *keltoi,* perhaps from a native word meaning "hidden people," by the Greek Hectaeus (ca. 517 B.C.), the Celts had already begun to migrate through Europe from their original homeland at the headwaters of the Danube, Rhine, and Rhône (all three rivers still carrying their Celtic names). It is thought that they were called "hidden people" because of the prohibition by their religion to commit anything to written record. The etymology of the word may well be the same root that gives us *ceilt,* an act of concealment, and *kilt,* the short male skirt of Celtic dress.

The Celts began their expansion through Europe around the start of the first millennium B.C., at which time they possessed great metalworking skills, especially in the use of iron (itself a Celtic word borrowed into the German languages, *iarn*). This metal was only just becoming known to craftsmen of the Classical world. With their iron weaponry and tools, the Celts were able to cut through the impenetrable forests of Europe.

By the sixth century B.C. they were established in France and Spain, as far south as Cadiz, and in the Po Valley of Northern Italy. It is believed that the Goidelic form of Celtic was the more archaic form and that it was Goidelic speakers who had settled in Spain, Ireland, and Britain by at latest the start of the first millennium B.C. Brythonic, or P Celtic, is regarded as a later modification of the Goidelic form.

It is believed that the two linguistic groups (Goidelic and Brythonic) diverged over 2,500 years ago. The Brythonic group began to simplify itself in its case endings and in the loss of the neuter gender and dual number. The two groups also differed in the matter of initial mutation and aspiration. There is the famous substitution of "P" for "Q" in the Brythonic languages—hence the designation of "P" Celtic and "Q" Celtic. Thus the word "head" in Irish, *ceann,* becomes *pen* in Welsh; the word "worm" in Irish, *cruimh,* becomes *pryf* in Welsh, and so forth.

The Celts dominated Northern Italy for a time, defeating the Etruscan empire and then Rome itself in ca. 390–387 B.C. Other Celtic tribes pushed further east and were met by Alexander the Great on the Danube in 335–334 B.C. in a peaceful conference. Not until after Alexander's death did the Celts invade Greece and sack the holy shrine at Delphi, pressing on to establish the state of Galatia on the central plain of Turkey. It is the Galatian state that provides us with our first accounts of how a Celtic state was governed.

It was in the third century B.C. that the Celts achieved their greatest expansion before the rise of Rome halted them and they, in turn, began to be pressed backwards by Roman expansion. Defeating the Celts of Northern Italy, then Spain, the Roman legions pushed into Gaul. At the same time the eastern Celtic areas in Rumania, the Balkans, Czechoslovakia, Austria, and Switzerland were being conquered and the people absorbed. The Galatian state also fell to Rome, although Gaulish Celtic was still spoken there, according to St. Jerome, who visited Ancyra (Ankara), which was a Celtic capital.

The Celts were an exciting and inventive civilisation with a highly developed religion that unified all their tribes from Ireland to Galatia. They had a sophisticated law system and were among the first to develop the concept of immortality of the soul, a fact that made the change to Christianity an easy process with, significantly, no Celtic martyrs being registered in the change. The Greeks Aristotle, Sotion, and Clement acknowledged that much of early Greek philosophy was influenced by the Celtic druids. The Celts of Cisalpine Gaul (northern Italy) and many from Spain actually contributed to Latin literature. Being forbidden to write in their own languages by religious prohibition, they wrote in Latin. Writers such as Gaius Valerius Catullus, Valerius Cato, M. Terentius Varro, Caecilius Statius, Lucius Pomponius, Cornelius Nepos, Trogus Pompeius, the famous Virgil, and many others were, in fact, Celts. While from Spain, Marcus Valerius Martialis, well known as Martial, made a frank assertion of his Celtic identity, as did the teacher of rhetoric Marcus Fabius Quintilanus. Like their descendants in more modern times, these Celts contributed to the language of their conquerors rather than their own.

Only Ireland and the Isle of Man, of the Celtic lands, were not conquered by Rome. Although the northern part of Britain was invaded, it never settled under Roman administration. As a major European people, Celtic civilisation was smashed first by the Romans and later by the expansion of the Germanic tribes. The emergence of the medieval Celtic kingdoms was also short-lived, as they quickly succumbed to the expanding English and French empires. See under the individual Celtic countries.

Celtchair. [I] A Red Branch hero who, having violated the laws of hospitality, has to undertake a task in compensation. He has to rid Ireland of three terrible scourges. He is successful except with the last scourge, which is in the form of a dog. He kills it but a drop of blood trickles from his spear onto his flesh and Celtchair is killed by its venom.

Celtiberia. See **Iberia.**

Celtic Church. Although popularly referred to, the term "Celtic Church" is not a strictly accurate one because the early Christian churches among the Celtic peoples were, in most essentials, part of the Roman Catholic Church. There was no identifiable church with a central leadership. However, for 150 years during the early Christian period the insular Celts of the British Isles were cut off from strict Roman influence. While Rome began to reform many of her customs during the fifth century A.D., especially the dating of Easter, the Celts clung to old computations and freely mixed pre-Christian traditions and social concepts into their Christian philosophies and thus developed as a distinct entity within the wide Christian movement.

The Celtic Church's views on social order and land tenure, which were contrary to hereditary rights and absolute ownership of land and property, brought it into early conflict with Rome. Absorption was inevitable; inevitable because of Celtic individualism and its lack of cohesion and centralism. However, Celtic Christian monks began to move through the Europe of the "Dark Ages," bringing literacy and learning to many. The Irish, in particular, were seized by a *peregrinatio pro Christo*. It was Irish monks who converted the pagan English kingdoms. When the Synod of Whitby in A.D. 664 opted for Roman custom instead of Celtic, it was not the end of Celtic Church influence in England, and another full century elapsed before Celtic missionaries ceased to be welcome among the English.

Celtic monks took their teachings as far east as Kiev, north to Iceland, and south even into Italy, where they established their own monasteries and churches. Their philosophers, such as Pelagius, Hilary, and others, added to the store of Christian wisdom. Eriugena the Irishman (ca. A.D. 810–877) is considered the most considerable philosopher in the western world between Augustine of Hippo and Thomas Aquinas.

In Latin and in Celtic languages, there survive many *Lives* of the founding fathers (and mothers) of Christianity among the Celts. These *Lives* are a typically Celtic mix of allegory and legend—often the stories of the Celtic saints are mixed with former traditions so that the *Lives* become part of Celtic mythology itself. St. Brigid, for example, is often mixed with the traditions of the goddess of fertility, and many saint's days were grafted onto existing pagan feast days. The saints of the Celtic Church are numerous, for the designation "saint" was given to all missionaries and teachers of distinction, signifying that they were eminent men and women.

It was, of course, under the auspices of the monks and scholars of the Celtic Church that the mythology of the Celts began to be written, and, unfortunately for posterity, many of the monks, with their newfound Christian zeal, sought to bowdlerise the myths with Christian images and morality. Nevertheless, the uniqueness and vitality of pre-Christian Celtic mythology and philosophy still shines through the thin Christian veneer.

By the twelfth century the Celtic Church had been absorbed into Rome, although as late as the fourteenth century in Scotland there were still bodies of Celtic monks (Culdees, or Céile Dé, servants of God) clinging to the old cultural customs. The Céile Dé order was a monastic one that sought to revive the purity and austerity of early Celtic monasticism. It is said they were founded by Mael Ruain, founder of the monastery of Tallaght (d. A.D. 794).

Cenferchyn. [W] In the "Dream of Rhonabwy" it is mentioned that Owain had been given 300 ravens by Cenferchyn and that whenever he went forth with this army he was victorious.

Ceridwen. [W] Wife of Tegid Foel and mother of Afagddu, who is so ugly that she resorts to magic in order to make him wise above all others. She sets Gwion Bach and Morda to tend the magic cauldron while she prepares the potion, but drops fall onto Gwion Bach's finger, which he sucks. Thus he attains wisdom and not Afagddu. In fury, Ceridwen pursues him, and while he is hiding in the form of a grain of wheat, she overtakes and eats him. She then gives birth to the poet and druid Taliesin, who is Gwion Bach reincarnated. She hides him in a leather bag and casts him in a river. She has another son, Morfan, who is so ugly no man would fight with him at the battle of Camlann because they thought he was a devil. Her daughter is Creirwy (dear one).

Cernunnos. "The Horned One," found in Gaul and Britain. He is sometimes equated with the Dis Pater and therefore the Dagda in Irish myth. Representations of him show a characteristic Buddha posture, although he is also shown with a club. He is also represented as "lord of animals," especially of the bull and stag. The hill figure at Cerne Abbas, in southwest England, which is also a near replica of a carving found at Corbridge, Northumberland, is thought to represent Cernunnos. It is 55 meters high and 51 meters wide.

Cesair. [I] Granddaughter of Noah and daughter of Bith. Bith was denied a place in the Ark and so Cesair advised him to build an idol. The idol advised them to build a ship as Noah had done and take refuge in it. After seven years they came to Ireland, where Cesair became the wife of Fintan. She perished with most of her followers, but Fintan escaped the Deluge by changing into a salmon.

Ceugant. [W] The concept of infinity, the outer of three concentric circles representing the totality of being in Welsh cosmogony.

Chariots. While chariots were popular in the Celtic world, and Julius Caesar was greatly worried by British war chariots during his campaign, they only feature prominently in the Red Branch Cycle of Irish mythology. In the Fenian Cycle there is scarcely any reference to them. The chariot usually contained a warrior and a charioteer—

demonstrated in the tales of Cúchulainn and his charioteer Laeg. While the charioteer concentrated on driving, the warrior could run along the yoke between the horses and cast his spear over the heads of the galloping beasts before returning to the car. Caesar witnessed this tactic during his campaigns in Britain. It is interesting that most words for chariots in Latin are Celtic loan words—*carpentum* (from which derives our modern "car" as well as "carpenter") and *carruca, carrus,* and *rheda,* and the *essendum,* the war chariot most popularly used by Gauls and Britons.

Chruinnaght, Yn. [W] Manx "Gathering" similar to the Welsh Eisteddfod but not on such a grand scale. It was revived as an annual event in 1977 after a lapse since 1939. It is held in July each year.

Cian. [I] A son of Dian Cécht, the god of medicine. Balor had stolen his cow and when he went to recover it he found Ethlinn locked in a tower by her father, Balor of the Evil Eye. It had been prophesied that Balor would die by the hand of his grandchild and he sought to keep his daughter Ethlinn away from men. But Cian entered the tower and seduced Ethlinn, who eventually bears him a son, Lugh Lámhfada, who fulfils the prophecy.

Cigfa. [W] Daughter of Gwynn Gohoyw and wife of Pryderi. She shares the tale of Pryderi, Rhiannon, and Manawydan during the enchantment of Dyfed.

Cildydd. [W] "Of the Hundred Holds." One of Arthur's warriors asked to accompany Culhwch.

Cilgwri, Ousel of. [W] An ancient bird who had pecked a smith's anvil to the size of a nut, so long had she lived. But she is unable to help Culhwch in his search for Olwen.

Clas Myrddin. [W] An ancient name for Britain, "Myrddin's Enclosure," referred to in the *White Book of Rhydderch.*

Cliodhna. [I] Goddess of beauty who fell in love with a mortal named Ciabhan of the Curling Locks. They fled from the wrath of Manannán Mac Lir and landed in Glandore, Co. Cork. While Ciabhan went to hunt, Cliodhna was lulled asleep by beautiful music played by Manannán, who then sent a great wave to sweep her back to the Otherworld, leaving Ciabhan desolate.

Clothra. [I] She drowned her own sister Ethné while she was pregnant. She had an affair with her three bothers and bore a son to them who became the High King Lugaid Riab nDerg ("of the Red

Stripes"), each section resembling one of her brothers, thereby proclaiming him to be the son of all three.

Clud. British goddess who gave her name to the Clyde (also in the form of Clòta and Clwyd).

Clust. [W] "The Hearer." He could hear an ant move at fifty miles distant. He is asked to accompany Culhwch on his quest.

Cobhthach Coel. [I] The king of Bregia who was jealous of his brother, the king of Leinster. He killed him and forced his nephew to eat the heart of his father, an experience that struck the boy dumb so that he was afterwards called Móen (dumb). Cobhthach became king of Leinster, but when Móen grew to manhood he returned and exacted vengeance.

Conaire Mór. [I] High King who was the son of Mess Buachalla and the mysterious bird god Nemglan. He was slain in the attack on Da Derga's Hostel, which is one of the most popular tales concerning the wrath of the gods when a *geis* is broken.

Conall. [I] Of the several Conalls in Irish myth, the best known is Conall Cearnach, "Of the Victories." It is he who avenges the death of Cúchulainn and is also instrumental in bringing about the death of Conchobhar Mac Nessa by a weapon he has devised by crushing the brain of Mac Da Thó, who he slays, and mixing it with lime to make a magical slingshot. This lodges into Conchobhar's head and causes his death seven years afterwards. Conall Cearnach is one of the great Ulster champions and many adventures are attributed to him.

Conan. [I] Of the warriors called Conan who appear in Irish myth, Conan Mac Morna or Conan Maol (bald), the brother of Goll, is well known. He appears as a buffoon, a glutton, and a coward, as well as foul-mouthed and a braggart.

Conchobhar Mac Nessa. [I] King of Ulster throughout the Red Branch Cycle. His mother, Nessa, promised to marry Fergus Mac Roth on condition that he give up the throne of Ulster for one year to her son, Conchobhar. At the end of the year, Conchobhar refused to return it and Fergus is driven into exile. Conchobhar appears in the sagas as something of a despot. He lusts after Deirdre and kills her lover Naoise. He is victorious in the war of the Táin. Eventually Conall of the Victories strikes him with a magical slingshot, which lodges in his brain. He is not killed but neither can the "brain ball" be extracted. After seven years Conchobhar loses his temper and the "brain ball" splits and kills him.

Condatis. Gaulish god of confluence.

Condwiramur. [W] A maiden who in some versions of Peredur, Perceval, or Parzival and the Grail marries him and bears his son Lohenergrain.

Conlaí. [I] A son of Cúchulainn by Aoife of the Land of Shadows. Cúchulainn, not recognising him, slays him.

Conn. [I] While there are several characters of this name, including a son of Lir, it is Conn of the Hundred Battles, the High King, who usually comes to mind. Associated with him are tales concerning the appearance of Lugh, who foretells his destiny, and of a beautiful goddess who represents sovranty.

Connachta. [I] The province of Connacht, an ancient kingdom, also known as the kingdom of Cruchain. It is often in rivalry with Ulster, especially during the Táin War. Medb is said to have ruled there for eighty-eight years.

Coraniaid. [W] From *corr,* "dwarf." A group of small beings who wrought a plague in Britain in the tale "Lludd and Llefelys." According to the tale "so great was their knowledge that there was no discourse over the face of the island, however low it might be spoken, that they did not know about if the wind met it." Their plague was but one of three that befell Britain. The second was a terrible scream raised by a dragon in contest with a foreign dragon on Beltaine that left all animals, trees, and waters barren. The place of their contest was under the midpoint of Britain, according to Lludd (in Geoffrey of Monmouth's *Historia*), at the site of Oxford. The third plague was that of a giant who stole all the food prepared for the king's court, except that consumed on the first night. The Coraniaid tale bears a similarity to the despoiling of the Irish Tuatha Dé Danaan by the Fomorii. The Coraniaid seem to be connected with the Corriganed, which have passed into Breton folklore as a group of invisible fairies who inhabit Brittany and are more generally known as the *corrigan* or *korrigan*. Professor J. Loth equated the *corrigan* with the Welsh *Tylwyth Teg*.

Cormac. [I] The most famous of the three warriors named Cormac in Irish myth is Cormac Mac Art, the High King, said to have ruled in the historical period A.D. 254–277. He was the patron of the

Fianna, the royal bodyguard, during their adventures under Fionn Mac Cumhail. Several tales are associated with him, including a trip to the Otherworld. His son Cairbre succeeded him and destroyed the Fianna.

Cornish. (Kernewek) The language of Cornwall, deriving from British Celtic (Brythonic), was the ancestor tongue also of Welsh and Breton. Cornish died as a generally spoken community language in Cornwall in the late eighteenth century, although a native knowledge of it was retained by some individuals until the start of the twentieth century, when a language revival was started by enthusiasts. Earliest forms of it as a distinct language occur from ninth century texts. The *Vocabularium Cornicum* is a twelfth century Latin/Cornish lexicon, also known as the "Cottonian Vocabulary." The main corpus of early Cornish literature is contained in a number of medieval religious plays, such as *Buenans Meriasek,* the life of St. Meriasek, the *Ordinalia* cycle of three dramas, plus the *Pascon agan Arluth* (Passion Poem).

While tradition has placed the provenance of the Arthurian legends and the romance of Tristan and Iseult to a Cornish setting, there are no surviving Cornish manuscripts that record any of the stories. Yet there is an intriguing indication that such sources might have existed. [Some works on the Cornish provenance of the Arthur saga are contained in Henry Jenner's "The Arthurian Legend," *Journal of the Royal Institute of Cornwall,* vol. LVII, and P. A. Lanyon Orgill's "Cornwall and the Arthurian Legends," *Cornish Review,* No. 6, Winter, 1950.]

The second great romantic saga connected specifically with Cornwall is Tristan and Iseult. Again, no early Cornish manuscripts survive with the tale. Indeed, the earliest full-length version in a Celtic language is the sixteenth century Welsh *Ystoria Trystan,* now in Cardiff Library. However, Joseph Bédlier [*Le Roman de Tristan par Thomas,* Paris 1902–1905] was the first scholar to demonstrate that all the stories of Tristan and Iseult could be traced back to a single poem—one written by Thomas, a French poet of the twelfth century. Professor Joseph Loth believed that Thomas had acquired the poem from a Cornish source. [Joseph Loth, *Revue Celtique,* vol. XXXIII, 1912, and also *Des Nouvelles Théories sur l'origine des Roman Arthurian,* Paris, 1892. For a further exposition, see also

Henry Jenner, "The Tristan romance and its Cornish provenance," *Journal of the Royal Institute of Cornwall*, vol. XVIII.]

Cornwall abounds with folktales, many of which are comparative with other Celtic cultural traditions. [See Robert Morton Nance, *Folk Lore recorded in the Cornish language*, Camborne, n.d. Nicholas Boson's "The Dutchess of Cornwall's Progresse" is basically a survey of West Penwith folklore (Bodleian Library ms. 10714). An excellent study of this is A. K. Hamilton Jenkin's "The Dutchess of Cornwall's Progress," *Journal of the Royal Institution of Cornwall*, 1924. A survey of Cornish folktales was made in Robert Hunt's *Popular Romances of the West of England*, 1865, and in William Bottrell's three volumes, *Traditions and Hearthside Stories*, 1880.]

Cornwall. (Kernow). Known to the Anglo-Saxons as "the land of the *Kern-weahlas*"—Kern-foreigners—hence Cornwall. It is the setting for much of the Arthurian saga and for the story of Tristan and Iseult. It does feature prominently in several Celtic myths. It emerged as a separate kingdom after the disintegration of Dumnonia in the eighth century. The Irish raided and settled parts of Cornwall during the sixth and seventh centuries, and also during this time missionaries of the Celtic Church, from Ireland and Wales, established many foundations in the country. At Castle Dor, Fowey, stands a monument dated to the sixth century A.D. showing there really was a King Mark and a Tristan in Cornwall. Warfare between the Cornish and the expanding Wessex kingdom continued until the Cornish kings finally submitted to Athelstan (A.D. 925–939) and accepted him as suzerain ruler. It was Athelstan who finally fixed the fluctuating border as the Tamar. In a charter of A.D. 944 Edmund of England styled himself "King of the English and ruler of this British province." After the Norman invasion the native rulers of Cornwall were known as *eorls*, or earls. At this time the earl was Cador (sometimes given as Condor), who was a descendent of the Cornish kings. He was deposed by William of Normandy. But Cador's son, Cadoc, was later restored as "earl of Cornwall." His daughter Avice married Reginald Fitz Henry, son of Henry I, who held the earldom by right of inheritance through his wife.

In 1337 Cornwall was created a duchy with the eldest son of the monarch as the incumbent. Until Tudor times laws had to be enacted "in Anglia et Cornubia," showing that Cornwall was not considered part of England. With Tudor centralisation, the Cornish rose up in arms against English rule no less than three times. In 1497 came the famous An Gof and Flamank insurrection, with a Cornish army marching to Blackheath in Kent and threatening London before being defeated. Then came a short-lived insurrection led by Perkin Warbeck. In 1549 came the "Prayer Book" rebellion, with the English language being forced on the Cornish in religious services. In their declaration, preceding the uprising, it was stated, "we, the Cornishmen, whereof certain of us understand no English, utterly refuse this new English."

It took several centuries, however, before the Cornish language died out as a generally spoken community language (see **Cornish**). Cornwall, since the suppression of the last Cornish uprising, has become a generally accepted part of England and from 1889 has been regarded as an "English county" so far as political administration is concerned. Yet there are still questions about its legal position within the United Kingdom. One such contention is that of the Cornish Stannaries Parliament.

King John in A.D. 1201 granted the first charter to the Stannaries and allowed it to be the government of a state within a state, able to raise its own taxes and make its own laws. They were even granted a power of veto over the London Westminster Parliament in A.D. 1508. The Stannaries Parliament survived the repression after the uprisings, and as late as 1753 this power of veto was recognised by London. Throughout the nineteenth century, the Stannaries did not meet but were reconvened in 1974 by enthusiasts, acting in accordance with Stannary law. Meeting regularly since 1974, the first time the Stannary Parliament challenged the United Kingdom government in law was over the Community Charge or Poll Tax brought in by the Conservative Government, for Scotland in 1989 and for England and Wales in 1990. Tim Saunders, charged before Cardiff magistrates for nonpayment of the Community Charge, defended himself by stating that he was subject to the Stannary Parliament and that England had no right in law to tax him. "You have no jurisdiction in law concerning the force and effect of Cornish Law. As Cornish Stannary Law is a separate body of law, English courts are not competent to decide what is correct or incorrect according to that law." [A Tinner's Case, *Kernow,* June/July 1991.] After listening to the arguments, the case was adjourned *sine die.* [See also "The Cornish Stannary Parliament," by Paul Laity, *Carn,* No. 66, Summer 1989.] In the perception of many, Cornwall is still a Celtic country.

Cors. [W] "Of the Hundred Claws." A warrior of Arthur's asked to accompany Culhwch.

Creiddylad. [W] Daughter of Lludd Llaw Ereint. She was to marry Gwythyr, son of Greidawl (Ardent). However, Gwyn ap Nudd carried her off by force. Arthur set out after her and demanded that Gwyn set her free. A peace was made that Gwyn and Gwythyr were to meet each year on May Day in combat. The annual combat would go on until doomsday and whoever was the victor on doomsday would have Creiddylad.

Creirwy. [W] "Dear one." Daughter of Ceridwen and Tegid Foel.

Cromm Cruach. [I] A golden idol worshipped by Tigernmas (Lord of Death) on Magh Slécht (Plain of Adoration), where human sacrifices were offered.

Crow. Also raven. In Celtic mythology the crow or raven is always associated with the goddesses of death and battles. The birds hover over the battlefield. It is a favourite guise of the Mórrígán. The name of Badb, the triune goddess, means "crow" or "raven."

Cruachan, Cave of. [I] A famous entrance to the Otherworld, sometimes called the "Gate of Hell" by Christian scribes.

Cruithne. [I] The progenitor of the Tuatha Cruithne or the Picts. See **Pict.**

Cúchulainn. [I] Originally named Sétanta, he became known as the Hound of Culann. His mother was Dechtíre, daughter of the druid Cathbad, while his father was Lugh Lámhfada. He features in numerous tales of the Red Branch Cycle but is chiefly famous for his single-handed defence of Ulster during the war of the Táin, when Ailill and Medb of Connacht invaded the country to secure the Brown Bull of Cuailgne. His is a tragic tale for though he is constantly in love with women, he is forced to kill his own son, lose several of the women he loves, and slay his best friend, Ferdia.

Although he is armed with magical weapons and adventures with impunity in the Otherworld, he arouses the wrath of the goddess of death and battles, the Mórrígán, by rejecting her love. His doom at the Pillar Stone is ordained, and when he dies the goddess, in the form of a raven, perches on his shoulder while an otter drinks his blood. His faithful companion through most of the sagas is his charioteer, Laeg, and among his mystical weapons are his sword, Caladín, and his spear, the Gael-Bolg. Although he knows many women, including the goddess Fand, the Pearl of Beauty, wife to the sea god Manannán Mac Lir, he constantly returns to Emer, the daughter of Fogall the Wily, who entreats him piteously not to go forth on his last battle foray.

Culann. [I] The smith who forged Conchobhar's weapons and who is regarded as Manannán Mac Lir in human form. When young Sétanta killed his hound, Culann was angry until Sétanta offered to be his hound until he found a new one. Thenceforth Sétanta was known as Cúchulainn, the Hound of Culann.

Culhwch. [W] Son of Cilydd and Goleuddydd. When his mother died and his father remarried, his stepmother so hated him for refusing to marry her daughter that she pronounced a curse for his destiny. He could only marry Olwen, daughter of the giant Yspaddaden Pencawr. He set off to Arthur's court to learn how to fight and how and where he might find her.

Cei, surly as usual, did not wish to allow him entrance (in some versions it is Glewlwyd of the Mighty Grasp who refuses to open the gate). Eventually he sees Arthur, who grants him help. He is joined by several heroes and they set off in search of Olwen. After many adventures they come to Yspaddaden's land. The sister of Goleuddydd, Culhwch's mother, is married to Custennin (we are told he is Yspaddaden's brother), and they arrange a meeting with Olwen and Culhwch. The two fall in love, but first Culhwch must overcome her fearsome father.

He is then given a long series of tasks that he eventually fulfils with the help of his companions. The giant acknowledges defeat and Goreu, son of Custennin, cuts off his head. Olwen and Culhwch marry and the warriors of Arthur disperse.

Cumal. [I] Son of Trenmor, chief of Clan Bascna, and leader of the Fianna. He fell in love with Murna of the White Neck but her

father, Tadhg, a druid, objected. They eloped. Tadhg ordered Goll
Mac Morna to kill Cumal, which he does, but not before Murna
becomes pregnant and gives birth to Cumal's son Fionn Mac
Cumhail. It is interesting to note that Cumal signifies "sky." It
seems cognate with the British name Camulos, who was also known
among the Gauls as a god of war. Camulodunum, the fort of
Camulos, was the Celtic name for Colchester. Camulosessa was the
name for Almonbury, Yorkshire. The name might be the origin for
Arthur's mythical court of Camelot.

Cumbria. Now a county of England. The British Celts were cut off in
this area after A.D. 655. Cadwallon of Gwynedd had managed to
reunite the Welsh and Cumbrians briefly in A.D. 633, but in A.D.
655 came Winwaed Field, after which the Saxons controlled the
territory between Cumbria and Wales, isolating Cumbria. Like
their Welsh compatriots, they called themselves Cymry (compatriots or fellow-countrymen) and their country Cymru (Cum-ree)
(land of comrades), which was Anglicised as Cumbria.

While the *Annales Cambriae* mention that Cumbrian poets were
well respected in the Celtic world, nothing that can be really
identified as Cumbrian can be discerned in early medieval Welsh
literature. After the defeat of the Celtic confederation at
Brunanburh, Edmund (A.D. 940–946) invaded Cumbria, but the
Cumbrians sought help from their Celtic neighbours of Alba
(Scotland). Edmund was forced to hand over Cumbria to Maol
Callum I (A.D. 943–954), and Cumbria, under petty kings, became
a province of Scotland with its capital at Caer Llywelydd (Carlisle),
originally Luguvallos, named after the Celtic god Lug. In A.D. 1092
William Rufus of England defeated Dumnail (Dòmhnuil), king of
Cumbria, and annexed it to England. Saxon colonists were encour-
aged to move into the fertile valleys, while the Celts took to the
inhospitable hills.

Celtic, however, was spoken in the Eden Valley area until the
fourteenth century. The original form of Eden was Ituna, after a
Celtic deity. An Irish record refers to a British god Eiturn, which it
is thought cognate with the Gaulish Taranus, a god of thunder. In
Welsh myth, Gluneu, one of the seven survivors of Bran's battle
with Matholwch, was son of Taran.

It is fascinating to note that Cumbrian shepherds used the old Celtic numerals to count sheep until the beginning of this century. While some observers thought they were using "gibberish," a comparison with other British Celtic forms shows the numerals to be fairly undistorted.

	CUMBRIAN	WELSH	CORNISH	BRETON
1	yau	un	onen	un
2	tau	dau	deu	daou
3	tethera	tri/tair	try	tri
4	methera	pedwar	peswar	peder
5	pimp	pump	pymp	pemp
6	[missed]	chwe-ch	whegh	c'hoéc'h
7	sethera	saith	seyth	seic'h
8	lethera	wyth	eth	eiz
9	nothera	naw	naw	na
10	dothera	deg	dek	dék
10	dick	deg	dek	dék

It will be observed that the number 6 has been missed in the Cumbrian tradition. Looking at the Welsh, Cornish, and Breton comparisons, it is obvious that 6 is a very difficult and un-English sound. Therefore the sound was not retained in memory as the knowledge of the language and its sound system became lost. To make up the first ten numerals, the number 10 was simply repeated with a variation. Like the other Celtic languages, the Cumbrians retained the unit of 20 for counting. Other numerals have been recorded up to 20, including 15, which is *pimptheg—pymptheg* in Welsh, *pempthak* in Cornish, and *pemzak* in Breton. [See D. B. Gregor, *Celtic: A Comparative Study,* Cambridge, 1980; see also *Times Literary Supplement,* July 14, 1979, p. 799.]

Cunedda. [W] Cunedda and his eight sons settled in Wales and founded the Welsh kingdoms. His story is similar to the story of Míl and his eight sons, who went to Ireland and founded the kingdoms there. Tybion, Cunedda's eldest son, for example, like Donn, eldest son of Míl, dies before the family settles in Wales, although his son Meirion takes his father's place (as Lugaid, son of Ith, does in Irish myth). Cunedda is the eponymous founder of the dynasty of Gwynedd, while his sons form other kingdoms such as Ceredigion (Cardigan).

Curad-mir. [I] "The Hero's Portion," a motif that features in such tales as "Mac Da Thó's Boar" and "Bricriu's Feast." It is a choice cut of meat, usually a piece of thigh, reserved for the greatest champion attending a feast, and therefore this apportionment was often the start of a quarrel between the warriors.

Cú Roí. [I] Son of Daire and a king of Munster. In one of the prototype versions of the theme that became famous in the story "Sir Gawain and the Green Knight," it is Cú Roí who presents himself to the Red Branch warriors and challenges them to cut off his head and then to let him retaliate. In most of the stories in which he appears there is nothing supernatural about him and he is finally slain by Cúchulainn after he kidnaps Blathnát, daughter of the king of Inis Fer Falga.

Curragh. [I] Cognate with the Welsh *cwrwgl* (coracle). The most popular of boats used in the sagas and tales.

Custennin. [W] A giant shepherd in the territory of Yspaddaden the Giant who, with his wife, helps Culhwch in his quest for Olwen. They arrange for Olwen to meet Culhwch at their house. There is a further symbolism here, for Custennin's wife is actually Culhwch's aunt (his mother's sister), and in their house two worlds meet—the real world and the world of giants. In some versions he is made the brother of Yspaddaden.

Cwn Annwn. [W] The hounds of the Otherworld, perhaps translated as "hounds of hell." They first appear as the hounds of Arawn in the story where Pwyll chases then off a deer so that he might claim it. Then Gwyn ap Nudd has domain over them. Folklore in Wales has created many evil creatures with white bodies and red ears, racing through the countryside on dark, stormy nights, pursuing the souls of unshriven men or unbaptised children. The folk tradition of the "hounds of hell" emanating from Celtic myth is fairly widespread even in non-Celtic areas.

Cwrwgl. [W] See **Curragh.**

Cwy. [W] A mysterious person referred to by Taliesin:

> *I will not allow much praise to the spiritless.*
> *They know not on what day, or who caused it,*
> *Or in what hour of the serene day Cwy was born,*

Or who caused that he should not go to the dales of Defwy,
They know not the brindled ox with the broad headband,
Whose yoke is seven-score handbreadths.
When we went with Arthur of mournful memory,
Except seven, none returned from Caer Fandwy.

No one has satisfactorily discovered the meaning of this verse.

Cyfarwydd. [W] A professional storyteller like the *seanchaidhe* (or *seanchaí)* of Ireland.

Cyfwlch. [W] One of three warriors who possess the brightest and sharpest weapons at Arthur's fortress. The others are Bwlch and Syfwlch.

Cymidei Cymeinfoll. [W] "The big-bellied battler." The wife of Llasar Llaesgyfnewid. She and her husband appear to be deities of war for they own a magic cauldron. If a slain warrior were cast into it he would come forth alive again except that he would have no power of speech. When they were in Ireland, Cymidei would give birth to a fully armed warrior every six weeks. Matholwch of Ireland tried to destroy them but they escaped to Britain where Bran gave them refuge. In return they gave him the cauldron. When Efnisien insulted Matholwch on the eve of his wedding to Branwen, Bran gave him the cauldron as a means of atonement.

Cymon. [W] A warrior at Arthur's court. He appears in a Welsh version of "Le Chevalier au lion" of Chrétien de Troyes. He comes across a black man with one foot and one eye, bearing a mighty club, in a glade in a forest with wild animals, stags, and serpents feeding by him. Cymon was looking for a combat and the man told him to go to a fountain, take a silver bowl he would find there, and fill it with water. The water must then be thrown on a nearby marble slab. A thunderstorm would follow, and the singing of enchanted birds, and a Black Knight would appear. Though couched in medieval guise, many things about the tale are of earlier Celtic origin. The Black Knight defeats Cymon, who returns to Arthur's court where Owain ap Urien is fired by his tale and sets out to defeat the Black Knight. The rest of the story belongs to Owain, except for when, after he had been missing from the court for three years, Arthur and Gwalchmai and a band of warriors, with Cymon as their guide, set forth to find him. They eventually find him well and prospering in the Castle of the Fountain.

Cymric. Pertaining to Wales or sometimes more widely to British Celtic. The ancestor language and culture of Welsh, Breton, and Cornish.

Cymru. The land of comrades or of fellow-countrymen. It derives from the British *combrogos,* "compatriot." See **Cumbria** and **Wales.**

Cynddelig. [W] A member of Arthur's retinue who guides Culhwch in his quest for Olwen.

Cynddylan. [W] Son of Cyndrwyn, lord of Pengwern. He is mentioned in a seventh century elegy but also features in the later saga literature.

Cynghanedd. A metrical system of multiple alliteration and rhyme within every line of the Welsh strict poetic metre.

Cythrawl. [W] Identified as two primary existences, destruction and life.

Cywydd. A form of strict metre in Welsh poetry and a dominant form until the eighteenth century.

D

Da Derga's Hostel. [I] "The Destruction of Da Derga's Hostel" is one of the most popular tales of a king ignoring the prophecy of his fate. A hostel by the River Dodder owned by a Leinster chieftain, it is the place to which Conaire Mór, the High King, travels in spite of warnings of impending doom on the way. He contrives to break all his taboos (*geis*). The hostel is besieged by Conaire's enemies. Although Conaire and his men wreak great destruction before perishing, he is slain.

Dagda, The. [I] Father of all the gods. His name signifies "the good god." He is also known as Eochaidh Ollathair (All-Father), as Aedh (Fire), and as Ruad Rofessa (Lord of Great Knowledge). He is also the patron god of druidism. He is the equivalent of the Dis-Pater, also identified in British tradition as Ceraunnos. He is visualised as a man clothed in rustic garb carrying a gigantic magic club, which, in Irish tradition, he drags on wheels. With one end of the club he can slay his enemies and with the other he can heal them. He has a black horse, Acéin (Ocean), and his cauldron, from the city of Murias, was one of the major treasures of the Dé Danaan. No man went away from it hungry. He also possessed a magic harp, once stolen by the Fomorii. With Ogma ad Lugh he set off in pursuit and recovered it.

After the defeat of the Tuatha Dé Danaan, it was the Dagda who allotted spiritual Ireland to his children, giving a *sídhe* to each of them. Only the love god was not allotted a *sídhe,* because the Dagda wanted Bruigh na Boinne, Aonghus Óg's palace, for himself. But Aonghus Óg tricked the Dagda by subtle wording into obtaining possession of the palace for eternity.

As the Dé Danaan departed to their underground *sídhe* (eventually to change, in the people's imagination, from gods to fairies), the Dagda resigned as their leader. A council was held at which his son the Bodb Dearg was chosen as leader. All accepted the decision except Manannán Mac Lir, who simply left the proceedings, and Midir the Proud, who started a war against the Bodb Dearg. In this war between the gods, the Fianna were enlisted on Midir's side. The Dagda no longer took any significant part in the affairs of Ireland.

Daireann. [I] Daughter of the Bodb Dearg and sister of Sadb. She falls in love with Fionn Mac Cumhail, but when he rejects her she gives him a cup of poison that drives him insane. The Fianna desert him but Cáilte persuades them to return when the madness passes. Daireann's sister, Sadb, becomes Fionn's lover and bears his son Oisín.

Damnonia. See **Dumnonia.**

Damona. Gaulish goddess. "The Divine Cow."

Dana. [I] Sometimes given as Danu and cognate with Anu. She is found in Welsh as Don. A mother goddess from whom the Tuatha Dé Danaan take their name. If her counterpart in the Welsh tradition is anything to go by, her husband was Bilé, god of death. The Dagda is her son. However, her husband is never mentioned in Irish tradition, although in some texts it is she, not Brigid, who is the mother of the children of Tuireann.

Dán Dírech. An ancient Irish poetical system equivalent to the Welsh Cynghanedd, a metrical system of multiple alliteration and rhyme within every line of the strict metre.

Dea Arduinna. Gaulish. She is shown seated on a wild boar and may be cognate with the Irish Flidhais, who ruled over the beasts of the forest and herded wild deer.

Dea Artio. Gaulish. Perhaps connected with Art, the Irish "bear."

Dechtiré. [I] Daughter of Cathbad the druid and Maga, daughter of the love god Aonghus Óg. She was mother of the hero Cúchulainn. At her wedding feast, celebrating her marriage to an Ulster chieftain, Sualtaim Mac Roth, a fly flew into her cup and she drank it. She fell into a deep sleep and was taken to the Otherworld, where the god Lugh Lámhfada became her lover and she bore him a son called Sétanta. She returns to Ulster, and Sualtaim accepts the child as his own. Sétanta eventually is given the name Cúchulainn.

De Excidio et Conquestu Britanniae. Attributed to Gildas (ca. A.D. 500–570). "On the Ruin and Conquest of Britain," a contemporary account of the Anglo-Saxon conquest of Britain that mentions the annihilation of the Celtic populations in those areas that became England. The work also speaks of the mass migration of British Celts to other lands. Arthur Wade-Evans makes an assertion, echoed by some other scholars, that *De Excidio* was not written by Gildas but by an anonymous monk born in the year of the battle of Badon (ca. A.D. 518) and designated "Auctor Badonicus."

Deirdre. [I] Deirdre of the Sorrows. Daughter of Felim Mac Dall, a chieftain of Ulster. Cathbad cast her horoscope at birth and foretold she would become the fairest of all women in Ireland. On hearing this the Ulster king Conchobhar Mac Nessa insists that she will marry him when she comes of age. However, the horoscope adds that because of her only death and ruin would come on the land.

When she grows to marrying age, she finds she is not in love with the elderly Conchobhar but with Naoise, son of Usna, a hero of the Red Branch. They elope, with Naoise's two brothers as companions, and flee to Alba. The years go by and Conchobhar sends Fergus Mac Roth to them, saying that he has forgiven them. Deirdre foresees their doom but Naoise believes that he can trust Fergus Mac Roth. They return to Emain Macha, the capital of Ulster.

Conchobhar gives the order to attack the hostel of the Red Branch where they are staying, and Naoise and his brothers are killed. Deirdre is now forced to wed Conchobhar and remains his unwilling wife, never smiling, for a year. Angered, Conchobhar gives her to Eoghan Mac Durthacht, who was the warrior who killed Naoise. With her hands bound to prevent her escaping, Deirdre contrives to throw herself from Eoghan's chariot and dash her head against a rock, which kills her. From her grave a pine grows and from Naoise's grave grows another pine. They intertwine over the graves and nothing can part them. Deirdre's story is one of the great love stories from the myths.

Delbchaem. [I] Fair shape. Daughter of Morgan, king of the Land of Wonder, and his wife, Coinchend, a terrible warrior woman. Imprisoned by her parents in a tower, she is rescued by Art, son of Conn, who slays her parents and takes her back to Ireland to wed.

Deluge. The story of the Great Flood occurs in the legends of many lands. We find the world destroyed and a human being who has survived through the good will of a god. The story of Noah, the most famous of these tales, is predated by the Babylonian tale of Utnapishtim, told in the epic of Gilgamesh. In Hindu mythology, Vishnu appears to Manu, the first man, and warns him of the coming flood. In Greek myth, the story of Deucalion, son of Prometheus, parallels that of Noah, with Deucalion and his wife, Pyrrha, being saved to repopulate the world. In Irish myth we also find a story of a deluge. It has been argued that Christian missionaries were responsible for introducing the story into Irish tradition. Certainly they embellished the story, but it is arguable whether we have simply another parallel flood tale. The Irish story does have some unique qualities in that it lists four survivors outside of the Hebrew Ark who escape the flood. Most notable is Fintan, who turns himself into a salmon to escape destruction.

Derbhorgill. [I] Daughter of a king of Lochlann. She is given to the Fomorii in lieu of tribute, but Cúchulainn rescues her and she falls in love with him. She follows him adoringly in the shape of a swan. Cúchulainn is out hunting with a companion, Laoghaire, when swans fly overhead. Laoghaire casts a slingshot that brings down Derbhorgill. Cúchulainn sucks the stone out of the wound and heals her, but now united by blood, he and Derbhorgill cannot wed. Cúchulainn gives her to Laoghaire to wed.

Dési. [I] Sometimes given as the *decies*. A clan of Bregia in the province of Mide. The clan features in the tale "The Expulsion of the Dési," which is stylistically dated to the third century by Professor Kuno Meyer. For disfiguring Cormac Mac Art, Aonghus of the Terrible Spear and his tribe, the Dési, are expelled from their lands. Some settle in Munster, the rest are pursued from Ireland and, after a voyage of many adventures, settle in Dyfed in Wales. The Dési settlement is a historical one. There is an Ogham inscription, surviving in the Carmarthen Museum, dated to the sixth century A.D. It is to Voteocorigas, a Dési ruler, who is believed to be the Voterporius whom Gildas attacks as a tyrant.

Dian Cécht. [I] The god of medicine. After Nuada lost his hand at the first battle of Magh Tuireadh, Dian Cécht supplied him with a silver hand. Miach, Dian Cécht's son, proved a better physician by eventually supplying Nuada with a flesh and blood hand. Miach actually did an eye transplant, replacing a human eye with that of a cat. In jealousy, Dian Cécht slew his son. Among the Brehon law tracts is one called "The Judgments of Dian Cécht," relating to the practise of medicine, which Professor Binchey dates as early as the sixth century A.D. [*Eriu,* Vol. XX].

Diarmuid. [I] There are three notable Diarmuids in Irish myth: a king whose wife, Bec Fola, visits the Otherworld; a son of Fergus Cearbaill who is cursed by St. Ronán; and, lastly, most famous of all, is Diarmuid Ua Duibhne (Of the Love Spot), the most handsome warrior of the Fianna. Gráinne, who is about to wed Fionn Mac Cumhail, persuades Diarmuid to elope with her and thus begins the most famous chase, "The Pursuit of Diarmuid and Gráinne," which lasts sixteen years. While Diarmuid is not exactly in love with Gráinne at the start, he does grow to love this capricious woman of the myths. When the love god Aonghus Óg and the High King eventually persuade Fionn Mac Cumhail to make his peace with them, Fionn still nurses a grudge.

Out hunting on Ben Bulben, Diarmuid meets his fate in the form of a magic boar. This is the child of Roc, Aonghus Óg's steward, by Diarmuid's own mother. Diarmuid's father, Donn, learning of his wife's affair with Roc and discovering the child, kills it. Roc, however, transforms the dead child into a great boar and orders it to bring about the death of Donn's son, Diarmuid. The boar now fulfils its destiny by goring Diarmuid. Mortally wounded, only Fionn can save him. But he does not and Diarmuid dies.

Diarmuid's grandfather, the love god Aonghus Óg, takes the body to Bruigh na Boinne and each day he sends a soul into the body so that he might talk with Diarmuid. But this "resurrection" is only for a few moments each day.

Fionn eventually succeeds in his ambition to marry Gráinne.

Dinas Emrys. [W] A hill fort at Bedgelert associated with Vortigern, according to Nennius. The fort is named after Emrys (Ambrosius), who overthrew Vortigern. Certainly, although mainly constructed in the pre-Roman period, defences were built here in the fifth and sixth centuries A.D. It is now dominated by a twelfth century tower.

Dinnsenchas. [I] "The lore of prominent places." A comprehensive topography of Ireland and a guide to geographical mythology. It is contained in the twelfth century *Book of Leinster.*

Dinodig. [W] The land over which Lleu and Blodeuwedd ruled.

Dis Pater. The Gaulish god whose Celtic name is not revealed by Caesar. "The Gauls all claim to be descended from Dis Pater, and say that this is the teaching of the druids. For this reason they measure the passage of time not by days but by nights." This would indicate that the Dis Pater was not a purely chthonic deity but reigned in the Otherworld and was compared to the Roman Pluto. The idea of common descent from an ancestor was essential to Celtic ideology. The analogous god to the Dis Pater in Irish mythology is thought to be Donn, while others regard him as identical with The Dagda.

Dissull. [W] A giant, the hair of whose beard could create the only leash for the dogs in the hunting pack that Mabon controls in the hunt for Twrch Trwyth. Cai and Bedwyr overcome him and pluck out his beard.

Divination. The art of foretelling the future is an essential part of the Celtic myths. In most cases the hero or heroine has his or her fate foretold at birth. Such was the case of Deirdre, whose horoscope was cast by Cathbad the druid. More often than not it is in an effort to escape their fate that the protagonists set out on the adventures that will eventually lead them to the very fate they seek to avoid. In some cases, particularly in the Irish tales, the fate seems unlikely, but circumstances always contrive to make it so. The art of divination was widely practised in all Celtic societies and came in many forms—astrology, dreams, signs and omens from nature, and unusual occurrences. One form was the casting of yew wands inscribed with mystic words in Ogham. Divination was the prerogative of the druids, both male and female. See **Astrology.**

Diwrnach. [W] An Irishman, owner of a magic cauldron that Arthur manages to loot in a trip to Ireland.

Domnu. [I] Goddess of the Fomorii. The name seems to signify the abyss of the sea; the Fomorii, of course, translates as "undersea dwellers." Domnu appears to be a mother goddess and ancestor of all the Fomorii. The theme of many sagas is the struggle between the Children of Domnu (representing darkness and evil) and the Children of Dana (representing light and goodness).

Don. [W] Welsh equivalent of Danu, the "mother goddess." The fourth branch of the *Mabinogion* introduces the children of Don, who include Gwydion and Gilfaethwy, sons of Don, and Aranrhod, daughter of Don. She is given as the daughter of Mathonwy and is therefore sister of Math. She marries Beli, god of death, son of Manogan. Their children are Gwydion (science and light), Aranrhod (dawn goddess), Gilfaethwy, Amaethon (agriculture), Gofannon (smith-craft), Nudd or Lludd (sky god), Penardun (wife to Llyr), Nynniaw, and Peibaw. From Gwydion and his sister Aranrhod come Nwyfre (space), Lleu Llaw (the sun god), and Dylan (sea god), while Nudd's son Gwyn is the keeper of the Otherworld (Annwn).

Don is regarded as a bye form of Donwy, which occurs in Wales in the river names Dyfrdonwy and Trydonwy. The name is cognate with the goddess Danu in Irish and in the Rig Veda, where the name signifies "waters of heaven"—there are several rivers throughout the former Celtic world that bear her name. In England the rivers Don in Durham and Yorkshire are derived from her, while the name is also cognate with the Danube.

Donn. [I] There are several people who bear the name in Irish mythology, but the most important one is the god of the dead, whose abode was at Tech Duinn (House of Donn), which is placed on an island off the southwest of Ireland. He is said to be the eldest son of Midir the Proud. Another important Donn was the eldest son of Milesius, whose tradition is somewhat mixed with the god of the dead. His doom was foretold by the goddess Éire because he ignores her wish that Ireland be named after her. He drowns in the sea during an invasion. The father of Diarmuid Ua Duibhne was also named Donn, while the famous Brown Bull of Cuailgne is called Donn Cuailgne.

Dormath. [W] The hound of Gwyn ap Nudd. The name appears to mean "door of death."

Dragons. These mythical beasts, which are found in the mythology and folklore of innumerable peoples, likewise abound in Celtic mythology. Sometimes they guard palaces or fortresses, mostly they live at the bottom of lakes. In the story of "Lludd and Llefelys," a dragon has to be encountered, and Fraoch fought a dragon. Throughout the Celtic world dragons are a traditional motif and a dragon was displayed on the war banner of Macsen Wledig. This is thought to be the origin of the red dragon banner of Wales. Arthur's father, in later tradition, becomes Uthr Pendragon (*pen* meaning "head" or "chief").

Drem. [W] The seer who could see any happening from Cornwall in the south to Alba in the north.

Drudwyn. [W] Whelp of Greid. Chief of the pack of hounds that hunted Twrch Trwyth. Only Mabon, son of Modron, could hold this hound.

Druid. The druids not only presided at religious functions but were important figures in the Celtic world—advisers, judges, teachers, and ambassadors between rulers. The philologist Rudolf Thurneysen believed the word came from the roots *dru-vid,* "thorough knowledge." Others believe that the word came be coined from *draoi-id,* "oak knowledge." Whatever the meaning of the word, druids, who were both male and female, held a position of exceptional power in Celtic society.

It took up to twenty years to learn all the druidical laws and canons, according to Julius Caesar. They were accounted philosophers, natural scientists, and teachers and, more importantly, were able to give legal, political, and even military judgments. They were trained in "international law" as well as tribal law. They could prevent warfare between tribes, for their moral and legal authority was greater than that of chieftains or kings. Even the High King could not speak at an assembly before his druid had spoken.

Whereas most of our knowledge of Continental and British druids has come down to us through the distortions of the Greek and Latin writers, there is a corpus of native Irish writing describing the role of the Irish druids. The *Dinnsenchas* describes the various roles and offices of the druids. Whereas this was written by Christian monks, and so contains a Christian veneer and outlook, there are many similarities to the eastern Zen masters. Their role in Celtic mythology seems confined as masters of the supernatural arts instead of as learned men.

While the druids of the Britons and the Continental Celts seemed to observe the strict prohibition against committing anything to writing, it can be observed in the Irish myths that the druids are always writing things down in Ogham on wands of wood.

From the myths we find that the Irish druids had a tonsor, as did the early Celtic Christian monks. They cut their hair in a mystic figure called *airbacc Giunnae* (perhaps, "fence cut of the hair")—a tonsor running from ear to ear, instead of the circular form on the crown of the head. The Celtic monks followed this form, which became a point of dispute with Rome, and the Roman tonsor eventually replaced the Celtic one.

Druids have long been the subject for myth making, from the time of the Latin writers, who were not exactly sympathetic to the Celts or the druids, until the nineteenth century romantic revival, which accorded all manner of weird and wonderful powers to the druids. Latin writers maintained that the druids were practitioners of human sacrifice, with particular reference to the Celts of Gaul. Cicero, Dionysius, and Pomponius Mela recite human sacrifice stories ad nauseam, which were taken up by such early Christian leaders as Tertullian, Augustine, and Lactantius. However, it must be pointed out that there is no native tradition of this. One would have thought that if there had been some hint of such a tradition then the Christian scribes would have undoubtedly seized upon it in an effort to denigrate the older religion and its practices, as they did with the story of Cromm Cruach, an idol who demanded sacrifice but who is portrayed as an aberration and not the norm in Celtic society.

The transition of moral and legal authority from the druids to the "saints" of the early Celtic Christian Church was an easy one. No martyrs are recorded. The answer seems to rest in the fact that the early "saints" *were* druids and that the new religion was seen simply as an extension of the old one. Illtyd, for example, is described in an early *Life of St. Samson* as "a most wise Magus Druid and a fore-knower of future events." Taliesin makes the point that the druids believed in "Christianity" before it was brought to the Celts by missionaries. In others words, the doctrines of the druidic religion were little different from those of the new one.

Drunemeton. A place in Galatia referred to by Strabo. The name means "sanctuary of oaks," a religious gathering place for the Galatian druids.

Dubh. [I] Wife of Enna and a druidess. When Enna was having an affair, she drowned her rival by magic. Enna slew her in revenge with a slingshot and she fell into a pool that became Dubh's pool—*Dubhlinn,* now the more popular name given to Ireland's capital city. The usual name in Irish, however, is Baile Atha Cliath, the town of the hurdle ford. In early times an artificial ford of hurdles was constructed across the River Liffey around which the city was built.

Dubhthach Doéltenga. [I] A warrior of the Red Branch who is described as "a man who never earned the thanks of anyone." The name Doéltenga signifies "backbiter," and this is precisely his role, to stir up trouble. He is present at "The Destruction of Da Derga's Hostel" and at "Bricriu's Feast" to ensure dissension among the guests.

Dumnonia. As the Anglo-Saxons established themselves in the island of Britain and began to push the native Celtic inhabitants westward, Dumnonia emerged as an independent kingdom for several centuries. Its eastern border with the Saxons fluctuated almost yearly following the Celtic defeat at Charford in Hampshire by Cerdic the Saxon in A.D. 521. From Hampshire into Dorset the Celtic borders receded westward to Devon, where, for a time, they stabilised. Indeed, in the place-name Devon (Defnas) we have a vestige of the name of Dumnonia, and in that name is traced the Celtic aborigines—the Dumnonii. Mid-Somerset had been annexed by the end of the seventh century, and Exeter fell to the Saxons in A.D. 710. Gereint was then ruler and he was the recipient of a famous letter addressed to him by Bishop Aldhelm (ca. 640–709). Aldhelm, who became canonised, was bishop at Sherborne and wrote a denouncement of the Celtic Church, arguing for the new Roman doctrines. Over a hundred years before the poem *Y Gododdin* mentioned a Geraint "of the south" taking part in the raid against the Anglo-Saxons at Catterick (Catraeth) In 721–722, the Dumnonians rallied briefly and won a victory over the West Saxons at Camel. But defeats in 825 and 838, the latter at Hingston Down, near Callington, caused Dumnonia to disappear. The Celts were then confined beyond the Tamar into the kingdom of Cornwall.

Dún. A fortified place, a word common to all the Celtic languages, including continental Celtic. Dynas in modern Welsh. Lyon, in France, was named Lugh's fort, Lugdun(um), the "um" being a Latin ending. Each king or champion had a dún. Many of these fortresses had magical properties themselves. They sometimes revolved, or hid their gates, or held all manner of devices to trap the unwary.

Dunatis. Gaulish god of the fortified place.

Dyfed. The southwestern kingdom of Wales that, in Welsh myth, seems to occupy the same role as Munster in Irish myth. Like Munster it has a mysterious realm within or beside it. Annwn, the Otherworld, is just to the west of Dyfed. The island of Gwales, off the west coast of Dyfed, seems comparable to the House of Donn off the west coast of Munster. It suffers a magic enchantment as a revenge by Llwyd for the affront given to Gwawl when Pwyll wins the hand of Rhiannon.

Dylan Eil Ton. [W] "Sea, Son of the Wave." The yellow-haired son of Aranrhod and twin to Lleu. At the moment Aranrhod gives him birth, Dylan makes for the sea and receives the sea's nature, able to swim as well as any fish. He is eventually slain by his uncle Gofannon, a story that seems cognate with the tale of the death of Ruadán caused by Goibhniu. The story of Lleu and Dylan seems remarkably similar to the tale of Krishna and Balarama in Hindu mythology. In this tale it is Balarama who disappears into the sea.

E

Eachtra. [I] Adventure. A class of tales in mythology usually connected with a mortal's journey to the Otherworld. The *eachtra* became very popular in Irish literature in the fifteenth to seventeenth centuries.

Eagle of Gwern Abwy. [W] One of the oldest living creatures.

Easal. [I] King of the Golden Pillars who befriended the sons of Tuireann and gave them seven magic pigs that, when killed and eaten at the nightly feasts, were found alive the next day. Anyone eating of their flesh was never afflicted with disease.

Eber. [I] Though several people bear the name Eber, such as Eber Scot, son of Esru, son of Goidel, son of Scota, the more famous is Eber Finn. He was a son of Milesius who quarrelled with his brothers over the division of Ireland. He attacked his brother Eremon but was slain by him.

Edeirnion. [W] North Wales.

Ederyrn. [W] Son of Nudd and brother of Gwyn. He appears in the Red Book stories such as "Culhwch and Olwen," "Dream of Rhonabwy," and "Geraint, son of Erbin." He is a warrior of Arthur's and slays three giants. A catalogue of Welsh saints actually lists him as a bard, and his name seems to have survived near Holyhead (Anglesey) at Bodedyrn.

Efnisien. [W] Half brother of Bran, Branwen, and Manawydan, the children of Llyr. Son of Eurosswyd and Penardun. He always creates hostility, while his brother Nisien is a peacemaker. Efnisien features in the tragic tale of Branwen's marriage to Matholwch of Ireland.

Efrawc. [W] Father of Peredur.

Eiddig. [W] Used as the name for any jealous husband in medieval Welsh love poetry.

Eidoel. [W] A secret prison in Glini.

Éire. [I] The goddess who gave her name to Ireland. She became the wife of Mac Gréine, son of Ogma. When the Milesians landed in

Ireland and killed their husbands, Éire and her sisters went to them and asked that their names be given to Ireland. If so, then the Milesians would be given the land. Donn, however, treated Éire and her sisters with little respect, provoking a war between the Milesians and the gods. Donn perished in this war. Amairgen, however, promised the goddess that Éire would be the country's principal name. Banba and Fótla have also been used by Irish poets over the centuries as synonyms for the country. Éire remains the modern Irish name for Ireland, and in its genitive form this becomes Éireann, Erin, Erinn, etc.

Éirinn. [I] Given as the mother of the triune goddess of sovranty— Éire, Banba, and Fótla—by Delbáeth.

Eiscir Riada. [I] The traditional boundary line dividing Ireland into two halves, running along a broken ridge of low mounds from Dublin to Galway Bay. *Eiscir* = sand hill; *riada* = to travel by horse or chariot. From mythological times there are references to the two halves of Ireland, divided originally between Eremon and Eber Finn.

Eisirt. [I] The poet of Iubdan, king of the Faylinn, a diminutive people. It was Eisirt who persuaded Iubdan to go to Emain Macha, which resulted in the king being held prisoner there.

Eisteddfod. [W] "A session"—from *eistedd,* "to sit." A gathering involving contests in the arts and crafts, especially poetry and music. The first historical Eisteddfod is recorded in A.D. 1176, at Christmas, at Aberteifi (Cardigan), organised by Rhys, Justiciar of Deheubarth. It was proclaimed not only in Wales but in Ireland and Scotland. Such gatherings were held regularly in medieval Wales, and in 1568 Elizabeth I granted licences to the bards to distinguish them from vagabonds. In 1789 the Eisteddfod was revived on a regular basis, the prime mover being Thomas Jones of Corwen. A new period of its life opened in 1880 when the National Eisteddfod Association came into existence. The Eisteddfod is now the major national cultural festival of Wales.

Elatha. [I] A Fomorii king who had an affair with Eri, wife of Cethor. She gave birth to a son, Bres, who was to become king of the Dé Danaan. Disposed by the Dé Danaan, Bres sought Elatha's aid, and thus began the second battle of Magh Tuireadh.

Elcmar. [I] Husband of Boann. The Dagda sent him on a journey so that he could sleep with Boann. The Dagda weaved an enchantment that nine months passed as one day for Elcmar, and thus he did not know that Boann had borne a son to the Dagda. The son was the love god Aonghus Óg.

Elen. [W] Sometimes given as Helen. Daughter of Eudaf, from whom the kings of Cornwall claimed descent. Elen Lwddog (Elen of the Hosts) married Macsen Wledig and on his death devoted herself to Christian work, founding monasteries at Llanelen in Monmouth, at Llanrihidion in Llanelen, at Capel Elen, Penrhosllugwy, Anglesey, and many other places. Her children also distinguished themselves. Plebig became a disciple of Ninian and founded Llanbeblig, the first monastery in Wales; Owain ap Macsen founded a dynasty in south Wales; Demetus founded the dynasty of Dyfed; Leo founded the dynasty of Kent; Antonius went to the Isle of Man; and Cystennin ap Macsen has his tomb at Segontium. Her daughter Sevra married Vortigern, and their son Brydw was blessed by St. Germanus of Auxeree during his visits to Britain. In some traditions Elen appears as the wife of Myrddin (Merlin).

Elffin. [W] Son of Gwyddno, an unlucky youth who was fishing with his father when they caught a leather bag. Inside was the baby Taliesin, whom they decided to raise. The first poem Taliesin composed was in praise of Elffin, who grew in riches and won favour with King Arthur. Elffin boasted that his wife was the most virtuous in the land and that his bard was more skillful than any of Arthur's poets. Angry, Arthur's servants had Elffin flung into prison. Rhun is then sent to seduce Elffin's wife and bring back proof of her folly. But Taliesin helps Elffin's wife trick Rhun and he mistakes her maid for her. Arthur was angry that the test had not worked. Then he challenged Taliesin to come before him. Taliesin pouted his lips and put a finger to his mouth saying "Blerwm blerwm," whereupon all that Arthur's bards could utter was these words. Then he sang, suggesting he was Merlin, and there is a similarity to the song of Amairgen, in which Taliesin claims to have been part of eternity, being with God "on the fall of Lucifer into the depth of hell." Elffin is brought from prison, but his chains fall away at Taliesin's song.

Eli. [W] One of Arthur's two huntsmen, the other being Trachmyr.

Ellan Vannin. Isle of Man. See **Mannin.**

Elphin. [W] See **Elffin.**

Emain Abhlach. [I] Emain of the Apple Trees, an island paradise ruled by Manannán Mac Lir.

Emain Macha. [I] The seat of the kings of Ulster, which features prominently in the Red Branch Cycle. It is the best known of royal residences after Temuir (Tara). It is identified with Navan, a phonetic rendering of *'n Emain,* two miles west of Armagh, where there are still the remains of circular ramparts. It was founded by Macha Mong Ruadh, who is said to have marked out the boundaries of the city with her brooch and forced captive enemies to build it. A fascinating echo of the myths here is the townland of Creeveroe, which is the Anglicised form of Craobh Ruadh, the Red Branch, the élite warriors who were the bodyguards to the kings of Ulster who resided at Emain Macha.

Emer. [I] The wife of Cúchulainn. She was the daughter of Forgall Manach. Their courtship was stormy and all was not "smooth" in their subsequent relationship, for Cúchulainn was loved by many women, including Fand, the wife of the sea god. Just before Cúchulainn's death at the Pillar Stone he had a vision of Emer's body being tossed from the flaming ramparts of Emain Macha. He hurried to his fortress and found her alive and well—it was a warning of his own impending doom. Emer tried to persuade him to stay with her, but he set off on the road that would lead him to his doom.

Emrais. [W] Sometimes occurring as an alternative name for Snowdonia.

Enid. [W] The daughter of a chieftain fallen on evil days who is wooed by Geraint. He doubts her loyalty to him and treats her spitefully, but in bitter tests she proves her love and loyalty. She is best known to the English-speaking world in Tennyson's "Enid."

Englyn. [W] A Welsh verse in strict metre in three or four lines with one rhyme. Since the thirteenth century most *englynion* use the four-line system.

Eochaidh. [I] The name signifies "horse," and it is argued that the English word "jockey" comes from this word, which is pronounced "y'ockey." No less than fifteen major characters named Eochaidh appear in the Irish myths, including Eochaidh Mac Erc, a king of the Firbolg whose daughter was Tailtu and who was defeated by the Dé Danaan at the first battle of Magh Tuireadh. There was Eochaidh Airemh, the High King who outwitted Midir the Proud to retain his wife Étain, the daughter of Etar, journeying to the Otherworld to rescue her. Then there was Eochaidh Allmuir of the

Dési, who fought seven battles with Cormac Mac Art before his clan was forced into exile because of the action of Aonghus of the Terrible Spear. There was also a king of Leinster who married the daughter of the High King Tuathal Teachtmhaire (A.D. 130–160) but wanted to marry her younger sister. He pretended that his first wife had died and married; when the two sisters found out what had happened they died of shame. Tuathal went to war with Eochaidh and forced him to agree on an annual tribute called the Bóramha. To exact the tribute once in a reign was a point of honour with a High King. The last to do so was Brían (1002–1014), who became known as Brían Bóramha, Anglicised as Brian Boru.

Eoghan. [I] There are four Eoghans who appear in Irish myths. One of them appears as a king of Connacht who is killed by Ulster warriors and buried on the Connacht border, facing Ulster, so that he could protect the kingdom from attack. The second is a king of Munster whose story resembles that of Art. There is Eoghan Mór, the true name of Mug or Mag Nuadat, king of Munster, who forced the High King Conn to split Ireland into two. He then ruled Mug's Half, the southern half of Ireland. He was eventually defeated and slain by Conn. The most famous was Eoghan Mac Durthacht, a champion of the Red Branch, who slew Naoise and his brothers at the request of Conchobhar Mac Nessa. Conchobhar gave him Deirdre, but she threw herself from his chariot and killed herself.

Epona. "The Divine Horse." One of the more important Gaulish deities, winning favour with the cavalry of the Roman army stationed in Gaul. She may be cognate with Edain Echraidhe in Ireland. She is, in fact, the only Celtic goddess known to have been worshipped in Rome. [See "Le mythe d'Epona," Henri Hubert, *Mélanges linguistiques* offerts à M.J. Vendryes, Paris, 1925.]

Erechwydd. [W] Sometimes Yrechwydd. An unlocated kingdom in sixth century A.D. north Britain.

Eremon. [I] Sometimes given as Heremon. The first Milesian king of Ireland. He was the eldest of the surviving sons of Milesius. Amairgen the druid decreed that he should rule Ireland. His brother Eber refused to accept this and the brothers fought. Eremon slew Eber.

Ergyng. [W] Herefordshire, west of the Wye.

Eryri. [W] Snowdonia in Gwynedd.

Esus. A Gaulish god whom Lucan refers to as "uncouth Esus of the barbarous altars." According to the Romans, sacrifices were made to Esus, the victims being suspended from trees and ritually wounded. Esus appears in the guise of a woodcutter on a relief dedicated to Jupiter, ca. A.D. 14–37, rediscovered in 1711 under the choir of the Notre Dame cathedral in Paris. A similar relief of the same period was found at Trèves.

Esyllt. [W] "Of the white neck." More commonly given as Iseult or Isolt. See **Trystan.**

Étain. [I] There are several Étains in Irish myth, ranging from the wife of Ogma, daughter of Dian Cécht, to the daughter of Olc Acha the Smith, who is the mother of Cormac Mac Art. The most famous Étain was the daughter of Ailill of Echraidhe. Midir the Proud fell in love with her and asked his foster son, the love god Aonghus Óg, to make the arrangements. Aonghus Óg had to perform three tasks before Ailill allowed her to go to Midir. Fuamnach, Midir's first wife, became jealous of Étain and turned her into several things, a pool, a worm, and then a fly, in order to destroy the marriage. She caused a strong wind that blew the fly away and, after seven years, she came to the palace of Aonghus Óg. The love god recognised Étain and went to fetch Midir. But Fuamnach sent another wind. Blown across the generations, the fly fell into the cup of the wife of Etar, a champion of Conchobhar Mac Nessa, and she drank it and became pregnant. The daughter was called Étain and she was married to the High King Eochaidh Airemh. Eventually Midir found her and returned her to the Otherworld. But Eochaidh forced Midir to give her up, and she returned to live with him and gave birth to a daughter, Étain Óig. It was Étain Óig who became the mother of Mess Buachalla.

Ethlinn. [I] Daughter of Balor of the Evil Eye. Because of a prophecy that he would be killed by his grandson, Balor confined her in a tower. However, Cian, the son of Dian Cécht, the god of medicine, manages to enter the tower. Ethlinn bears a son, whom Balor orders to be drowned. The child is saved and fostered by Manannán Mac Lir. The child is Lugh Lámhfada and he fulfils the prophecy by destroying Balor.

Ethné. [I] There are several women named Ethné in Irish mythology, among them the daughter of Roc, the steward of the love god

Aonghus Óg. A Dé Danaan chieftain attempted to rape her, and as a result she became pure spirit. She lost her Veil of Invisibility, which not only hid Dé Danaans from mortals but gave them entrance into the world of immortality. Thus she was consigned to wander the earth listening to the sounds of the Dé Danaan kindred, disembodied voices in the air, searching for her in vain.

Ever Living Ones, The. A synonym for the gods of the Tuatha Dé Danaan.

Evnissyen. [W] See **Efnisien.**

Evrawc. [W] See **Efrawc.**

Ewais. [W] Sometimes Euas. A district in north Gwent.

Excalibur. See **Caliburn.**

F

Fachtna. [I] There are several of this name but the most famous is the king of Ulster who married Nessa, daughter of Eochaidh Sálbuidhe. Conchobhar Mac Nessa was brought up as his son, although the tradition has it that he was the natural son of the druid Cathbad, who had an amorous affair with Nessa.

Fand. [I] The Pearl of Beauty, wife of the sea god Manannán Mac Lir. When Manannán left her, she was attacked by three Fomorii warriors. Her brother-in-law sent her sister Lí Ban to bring Cúchulainn to the Land of Promise to protect her on condition that Fand would reward him by becoming his lover. Cúchulainn arrives, defends Fand from her enemies, and becomes her lover. He then returns to Ulster, where Emer, his wife, finding out about the affair, attempts to kill Fand when she makes an assignation to see Cúchulainn again. Manannán arrives and demands that Fand choose between him and Cúchulainn. She chooses her husband and Manannán shakes his cloak between Fand and Cúchulainn, thus ensuring they will not see each other again.

Fasting. The ritual fast, in Irish *troscad,* or hunger strike, frequently occurs in the sagas and myths. It is an ancient custom laid down by law as a means of compelling justice and establishing one's rights. It has a parallel in the Hindu practice of *dharnia.* In Welsh the *ymprydio* (fast) held the same intent. The person wishing to compel justice would notify the person complained against and would then sit before the door and remain without food until the wrongdoer accepted the administration of justice. The hunger strike or fast as a means of political protest has remained part of the Irish tradition into modern times.

Faylinn, The Kingdom of. [I] A country of diminutive people to whom even dwarfs appear as giants. It was ruled over by Iubdan and Bebo.

Féis. [I] A festival. The word also occurs in Manx and Scottish Gaelic.

In the Irish sagas there were three great festivals: Féis Temrach (Tara), Féis Cruachan (Croghan), and Féis Emna (Emain Macha). The gatherings at Tailltenn, Tlachtga, and Uisneach were fairs rather than festivals. The Irish also differentiated between the religious festivals, those of Imbolg or Brigid (February 1), Beltaine (May 1), Lughnasadh (August 1), and Samhain (November 1).

Female Champions. In early Celtic society women had an equality of rights with men, being able to be elected to any office, inherit wealth, and hold full rights of ownership under law. Many prominent female warriors or champions are to be found in the myths and sagas, from the grotesque Coinchend to the more attractive Scáthach and her sister Aoife. Credne was the female champion of the Fianna, while in another tale there emerge two female warriors named Bec and Lithben. Famous was Medb of Connacht, who led her armies in the Táin war. She was no mere symbolic leader, for she slew the hero Cethren with her spear. Scáthach ran a martial arts academy and taught many of the champions of Ireland, including the most famous of them all, Cúchulainn. The deities of death and battles—such as Mórrígán, the triune goddess—are invariably female.

In ancient history warrior queens appear among the Celts, including Cartimandua, the "sleek pony," queen of the Brigantes in Britain. Most famous of all was Boudicca (Boadicea to the Romans) of the Iceni, who rose against Roman rule in A.D. 60 and came close to driving them back into the sea. Her name means Victorious (in Irish *buadach,* in Welsh *buddogal).* Irish history abounds in such leaders as Ébha Ruadh Ní Murchú, Máire Ní Ciaragáin, and the famous Gráinne Ní Maillie.

Fenian Cycle. [I] Also known as the Ossianic Cycle. The tales are thought to date stylistically to the third century A.D. and concern the deeds of Fionn Mac Cumhail and his Fianna. The first bold synthesis of the eight major parts of the cycle into a cohesive whole appeared in the twelfth century tract *Acallamh na Senórach* (Colloquy of the Ancients). The Fenian Cycle, next to the Red Branch Cycle, is one of the longest compositions and became very popular with the ordinary people in Ireland during the medieval period. It is argued that the Arthurian sagas derived their themes and embellishments from these tales.

Ferdia. [I] The friend of Cúchulainn who grew up with him and was taught the martial arts under Scáthach with him. During the Táin war he took the side of Ailill and Medb but tried to avoid open conflict with Cúchulainn. Medb goaded him into single combat. After this, the greatest combat of all, Ferdia is slain by his friend. Disheartened by his act, Cúchulainn falls exhausted while the victorious Connacht army pours across the ford he has guarded so well, rejoicing with war songs.

Fergus. [I] There are at least ten personages named Fergus (sometimes given as Feargus) in Irish myth, but the most famous of them all was Fergus Mac Roth, who was king of Ulster, succeeding his brother Fachtna Fathach. He was in love with his brother's widow, Nessa, who promised to marry him if he gave up the throne for one year to her son Conchobhar. Fergus did so and then found himself betrayed, with Conchobhar clinging on to the throne after the time had come to return it. At first, Fergus serves Conchobhar, then after Conchobhar's betrayal of Naoise, he goes off into exile in Connacht.

When Ailill and Medb led the men of Connacht against Ulster in the Táin war, Fergus accompanies them with other dissident Ulstermen. It is Fergus' strategy that almost wins the day, until Cúchulainn reminds him of a personal oath, which forces Fergus to leave the battlefield, ensuring the defeat of the Connacht army. Tradition has it that it was Fergus who first set down the story of the Táin.

Fianna, The. [I] Popularly called the Fenians. A band of warriors guarding the High King of Ireland, said to have been founded in 300 B.C. by Fiachadh the High King. They consisted of twenty-five battalions. They were a military élite, and scholars suggest that it was from the Fianna that the later concept of the Arthurian Knights of the Round Table was derived. See **Knights.**

Fidchell. [I] "Wooden wisdom." An ancient Irish board game said to have been akin to chess in which a piece, known as a king, attempts to escape to the side of the board while the opposing player attempts to prevent this. It was played extensively by the gods as well as the heroes. It was a game said to have been devised by Lugh, the god of arts and crafts. In Welsh myth the game *gwyddbwyll* has the same meaning and is obviously the same game.

Filidh. [I] A class of poets, sometimes referred to as filí. Their duties included being learned in history, genealogy, as well as literature. They were honoured and respected in ancient Irish society and seem sometimes akin to Brahmins. The Brehon Laws note that it took a filidh twelve years of study to qualify.

Fin. Manx equivalent of Fionn Mac Cumhail.

Findbhair. [I] "Fair eyebrows." A daughter of Ailill and Medb who fell in love with Fraoch and helped him kill the water demon or dragon. She was offered to Ferdia by her parents in order to coax him into single combat with Cúchulainn during the Táin war.

Finegas. [I] A druid who taught Fionn Mac Cumhail. It was actually Finegas who caught the Salmon of Knowledge and gave it to Fionn to cook. Fionn burnt his thumb while cooking it and sucked the burn, thus acquiring knowledge. Finegas, realising that he was not destined to eat of the Salmon of Knowledge, gave it to Fionn to eat.

Fingal. Scots equivalent of Fionn Mac Cumhail. This form was made famous by MacPherson in his *Ossian* and by Mendelssohn with his overture movement "Fingal's Cave," which was not inspired by *Ossian* but rather by a visit to Fingal's Cave in Scotland. The name is not actually cognate with Fionn, for Fingal means "fair foreigner." The name was also borne by a king of the Isle of Man called Fingal Mac Godred (1070–1077), a name demonstrating the intermarriage between Gael and Viking.

Finnbhenach. [I] The White Horned Bull of Connacht, born into the herd of Medb of Connacht. The bull was originally the swineherd of Ochall of Connacht and archrival of the swineherd of the Bodb Dearg. Finnbhenach considered it unseemly that he should be born into the herd of a woman and so transferred himself to the herd of Ailill, thus starting off the chain of events that led to the war of the Táin.

Fintan. [I] First appears as the husband of Cesair, the first "invader" of Ireland. He survives the Deluge by changing himself into a salmon. It is argued that Fintan, the Salmon of Knowledge, is actually a separate entity. The fish ate of the Nuts of Knowledge before swimming to a pool on the River Boyne. Finegas the druid caught him but gave him to Fionn Mac Cumhail to cook. Fionn burnt his thumb while cooking the fish and thus acquired wisdom.

Fionn. [I] While there are many named Fionn who emerge in the Irish sagas, the most famous is undoubtedly Fionn Mac Cumhail, often

Anglicised as Finn Mac Cool. He is one of the most celebrated heroes in Irish myth, and the stories related to him have been argued as the basis of many of the Arthurian tales, which were developed in the medieval period when the tales of Fionn and the Fianna were at their most popular.

His father was Cumal of Clan Bascna. He fell in love with Murna but was opposed by her father, a druid. He eloped with her but her father sends Goll of the Clan Morna after him. Goll kills him, but Murna bears his son Demna. The child is so fair that he becomes known as Fionn. He received his education from the druid Finegas, who catches the Salmon of Knowledge and gives it to him to cook. Fionn burns himself while doing so and sucks his thumb, thus acquiring knowledge. He set out on his adventures, killing Lia, lord of Luachtar, the keeper of the Treasure Bag of the Fianna. He saves the life of Cormac Mac Art, the High King, and is made head of the royal bodyguard, the Fianna. From then on there occurs a series of adventures involving hunting, fighting, sorcery, love, and passion. Fionn has many romances but it is with the goddess Sadb that he begets his famous son, Oisín (Ossian). In the story "Cath Fionntragha" (Battle of Fionn's Strand, which is in Ventry, Co. Kerry), Fionn overcomes Daire Donn, the King of the World, in one of the great military exploits of his career. This is described in a fifteenth century manuscript now kept in the Bodleian Library.

Accounts of Fionn's death vary. Some tales record he was killed by Aichleach while trying to quell an uprising among his own Fianna. Another version contains a typical Celtic motif; the tale concludes that Fionn is not dead but sleeping in a cave, waiting for the call to help Ireland in her hour of need. This is, of course, paralleled in the legends of Arthur of Britain.

Fionnbharr. [I] A Dé Danaan assigned to the *sídhe* of Meadha (Knockma, five miles west of Tuam). He took part in the war between Midir and the Bodb Dearg. His wife was Oonagh. As the memories of the old gods faded, they degenerated in folk memory as fairies, and Fionnbharr and Oonagh became king and queen of all the fairies in Ireland.

Firbolg. [I] The name signifies "bag men." They came to Ireland after the Nemedians and may represent a genuine pre-Goidelic population of Ireland. In some accounts it is said they descended from the Nemedian survivors who had fled to Thrace, where they became enslaved. The name was given to them because they were made to carry bags of earth from the fertile valleys to the rocky hills during their enslavement. They came to Ireland in three groups, although all three took on the general name Firbolg. They play no spectacular part in the myths.

Fomorii. [I] The dwellers under the sea. A misshapen and violent people who are the evil gods of Irish myth and whose centre appears to be Tory Island. They reached Ireland about the same time as Partholón and battled with him, the Nemedians, and the Tuatha Dé Danaan. Sometimes they succeed in their battles and sometimes they fail. They often appear with only a single hand, foot, or eye. Their power was eventually broken for all time at the second battle of Magh Tuireadh.

Fosterage. An important feature of Celtic society that lasted in Scotland until the eighteenth century. Boys entered fosterage at the age of seven, when they were sent to the household of a distinguished druid, chieftain, or, later, Christian monk. Here they received their education. They would live and study with them until they reached the "age of choice," which was seventeen for a boy but fourteen for a girl. During the period of fosterage they would be taught many subjects—music, literature, poetry, the art of warfare, the virtues of single combat, and the high value of honour—and pursue such recreational pursuits as board games as well as team games. They were also taught to be efficient in the hunt. In Christian times they were taught Latin, Hebrew, and Greek in addition to their own languages. Fosterage as a concept occurs both in the Irish myths and the Welsh myths.

Fraoch. [I] The hero of the *Táin Bó Fraoch*. One of the most handsome warriors in Ireland. He fell in love with Findbhair, daughter of Ailill and Medb. While she returned this love, he could not persuade her to elope with him, nor could he pay the bridal price. Ailill and Medb plot his death and suggest he swim in a lake where a monster dwells. He does so. The monster eventually attacks him, but Findbhair comes to his rescue and they manage to kill the creature. Fraoch is wounded but is nursed by the gods and goddesses and Ailill and Medb are persuaded to consent to the wedding of their daughter.

There is a second part to the tale in which Findbhair and her three children and cattle herds are carried off and Fraoch sets out after them in the company of Conall Cearnach. They overtake the kidnappers and rescue Fraoch's family and possessions.

Freagarthach. [I] The Answerer. The sword of the sea god Manannán Mac Lir.

Friuch. [I] The swineherd of Ochall Ochne of Connacht, who is in perpetual rivalry with Nár, the swineherd of the Bodb Dearg of Munster. They fight through many reincarnations before being reborn as Finnbhenach, the White Horned Bull of Connacht, and Donn, the Brown Bull of Cuailgne.

Fuamnach. [I] The first wife of Midir the Proud who grew jealous when he took Étain Echraidhe as his second wife. She turned her into a pool, then a worm, and finally a fly in order to part her from Midir. Then she raised a tempest that blew the fly/Étain away from Midir's palace. Aonghus Óg slew her and took her head to his palace at Bruigh na Boinne as a trophy.

G

Gabalgline. [I] The ancient blind seer of Clan Dedad who was consulted by Ailill and Medb about the prophecy connected with the debility of the men of Ulster.

Gabhra, Battle of. [I] Anglicised as Gowra. The last great battle in which the Fianna took part and in which they were exterminated. Said to be fought on the site of Garristown, Co. Dublin, the battle is full of melancholy grandeur and a fitting end to the Fenian Cycle. The High King Cairbre, trying to curb the power of the Fianna following the death of Fionn Mac Cumhail, provokes the conflict. The hero, Oscar, commands the Fianna and slays Cairbre, but is himself mortally wounded. Fionn himself returns from the Otherworld to mourn his grandson, while Oisín and Celta carry Oscar's body from the field on a bier.

Gae-Bolg. [I] Cúchulainn's famous "belly spear," which was given him by the female champion Scáthach, who taught him the martial arts. It made one wound when entering and opened into thirty barbs once in the body.

Gael. [I] See **Goidel.**

Gaiar. [I] A son of Manannán Mac Lir who had an affair with Bécuma, which caused her expulsion from Tír Tairnigiri, the Land of Promise.

Galahad. [W] Originally Gwalchafed, "Falcon of Summer." He became famous in the medieval versions of the Arthurian sagas as the only knight to find the Holy Grail. See **Grail.**

Galan Mai. [W] Equivalent of Beltaine, Welsh spring festival on May 1.

Galatia. The first Celtic state about which we have evidence of how it was governed. Galatia, an area in central Turkey, was settled by the Celts in ca. 275 B.C. There were three main tribal groups, the Tolistoboii, the Tectosages, and the Trocmi. The Tolistoboii settled the upper valley of Sangarios (Sakarya), in which the famous city of Gordium (now Polatli) stood; the Tectosages settled around Tavium and eastwards. The Trocmi settled along the banks of the River Halys (Kizirmak), with Ancyra (Ankara) as their chief settlement. Strabo records that each tribe had four septs, making twelve septs altogether, all of whom sent a total of 300 elected representatives to an assembly at Drunemeton. Elsewhere it is recorded that Pessinus was their chief city, in the territory of the Tolistoboii, so perhaps this was the same as Drunemeton ("the sanctuary of oaks"). The Galatian Celts issued their own coinage. Galatia remained independent for 250 years until on the defeat of Deiotaros II, the last king, Galatia became a Roman province (25 B.C.). Paul of Tarsus made Galatia famous in Christian terms by visiting the land of the Tolistoboii and staying in Pessinus between A.D. 40 and 50. He later wrote his famous "Epistle to Galatians." St. Jerome, staying in Ancyra (Ankara) in the early fifth century, reported that the Galatians still spoke a Celtic language that was similar to that spoken in Gaul, with which he was familiar. At what period the Celtic language of Galatia, its culture, customs, and historical traditions ceased to exist is difficult to estimate. The language was probably dead by the eighth century, when the earliest records of modern Turkish are to be found. There seems, within Turkish culture and the surrounding Greek culture, to be little trace of the seven centuries of Celtic occupation in the area.

Galicia. Northwest Spain. During the fifth and sixth centuries A.D., as the Anglo-Saxons began to push into Britain to carve England out of the former Celtic territory, British tribes began to migrate. The major migrations were to the Armorican peninsula—Brittany. Others settled in Celtic pockets elsewhere, such as Brittenberg on the Rhine, while more groups went to Ireland. Other tribal groups arrived on the northern seaboard of Spain, in Galicia and Asturias, settling among a Latin-speaking population.

The settlers were recognised at the Council of Lugo in A.D. 567 as constituting the Christian episcopal See of Bretoña, whose bishop, Mahiloc, signed the *acta* of the Second Council of Braga in A.D. 572. The settlers have a Celtic name for the area—Galicia—argued to be the same root as Galatia. But these Brythonic Celtic–speaking settlements in Galicia and Asturias were quickly absorbed and the Celtic Church influence, which they had imported, ceased when Roman orthodoxy was accepted at the Council of Toledo in A.D. 633. However, the See of Bretoña existed until at least A.D. 830.

Celtic influence in the area had disappeared long before the ninth century A.D. Asturias, with its capital at Léon (name from the Celtic Lugdunum), became the centre from which the liberation of Iberia from the conquest of the Moors began in the eighth century A.D. There are some identifiable signs of a Celtic culture in Galicia today; some words of Celtic origin have survived in the Galician language, which is a Romance language, deriving from the same Hispanic dialect as Portuguese. Musical expression in the area also has an echo of Celtic forms. These Celtic elements came from the fifth and sixth century settlements and not from the pre-Roman conquest period of Celtiberia.

Gálioin. [I] Fir Gálioin, one of three groups identified as people of the Firbolg.

Gall. [I] The oldest meaning of the word was a person from Gaul. In subsequent usage, in Irish, Manx, and Scots Gaelic, it became the word for a stranger or foreigner.

Gallia Cisalpina. A Celtic country between the Alps and the Appennines, along the Po Valley. A confederation of Celtic tribes (including the Bituriges, Arverni, Senones, Aedui, Ambarri, Carnutes, Auelerci, Insurbres, and Taurini) had established themselves in the Po Valley by the sixth century B.C. Livy records their "invasion myth" in that they were led by Bellosvesos ("he who can kill"). They defeated the Etruscans in battle, particularly in 474 B.C. at Ticino. On July 18, 390 B.C., they defeated the Romans at the River Allia and went on to take Rome itself. The story is almost a part of Latin mythology.

By 349 B.C. the Celts were still ranging south as far as Apulia. Titus Livius, better known as Livy (59 B.C.–A.D. 17), grew up at Patavium (Padua) in the country of the Celts. His family were settlers during the aftermath of the Roman conquest of Cisalpine Gaul. His *Ab urbe condita libri* (History of Rome from its Foundation) is fabulous and epic, and unlike most Latin histories. Camille Jullian has suggested that it is made up of Celtic traditions, which Livy would have known well from his childhood. There is one episode concerning Marcus Valerius Corvus (Corvus = *crow*) that bears a remarkable likeness to an episode in the *Táin Bó Cuailgne.*

The Celts of northern Italy were continually at war with Rome, allying themselves with the Etruscans and Sabines, with Pyrrhus of Epirus, and later with Hannibal of Carthage. In 237 B.C. the Romans seized the Senones' territory at Picenum and began to colonise it. In 225 B.C. a Celtic army was defeated at Clusium, 85 miles north of Rome, which allowed the Romans to begin a full-scale invasion of Cisalpine Gaul during the following year. The battle of Clastidium was a major defeat for the Celts in 222 B.C. The Cisalpine Gauls made an alliance with Hannibal, and 10,000 warriors joined him during his campaign against Rome in 218–207 B.C.

With the defeat of the Carthaginians, in 198 B.C., Rome began a systematic conquest of Cisalpine Gaul. In 192 B.C. the chieftain of the Boii, the last major Celtic tribe, surrendered to the Romans and was slaughtered with his family to provide entertainment for one of the consuls. In 173 B.C. there occurs the last record of conflict between the Celts of the Po Valley and Rome. Rome began a systematic colonisation of the entire area. In 82 B.C. Cisalpine Gaul was declared a Roman province. Celtic was spoken in the area into Imperial times, and numerous Celtic place-names have been left throughout northern Italy.

Importantly for Latin literature, many Cisalpine Celts began to write in Latin. As early as the first century B.C. Rome recognised a school of Celtic poets from Cisalpine Gaul. A leading figure was Gaius Valerius Catullus (ca. 85–54 B.C.). His name is derived from *catos*—clever. Another member of the school was a Cenomani poet, Helvius Cinna, who actually introduced a number of Celtic words into his Latin. Furius Bibaculus (ca. 103–25 B.C.) was another member of the school whose work has only survived in epigrams. He refers to another Cisalpine Celtic poet, Valerius Cato. M. Terentius Varro (b. 82 B.C.) wrote among other things a war epic, *Bellum Sequanicum,* thought to have been about the conquest of his own people, the Sequani Celts.

In *Galli Transalpini,* Lucius Pomponius of Bononia (Bologna) satirises his fellow Celts—satire being a traditional Celtic literary form.

Perhaps the most famous of these Celtic writers in Latin was
Cornelius Nepos (ca. 100–ca. 25 B.C.), an Insubrean who wrote a
universal history, love poems, and biographical works. A Celt from
the Vocontii tribe was Trogus Pompeius (ca. 27B.C.–ca. A.D.14),
who also wrote a universal history in 44 books entitled *Historiae
Philippicae.* T. Catius, another Insubrean of the period, wrote on
philosophy. More contentious was Publicus Vergilius Maro, the
famous Virgil (70–19 B.C.). He was born and raised in Cisalpine
Gaul, but whether he was a Celt or merely of a Roman settler family
is not certain. According to Professor H. D. Rankin, "We need not
deny Celtic influences in the background of Virgil's life." His
poems are rooted in the life of the Po Valley Celts.

Certainly Livy, much influenced by Celtic cultural traditions,
was of a settler family. Episodes from Livy's history compare fas-
cinatingly with episodes in insular Celtic myth. [A critical
examination of the contribution of the Celts to Latin literature is
given in *Celts and the Classical World,* H. D. Rankin, Croom Helm,
London, 1987.]

Gann. [I] One of the five sons of Dela who led the Firbolg invasion.
Gann and Sengann divided the province of Munster between them.
They both also appear as Fomorii leaders fighting the Nemedians.

Garach, Battle of. [I] The final battle in the Táin saga, where the
armies of Ailill and Medb face those of Conchobhar Mac Nessa on
the Plain of Garach. It is here that the Ulster army defeats the
invading army of Connacht.

Gast Rhymri. [W] A dog whose cub hounds comprise the pack with
which Mabon has to hunt the Twrch Trwyd.

Gaul. Regarded as "the heartland" of the ancient Celts, covering
Switzerland, France, and Belgium. It is generally argued that the
Celts developed in the area around the headwaters of the Danube,
the Rhine, and the Rhône. All three rivers still retain their Celtic
names; the Danube is cognate with Don, Dana—the "mother
goddess"; the Rhine, from *renos*—"the sea"; the Rhône, from "road-
way river"; and even the Rhur retains its Celtic origin, from Raura,
along whose banks dwelt a Celtic tribe, the Raurici. The tributaries
of these rivers also retain Celtic names. Scholars believe that the
Celts were living in this region as an aboriginal population. Most
also believe in the "expansion" theory, that Celtic speakers moved
outwards at the start of the first millennium B.C. into northern

Italy, into Spain, into eastern Europe, and into the western fringes. The Greeks had established a trading colony at Massilia (Marseilles) in 600 B.C., making it into one of the great commercial centres of the Mediterranean world. In 125 B.C. the Romans saw an opportunity to interfere with this independent Greek city-state by offering military support to the Massilots against the surrounding Celts. The Romans conquered the Celtic tribes in this area and by 118 B.C. established their own colony at Narbo (Narbonne) and created a province called Gallia Narbonensis. It was later simply called "the province" and has remained Provence until modern times. Not only the Celts were absorbed into this part of the Roman Empire but also the Massilots.

It was not until 58 B.C. that the Romans seized an opportunity to enter Gaul proper. The Celtic Helvetii of Switzerland began one of the last great Celtic migrations westward at this time and Rome used the excuse to send an army into Gaul, under Julius Caesar, to turn them back into Switzerland. Caesar then used the opportunity to begin the conquest of Gaul. By 55 B.C. it was thought the Gauls had been defeated and Rome was in control. Caesar was able to launch two expeditions to Britain in 55 and 54 B.C. But in 54 B.C., during the winter, Gaul rose up in general insurrection against Rome. It was not until 51 B.C. that the last independent Celtic hill fort was destroyed. Nevertheless, insurrections continued in Gaul in 46 B.C., 44 B.C., 33–30 B.C., and 27–5 B.C., when Gaul was finally declared a Roman province.

The Celts of Gaul, pressed first by the Romans and then by the westward sweep of the Germanic tribes—particularly the Franks— finally disappeared, annihilated or assimilated. Only the peninsula of Amorica (the land by the sea, later to become Brittany), reinforced by Celtic migrations from Britain in the fifth and sixth centuries, retained its Celtic heritage. See **Gaulish** and **Gaulish Mythology.**

Gaulish. The language of Continental Celts, imperfectly known from inscriptions. The longest inscription in Gaulish was found in 1983 in L'Hospitalet du Larzac (Aveyron). It is written in Latin cursive on a lead tablet. [*Études celtiques,* vol. XXII, 1985.] Prior to this time the Coligny calendar (Musée des Arts, Lyons), dated to the first century B.C., was considered the most extensive document. Gaulish has been identified as similar to the Brythonic (British)

Celtic spoken during the Roman Occupation, from which Welsh, Cornish, and Breton derive. Close similarities can also be seen with Old Irish. For example:

GAULISH	OLD IRISH	ENGLISH
maros	mór	big
nertomaros	nertmar	powerful
senobena	senben	old woman
uxellos	uasal	high
vindomagos	findmag	fair/plain
vindos	fionn	fair/white

Gaulish was spoken throughout Celtic Europe, from what is now Belgium and France, through Switzerland and Northern Europe, Austria, Hungary, Czechoslovakia, and parts of the Balkans, to the Celtic state of Galatia in central Turkey. It is obvious that the people in these areas shared a common mythological tradition.

It is difficult to be specific as to when Gaulish vanished in Europe and Asia Minor. St. Jerome (Eusebius Hieronymous), during the fourth century A.D., spent some time in Ancyra (Ankara), capital of the Celtic Trocmi, and reported that the Galatians still spoke Celtic and likened it to the language of the Treveri (in Trèves, northern France). Jerome was not guessing, for he had also spent time among the Treverii. The Celtic language of Galatian probably vanished sometime between the fifth and eighth centuries A.D.

In the European areas in which the Celts settled, like northern Italy, the language seems to have vanished at a far earlier period.

In the area we now accept as "Gaul," modern France and Belgium, it is popularly thought that Gaulish vanished with the commencement of the Roman occupation. This is, of course, not so. Gaius Sollius Apollinaris Sidonius (ca. A.D. 430–ca. 480), bishop of the Arvenri, states that the leading families of Gaul were, in his day, still trying to throw off the "scurf" of Celtic speech, as he puts it. If the leading families of Gaul in the late fifth century A.D. were trying to distance themselves from speaking Celtic, then the language must have been pretty widespread among the ordinary people. Indeed, a considerable Celtic vocabulary has actually survived in modern French. See **Breton.**

Gaulish Mythology. Since the Gauls left no written literature, we cannot speak of their myths or religious attitudes with complete authority. What fragments we have, however, seem cognate with their insular counterparts whose culture has survived the millennia. With the gods of Gaul, unfortunately, we can only glimpse them through Greek or Roman eyes, especially the eyes of Lucan and Caius Julius Caesar, who tried to place Roman equivalents on them. Caesar refers to six gods, whom he equates with Mercury, Jupiter, Mars, Minerva, Apollo, and Dis Pater (Pluto). This unfortunate *interpretatio Romana* has merely confused their identity and functions, but some of them are clearly cognate with the gods of Britain and Ireland, Ogmios and Belenus, for example.

While the Irish and British Celtic "origin myths" have survived, we have no such myths about the origin of the Gauls. However, from Livy we can trace a story about the start of the Celtic spread through Europe. Livy, who was raised in Cisalpine Gaul, was undoubtedly recording a native Celtic tradition, and Henri Hubert believes his source was the Celtic writer Cornelius Nepos (ca. 100–ca. 25 B.C.). Livy says that the Celts were ruled by Ambicatos.

> Gaul was so fertile and populous that the immense multitude threatened to be hard to rule. So the King, being old and wishing to relieve his kingdom of its excess population, declared that he would send his sister's sons, Bellovesos and Sigovesos, who were energetic youths, to whatever country the gods should indicate by omens, and they could take as many men as they wished, so that no people should be able to resist their advance. The omens assigned the Hercynian Forests [central Germany] to Sigovesos, and to the more fortunate Bellovesos, the road to Italy.

Another Latinised Celtic historian, Trogus Pompeius, compared the Celtic migrations through Europe with the Roman *ver sacrum* (sacred spring), when, in times of emergencies, the overpopulated community expelled their members aged twenty years to go where they pleased and found new communities. The story of the early Celtic migrations through Europe was certainly accepted by the Celts of Cisalpine Gaul in Livy's time. It has become obvious that the fabulous and epic nature of Livy's histories, so unlike most Latin accounts, is full of Celtic traditions. It was first pointed out by Camille Jullian that Livy was born in Patavium (Padua) and grew up in Cisalpine Gaul among a Celtic population. One episode recounted by Livy, which he ascribed to an event in 345 B.C. during a campaign by the Romans against the Celts of northern Italy, is remarkably similar to an episode in the Irish epic *Táin Bó Cuailgne* in which the goddess of death and battles, the Mórrígán, in the form of a crow, attacks Cúchulainn, who has spurned her love. The crow, or raven, was the symbol of the Celtic goddess of death and battles. Livy has a crow attack a Celtic chieftain to protect a Roman and hide the Roman with its wings. Such examples could well indicate, on further research, that a strong case could be made for Gaulish traditions to be cognate with the Celtic traditions of Ireland and Wales that have survived in written form.

Gauvain. [W] Sir Gawain, a companion and fellow knight to Peredur (Perceval). While Gawain is best known through a Middle English poem, "Sir Gawain and the Green Knight" (written ca. 1370), the poem shows a strong Celtic source, though from Irish rather than Welsh. Written by an unknown poet, the story is a variation on part of "Bricriu's Feast" and its variants in Irish. It is regarded as the greatest single Arthurian legend in English and a masterpiece of Middle English writing. In the middle of a feast at Arthur's court a green giant on horseback bursts in and challenges the knights to chop off his head on condition that he be allowed to return the blow in one year. Sir Gawain accepts. Having chopped off the giant's head, the giant calmly picks it up and leaves. Gawain has to set out for the Green Chapel, where he is to present himself for the blow. He comes to a castle where he is entertained by Bercilak and his beautiful wife. The wife tempts Gawain. For two days he resists and then he accepts a gift of a green sash from the lady. Finally, at the chapel, the green knight strikes at his neck. Three times the axe descends; twice it is deflected (because twice he resisted the adulterous temptation), but the third time the axe nicks his neck because he accepted a gift from the lady. The green knight is Bercilak. The ruse is planned by Morgan le Fay, but Gawain has triumphed.

For the Irish version of the beheading game see **Uath Mac Imoman.**

Gawain. [W] See **Gauvain.**

Gawlgawd, Horn of. [W] Culhwch has to obtain it for Yspaddaden the Giant.

Gebann. [I] Father of Cliodhna, Irish goddess of beauty.

Geis. [I] See **Taboo.**

Geneir. [W] One of Arthur's warriors.

Geoffrey of Monmouth. (ca. A.D. 1100–1155). A Welsh cleric of Breton origin. His family appears to have followed William of Normandy into England but then established themselves in southern Wales. He was a cleric at Oxford and later became Bishop of St. Asaph in 1151. Among other texts, he wrote the *Historia Regum Britanniae* (History of the Kings of Britain), which is regarded as a founding text for medieval Arthurian saga.

Geraint. [W] He features in the rather sentimental love story as the lover who doubts the loyalty of Enid. It is thought he is based on the Dumnonian king who rode with the Gododdin to recapture Catraeth (Catterick) from the Anglo-Saxons, but he is not to be confused with the Dumnonian king (fl. A.D. 710) to whom Adhelm, bishop of Sherborne, wrote his criticism of the Celtic Church.

Giants. Giants occur in the myths and sagas quite frequently, and, indeed, some of the Celtic heroes and deities are referred to in the form of giants. Giant seems to be a Celtic metaphor for distinguishing a personage above the ordinary. In later legends Fionn Mac Cumhail is termed a "giant," while Olwen is the daughter of Yspaddaden the Giant.

Gildas. "The Wise." British Celtic saint (ca. A.D. 500–570). While he studied under St. Illtyd in southern Wales, he is thought to have been born either in the British Strath-Clòta (Strathclyde) kingdom or in Cumbria. He is accredited with writing *Epistola Gildae,* an open letter to rebuke the secular and ecclesiastical British Celts, and with *De Excidio et Conquestu Britanniae.* However, some scholars contest his authorship of *De Excidio,* claiming that a contemporary cleric, whose name is unknown, wrote it. Gildas is thought to have visited Ireland and then gone to Brittany, where he founded a monastery at Rhuys. In the twelfth century, the abbot at St.Gildas-de-Rhuys was Abelard. The tragic story of Abelard and Heloise is almost part of Celtic mythology itself. It has curious parallels to the Irish tale of Liadin and Cuirithir, surviving from a ninth century text. Gildas' work is a fascinating support to some Arthurian contentions. See *De Excidio et Conquestu Britanniae.*

Gilfaethwy. [W] Son of Don. He fell ill for the love of Goewin, daughter of Pebin, who was the current virginal foot holder to Math, son of Mathonwy. Gilfaethwy confided his feeling to his brother Gwydion. Gwydion promised to help him and went to Math and asked leave to go to Pryderi of Dyfed to ask for a gift of a herd of swine, which had been bestowed on him by Arawn, king of Annwn. Math, eager to own these magical beasts, agreed. Gwydion and Gilfaethwy went to Dyfed with ten companions. They came to Pryderi's court in the guise of bards, and Gwydion, after being feasted, offered to tell a tale. It was so good that Pryderi offered him anything in payment. He asked for the swine. Pryderi explained he was under a compact with Arawn not to sell or give them away until they had produced double their number in the land. Gwydion, using magic, presented an illusion of twelve magnificent horses and twelve hounds. Gwydion and Gilfaethwy make off with the swine. On the following day the illusion ceases and Pryderi, in rage, sets out to recover his property. Math, thinking Pryderi is invading his land, sets out to meet him. Only in times of war are the maidens allowed to abandon their task of holding his feet.

While Math departs with his army, Gilfaethwy seizes the opportunity to make an unwilling Goewin his wife. The dispute ends with a single combat between Gwydion and Pryderi and "by the magic and charms of Gwydion, Pryderi was slain." When Math returns he finds Gilfaethwy and Gwydion gone into exile. But they return. Math turns them into deer for a year, then swine, then wolves. Each year they return with a young one of the species, who is changed into human shape. At the end of this time they are deemed to have fulfilled their penance.

Gilla Stagshank. [W] The chief leaper of Ireland, who can leap across any distance. He is asked to help Culhwch in his quest.

Gilvarthwy. [W] See **Gilfaethwy.**

Giolla Gréine. [I] The daughter of a human father and a sunbeam. When told of her origins she jumped into Loch Gréine (lake of the sun), floated to Daire Gréine (oak grove of the sun), and died at Tuam Gréine (tomb of the sun).

Gíona Mac Lugha. [I] Son of the warrior-daughter of Fionn Mac Cumhail, he became a leader of the Fianna. But he was not a good leader, vain and selfish and lazy. His men laid down their weapons and refused to fight under him. Fionn eventually taught him how to become a good leader, and he did indeed become one of the Fianna's greatest champions.

Glas Ghaibhnenn. [I] The magic cow stolen by the Fomorii Balor of the Evil Eye and taken to Tory Island. Cian pursued and rescued it.

Glass Castle. [I] Conan's Tower. A tower of glass or crystal built by the Fomorii on Tory Island. The Nemedians stormed it and slew Conan Mac Febar, the Fomorii king. Balor of the Evil Eye is said to have imprisoned his daughter there. Glass towers tend to be often one of the sights encountered in the Irish voyage myths. In Welsh mythology Caer Wydyr, a glass castle, seems a synonym for the Otherworld.

Glewlwyd. [W] "Of the Mighty Grasp." A doorkeeper at Arthur's fortress.

Gluneu. [W] Son of Taran. One of the seven survivors of the ill-fated battle between Bran and Matholwch. Is Taran cognate with the Gaulish god Taranis and is there a similarity between him and "Etirun," which is recorded in Irish sources as a pagan god of the Britons?

Glyn Cuch. [W] The place where Pwyll encountered Arawn, king of Annwn (the Otherworld).

Glyn Rhosyn. [W] The spot where St. David lit the sacred fire after a ritualistic encounter with the druids, which bears a strong similarity to St. Patrick's encounter with druids and the lighting of a sacred fire at Tara.

Goddau. An unlocated kingdom in northern Britain during the sixth century.

Godeu. [W] A synonym for the "otherworld."

Gododdin, Y. The name of a poem ascribed to Aneurin in the sixth century. It contains the first literary mention of Arthur. It describes how the Gododdin tribe (obviously the Votadini of the Roman occupation), under their king Mynyddawg Mwynfawr, send 300 picked warriors south to retake Catraeth (Catterick) from the Anglo-Saxons. They all meet defeat and death. The capital of the tribe was at Dineiddyn (Edinburgh).

Gods. There is considerable confusion about the gods of the ancient Celts because of the fact that the myths were first set down by Christian monks who often altered things to fit their religious sensibilities. The Tuatha Dé Danaan are clearly the "immortals" of the world of Irish myths. In Celtic perception, the gods and goddesses are not creators of the people, they are the ancestors of the people. Caesar noted that the Celts regarded themselves as having descended from one central universal father. The gods, in fact, were ancient heroes, ancestors of the people, rather than their creators. In the lives of these "immortals" the lives of the ordinary people and the essence of their religious beliefs were mirrored. The gods and goddesses were subject to all the natural virtues and vices and were, therefore, totally human.

There are no hard-and-fast rules between gods and mortals—mortals can wound gods, and gods can die. J. A. MacCulloch [*The Religion of the Ancient Celts,* 1911, reprinted by Constable, London, 1991] put forward the following comparative table of possible cognates, which I have amended slightly for accuracy:

IRELAND	BRITAIN	GAUL
—	Anextiomarus	Anextiomarus
Anu	Anna	Anoniredi
Badb	—	Bodua
Bíle	Beli, Belinus	Belenos
Brigit	Brigantia	Brigantu
Bran	Bran	Brennus
Buanann	—	Buanu
Cumal	Camulos	Camulos
The Dagda	Cerunnos	Dispater
Dana	Don	—
—	Epona	Epona
Gobhniu	Gofannon	—
—	Grannos	Grannos
Lir	Llyr	—
Lugh	Lleu	Lugos
—	Mabon	Maponos
Manannán	Manawydan	—
—	Matres	Matres
Nemed	—	Nemetona
Nét	—	Neton
Nuada	Nudd/Nodons	—
Ogma	—	Ogmios
—	Silvanus	Silvanus
—	Taran	Taranis
—	Totatis/Tutatis	Teutates

This table can be improved on by more recent discoveries. For example, Ogma can also be identified in Britain as Ogmia.

Goewin. [W] Daughter of Pebin of Dol Pebin of Arfon. She is a virgin and foot holder to Math, son of Mathonwy. She is abducted and married by Gilfaethwy while Math is at war.

Gofannon. [W] Son of Don. His name bears a resemblance to the Irish Goibhniu (also Gobhniu), the donor of the Feast of Immortality and the divine smithy. It obviously derives from the same root—*gabha* in Irish and *gof* in Welsh mean smith. He slays his nephew Dylan and this seems cognate with the slaying of Ruadán at the hands of Goibhniu. He makes an appearance in the story of Culhwch and Olwen.

Gogigwr. [W] A doorkeeper at Arthur's fort, named with Huandaw and Llaesymin.

Goibhniu. [I] The smithgod. Founder of artistry and handicraft. He had two brothers, Cian and Samhan—again constituting the Celtic triune godhead. He could make a spear or sword by three blows of his hammer. He presided over the Otherworld feast of Fled Ghobhnenn, at which he served a special ale that rendered all who drank it exempt from disease and death. The word "smith" in all the Celtic languages has a common provenance: Irish, *gabha;* Scottish Gaelic, *gobha;* Manx, *gaaue;* Welsh, *gof;* Cornish, *gof;* and Breton, *gof.* In later Irish legend a figure called Góbhan Saer, the Wright, became a master mason and architect for the fairies.

Goidel. [I] Also given as Gaedhal and Gael. Son of Niul and Scota, daughter of the pharaoh Cingris. He is acclaimed as the progenitor of the Goidelic or Gaelic Celts (Irish, Manx, and Scots). In what seems to be a Christian embellishment, Goidel was healed by Moses, for his father had befriended Aaron during the Hebrew enslavement in Egypt. Goidel's son was Esru, whose son Sru was father or Eber Scot.

Goidelic. Usually given as the Gaelic language. The Q-Celtic branch of the Celtic languages spoken by the Irish, Manx, and Scots.

Golamh. [I] Original name of Milesius.

Golden Pillars, Kingdom of. [I] See **Easal.**

Goleuddydd. [W] Wife of Cilydd and mother of Culhwch. She is said to have gone mad and run into the forest to give birth to Culhwch. Knowing she was about to die, she had her grave measured and made Cilydd take an oath that he would not remarry until a briar with two heads grew from her grave. Only in the seventh years does such a briar grow and Cilydd takes another wife.

Goll. [I] The name means "blind of one eye" or "one-eyed," and therefore we meet several people of this name in Irish mythology, most of them unsavoury characters. We have the son of Garb the Fomorii, whose wife, Lot, has bloated lips in her breasts and four eyes in her back. His son was Cichol Gricenchos. Then there is Goll Mac Golb, ruler of Magh Mell, who abducted the wife of Fiachna Mac Retach. He was finally slain by Laoghaire Mac Crimthann, who rescued Fiachna's wife and married their daughter Dér Gréine (tear of the sun). But the most Goll of them all was Goll Mac Morna, leader of the Fianna before Fionn Mac Cumhail. He slew Fionn's father, Cumal, to gain leadership of the Fianna. He married Fionn's daughter, Cebha, and features prominently in the tales of the Fenian Cycle. Goll eventually slew Cairell, Fionn's son. He fled, was pursued, and was finally trapped by the Fianna. Refusing to surrender, he died after twelve days from lack of food.

Golwg Hafddydd. [W] "Aspect of a Summer's Day." Maid to Esyllt and lover of Kae Hir, a companion of Trystan.

Gonemans. [W] A warrior who trains Peredur.

Gorias, City of. [I] One of the four great cities of the Dé Danaan—Falias, Finias, Gorias, and Murias. It was from Gorias that Lugh brought his invincible sword.

Gorm Glas. [I] "Blue green." Conchobhar Mac Nessa's sword.

Gorsedd. A bardic gathering, thought to derive from *uerensed,* a high seat. In Welsh myth the Gorsedd of Arberth is mentioned and Taliesin is claimed as founding an Order of Bards of Britain. Edward Williams (Iolo Morganwyg) inaugurated a Gorsedd ceremony on June 21, 1792. In this he claimed to have revived the rituals of the druids in their nature worship. At Carmarthen, in 1819, the Gorsedd ceremony became an integral part of the Eisteddfod, in spite of criticism by scholars. Today, after two centuries, the Gorsedd Cymru has become, of itself, a historical tradition, presenting a unique and colourful national spectacle. In 1901 the Bretons inaugurated a Breton Gorsedd (Gorzez Breizh), and in 1928 the Cornish Gorsedd (Gorseth Kernow) came into being. In September 1971 it was agreed that the three Gorseddau—the Gorsedd of the Bards of the Isle of Britain—while retaining their independence in domestic matters, should recognise the supreme authority of the Archdruid of Wales.

Gortigern. [I] The language spoken by all mankind before the development of different languages. This is a parallel to the Tower of Babel story.

Grail. "The Holy Grail" is the cup that Jesus drank out of at the Last Supper. The quest for it features prominently in the Arthurian saga. The origin of the idea of a quest for this magical vessel lies in the original Celtic idea of the cauldron of abundance; one of the best examples features in the tale "The Spoils of Annwn." The mass of Grail literature, both ancient and modern, is enormous. The stories of Peredur, in the *Mabinogi,* is the most archaic form of the story. From Peredur comes Chrétien de Troyes' "Perceval" adaption and then Wolfram von Eschenbach's "Parzival." The main features of the later bowdlerisation of the Celtic myths is that Joseph of Arimathea caught some of Jesus' blood in the Grail at the crucifixion and carried it to Britain, where it was handed down from generation to generation. Galahad is the last descendent of Joseph and he is the noblest of Arthur's knights. He alone achieves the quest for the Grail and brings fertility back to the land. When he sees the uncovered chalice, he renounces the world and asks God to release him from his material existence. The story is best known from Malory's *Morte D'Arthur.*

Gráinne. [I] The daughter of Cormac Mac Art, the High King. She was promised to Fionn Mac Cumhail, who, though still a renowned warrior, had grown old at this time. On the night before the wedding, Gráinne speculated on which one of the younger, handsome Fianna warriors she could persuade to save her from marriage to an old man. Oisín was approached but refused. However, Diarmuid Ua Duibhne is beguiled by her and agrees to elope with her, having been placed under a *geis* by her to do so. Thus begins the famous "Pursuit of Diarmuid and Gráinne." They are pursued by an enraged Fionn and his Fianna. Diarmuid, who had been a friend of Fionn's, seeks to assure him that he has not slept with her, leaving subtle symbolic messages. Gráinne mocks Diarmuid for refusing to make love to her and eventually he does so. The pursuit lasts 16 years, until the love god Aonghus Óg intercedes and persuades Fionn to forget his anger. Diarmuid and Gráinne eventually set up residence close to Fionn at Tara (at Ráth Gráinne), where they have four sons and a daughter.

Fionn, however, still nurses thoughts of revenge, and Diarmuid is eventually slain by a magic boar, fulfilling the destiny ordained at his birth. Fionn could have saved his life but does not do so.

Gráinne at first swears vengeance and begins to train her four sons in skill with arms to kill Fionn. But Fionn woos her and bears her back to his fortress on the Hill of Allen as his bride. Gráinne is well drawn in the Irish myths, and is always consistent, as a wilful, ruthless, and passionate person, rather shallow and neurotic.

Grannos. Gaulish sun god and god of healing who, according to Dio Cassius, was invoked by the emperor Caracalla in A.D. 215. He was usually paired in Gaul with the goddess Sirona, whose name derives from the word for a star. Grannos could be cognate with the Goidelic word for sun—*grian.* He was invoked in Musselborough in England; in Auvergne, France, he is still remembered in a "nonsense chant" around harvest time. People dance around a harvest festival bonfire with a sheaf of corn, cut and set light to, while the chant is given: "Granno, my friend, Granno, my father, Granno, my mother."

Grec. [I] A Connacht warrior who rescues Cormac Mac Art, when a baby, from a pack of wolves.

Grey of Macha. [I] Liath Macha. One of Cúchulainn's two famous horses that were foaled at the same time as he was born. The other was the Black of Sainglenn. Before he went on his final battle foray, the Grey of Macha refused to be saddled and bridled by Cúchulainn and shed tears of blood. During the last fight the beast was wounded by Erc, king of Leinster, but still managed to kill fifty warriors with its feet, and thirty more with its hoofs before it died.

Grian. [I] A solar female deity. Her palace was at Cnoc Gréine at Pailis Gréine (Pallis Green), Co. Limerick.

Grianainech. [I] Synonym for the god Ogma, meaning "sunny countenance."

Gronwy Pedbyr. [W] Lord of Penllyn, lover of Blodeuwedd, wife of Lleu Llaw Gyffes. Their plot to murder Lleu fails and Lleu slays him.

Grúacach. [I] Often used as a term for an ogre or monster, also an enchanter or wizard. The name signifies hairy, long-haired, or mane.

Grudye. [W] Son of Muryel, one of the seven survivors of the battle between Bran and Matholwch.

Guinevere. [W] See **Gwenhwyfar.**

Gwalchmei. [W] "Hawk of May." One of Arthur's retinue who serves as a peacemaker between Trystan and March ap Meirchion. He was Arthur's nephew. He seems to have been transformed into Sir Gawain in the medieval sagas.

Gwales. [W] An island off the coast of southwest Wales (Grassholm) where the seven survivors of the war between Bran and Matholwch spent four score years on their journey back to the Island of the Mighty. They are oblivious of the passage of time until a forbidden door opens and allows them to continue their journey.

Gwawl. [W] "Light," son of the goddess Clud. The suitor of Rhiannon who is eventually overcome by Pwyll. His friend Llwydd takes revenge on Pwyll and Rhiannon for his ill treatment.

Gweddw. [W] Owner of a magic horse, Gwynn Mygdwn, the only horse that will bear Mabon.

Gwen. [W] "The White Swan," daughter of Cynwal Hundred Hogs. One of the most beautiful maidens in Britain.

Gwenhwyach. [W] Sister of Gwenhwyfar.

Gwenhwyfar. [W] Most popularly known as Guinevere, the wife of Arthur. The name is spelled in a variety of ways, including Guanhumara in Geoffrey of Monmouth's *Historia*. The name is an equivalent of the Irish Finnbhair. From her appearance in the Arthurian sagas, she has her counterparts in Helen of Troy and Persephone. Her beauty and abduction bring betrayal, war, and ultimate disaster. The name became very popular in Wales after the conquest of 1282.

Gwenlliant. [W] One of the most beautiful maidens in Britain.

Gwent Is-Coed. [W] See **Teyrnon.** Gwent is the area of southeast Wales.

Gwern. [W] Son of Branwen, daughter of Llyr, and of Matholwch of Ireland. On him is bestowed the sovranty of Ireland in an attempt to avoid battle between Matholwch and Bran. But he is cast into a blazing fire at the age of three by his uncle Efnisien and his death precipitates the great battle between his uncle Bran and his father Matholwch.

Gwion Bach. [W] Son of Gwreang of Llanfair. A boy who features in a tale about the origin of Taliesin. Taliesin is Gwion Bach reincarnate. He is seen as helping to stir Ceridwen's cauldron. She is making a magic brew which, after a year's boiling, will produce three drops, and whoever swallows the drops will know all the secrets of the past, present, and future. Ceridwen intends it for her son Afagddu, who is ugly and whom she desires to compensate by making him wise. There is a similarity here to the boyhood of Fionn Mac Cumhail and how he tastes of the Salmon of Knowledge. As he stirs the cauldron, the magic drops fall onto the finger of Gwion Bach, who puts his finger into his mouth and obtains wisdom. Realising his danger from the enraged Ceridwen, he flees from her, but she sets out in pursuit. During the chase he transforms himself into a hare, a fish, a bird, and a grain of wheat, and Ceridwen chases him in the appropriate form of a greyhound, otter-bitch, hawk, and hen. As the hen, she swallows the grain of wheat that is Gwion Bach. Gwion Bach is later reborn from Ceridwen as Taliesin.

Gwlwlyd. [W] He will not lend Culhwch his two dun-coloured oxen to plough the hill as one of Yspaddaden's tasks.

Gwreang. [W] Father of Gwion Bach, who eventually transmigrates as Taliesin.

Gwreidawl. [W] Father of Gwythyr.

Gwri. [W] "Gold hair." The first name given to Pryderi.

Gwrnach. [W] A giant and owner of a magic sword that Culhwch must win for Yspaddaden the Giant.

Gwrtheryn. [W] The fifth province of Wales "between the Wye and Severn" is said to have been the land of Gwrtheryn or Vortigern (*vawr-tigern*—overlord, or High King). Vortigern ruled Britain when the Jutes, Saxons, and Angles, ancestors of the English, first began to invade Britain in the fifth century. His son was Gwerthefyr (Vortimer), which also signifies "supreme king." [See *Transactions of the Honourable Society of Cymmrodorion*, 1946/7, 51.]

Gwyar. [W] Referred to as Anna by Geoffrey of Monmouth and Morgawse by Malory, she was the sister of Arthur and wife of Lludd.

Gwyddbwyll. [W] Wooden wisdom. An ancient Welsh board game. See **Fidchell.**

Gwyddno. [W] "Long Shank" who rules the "drowned kingdom." Culhwch has to get his hamper for Yspaddaden the Giant.

Gwyddno Garanhirtan. [W] The father of Elffin who finds the baby Taliesin in a stream and raises him. He is also referred to as Urien, king of Rheged, in a Taliesin poem.

Gwydion. [W] Son of Don. He is referred to as the best storyteller in the world. [*Pedeir Keinc y Mabinogi,* ed. I. Williams, Cardiff, 1930, p. 69.] He appears to be the father of his sister Aranrhod's son, Lleu Llaw Gyffes. He saves the child and rears him and through his art cures him when he has been wounded by Gronw. To help his brother, Gilfaethwy, obtain Goewin, the maiden who is the foot holder of Math, son of Mathonwy, he tricks Pryderi into going to war with Math. In the battle he slays Pryderi by trickery.

Gwydre. [W] A son of Arthur killed hunting the Twrch Trwyth.

Gwyn ap Nudd. [W] A king of the Otherworld who appears as a warrior and hunter in the saga of Culhwch and Olwen. He also features in the tale of Creiddylad, daughter of Lludd Llaw Ereint. He abducts Creiddylad, even though she is about to marry Gwythyr, son of Gwreidawl. Arthur besieges him in his fortress, and finally it is ordained that Gwyn and Gwythyr should fight an annual combat and whoever wins that combat on doomsday will be the victor. The name Gwyn is cognate with the Irish Fionn.

Gwyn Dun Mane. [W] A steer belonging to Gweddw that Culhwch has to obtain for Yspaddaden the Giant.

Gwynedd. The northwestern kingdom of Wales, which includes Ynys Mon (Anglesey). It is now a county covering 3,869 square kilometres. Math, son of Mathonwy, is Lord of Gwynedd.

Gwynfyd. [W] "Purity." The second of three concentric circles in Cymric cosmogony that represent good over evil.

Gwyngelli. [W] A companion of Arthur's who seizes the four feet of the Twrch Trwyth and plunges him under water during the hunt in the story of Culhwch and Olwen.

Gwynn Mygddwn. [W] A magical horse owned by Gweddw. It is the only horse Mabon can ride.

Gwythyr ap Gwreidawl. [W] His bride-to-be is abducted by Gwyn ap Nudd and he has to fight an annual combat with Gwyn, ordained by Arthur, until doomsday. Whoever is victor on doomsday may have the girl. See also **Creiddylad.**

Hafgan. [W] "Summer White." He is the rival of Arawn, king of Annwn. He is slain by Pwyll of Dyfed in what appears to be an annual contest between Arawn and Hafgan, when Pwyll changes shapes with Arawn.

Hag of Beara. [I] See **Cailleach Beara.**

Hallowe'en. See **Samhain** and **Calan Gaef.**

Hanes Taliesin. [W] "The History of Taliesin." A work compiled in the sixteenth century by Sion Llywelyn (1540–ca. 1615) from which Lady Charlotte Guest took material for her *Mabinogion* translation in 1849. Most recent works on the Mabinogion saga tend to leave out this material, specifically relating to the origins of Taliesin, as being of a too late origin.

Head, Cult of the. The head was revered by all ancient Celtic societies. It was in the head and not the heart that they located the souls of men and women. In battle they collected the heads of enemies as trophies, a custom that seems to have died out around the turn of the millennium. Livy described how the victorious Boii in 216 B.C. took the head of an enemy chieftain and placed it in a temple. He described how "some Gallic [Celtic] horsemen came in sight, with heads hanging at their horses' breasts or fixed on their lances and singing their customary song of triumph." It is Diodorus Siculus, the Sicilian Greek historian, writing ca. 60–30 B.C., who gives us a full description.

> They cut off the heads of enemies slain in battle and attach them to the necks of their horses. The blood-stained spoils they hand over to their attendants to carry off as boot, while striking up a paean and singing a song of victory; and they nail up the fruits upon their houses, just as do those who lay low wild animals in certain kinds of hunting.

They embalm in cedar oil the heads of the most distinguished enemies, and preserve them carefully in a chest,
and display them with pride to strangers, saying that for
this head one of their ancestors, or his father, or the man
himself refused the offer of a large sum of money. They say
that some of them boast that they refused the weight of the
head in gold; thus displaying what is only a barbarous kind
of magnanimity, for it is not a sign of nobility to refrain
from selling the proofs of one's valour.

The cult of the head is frequently mentioned in Celtic mythology, particularly in the Irish Ulster Cycle. Cúchulainn, returning to
Emain Macha after his first battle, is described as having three heads
hanging from his chariot and "nine heads in one hand and ten in
the other, and these he brandished at the hosts in token of his
valour and prowess." To enforce that the Celts believed that the soul
dwelt in the head and, therefore, the head could function without
the body, we have the example of Conaire Mór, who is slain in "The
Destruction of Da Derga's Hostel." His head is removed. But when
Conall, the warrior, pours water into the mouth, it speaks and
thanks him. In the Welsh tale about Bran the Blessed, Bran, having
been mortally wounded, asks his companions to remove his head
and take it back to the Island of the Mighty for burial. It takes them
many years on their journey and, all the time, Bran's head eats,
drinks, and speaks just the same as when he had been in life.
Archaeological finds give full corroboration to this cult.

Heber. [I] See **Eber.**

Hefydd Hen. [W] Father of Rhiannon. *Hen* signifies "ancient."

Heilyn. [W] Son of Gwynn, one of the survivors of Bran and
Matholwch's devastating war in Ireland. It is he who has the courage to open the magic door through which the seven survivors are
released from the island of Gwales.

Heinin. [W] The chief bard at the court of Arthur at the time when
Talisien arrives.

Heledd. [W] Daughter of Cynddylan.

Heremon. [I] See **Eremon.**

Hervydd Hen. [W] See **Hefydd Hen.**

High Kings. Of Ireland, see **Ard Rí.**

Historia Brittonum. Latin text written ca. A.D. 800 by Nennius, a Welsh historian. It is important in connection with the origins of Arthurian literature as he mentions Arthur's twelve victories over the Anglo-Saxons.

Historia Regnum Britanniae. (ca. A.D. 1137.) A Latin prose chronicle in 12 books by Geoffrey of Monmouth, a Welshman of Breton origin who was a cleric at Oxford. It is considered the source book of subsequent Arthurian sagas and the source book for Holinshed's *Chronicles of England, Scotland and Ireland,* ca. 1580. Geoffrey, in writing his *Historia,* says that he had only translated the work.

> Walter, Archdeacon of Oxford, a man skilled in the art of public speaking and well informed about the history of foreign countries, presented me with a certain very ancient book written in the British language. The book, attractively composed to form a consecutive and orderly narrative, set out all the deeds of these men, from Brutus, the first King of the Britons, down to Cadwallader the son of Cadwallo. *At Walter's request I have taken the trouble to translate the book into Latin.*

If we are to take Geoffrey's word, then the book to which he refers is now lost. Indeed, many cynical scholars doubt whether such a book ever existed, believing it to be a figment of Geoffrey's imagination. Though why Geoffrey also involves Walter, Archdeacon of Oxford, is curious. If it is a forgery, then Walter would have been a conspirator and party to it. Why should such a renowned churchman and scholar take part in the forgery?

The main reason to believe that the book was a forgery is that it has not survived and, as Sir John Lloyd points out: "No Welsh composition exists that can be reasonably looked upon as the original or even the groundwork of the *History of the Kings of Britain.*" But Geoffrey merely said it was written in "the British language." That term could equally have meant Breton or Cornish as well as Welsh. And could it have been written in Cornish? The theory is not so farfetched when one considers a poem produced by John of Cornwall in the twelfth century in Latin hexameters, which he says he has translated from an old Cornish manuscript. John, to our gratitude, produces some glosses from the original text of

Cornish words, which places the composition in Cornish to the tenth century. Furthermore, the work is called "The Prophecy of Merlin," while Geoffrey has a section entitled "The Prophecies of Merlin." The only known copy of John of Cornwall's manuscript is a fifteenth century one, dated 8 October 1474, and currently in the Vatican Library. [*Merlini prophetica cum expositione Joannis Cornubensis.* cod. membr. 8 Octob. 1474. Seac. XIV, Vatican Library. See also *Spicilegium Vaticanum,* Frauenfeld, 1838, p. 92; and Whitley Stokes, "Cornica," *Revue Celtique,* vol. iii.]

Huarwar. [W] "The Hungry." One of the three plagues of Cornwall.

Hy-Brasil. [I] See **Breasal.**

Hywel Dda, Laws of. The Welsh equivalent of the Brehon law system and the system of law under which the independent Welsh state was governed into medieval times. Hywell ap Cadell, called *Dda,* "the good," ruled from about A.D. 910 to 950. He gave his name to the Welsh law system only because, during his reign, he decreed that the laws of Wales be gathered together in one unified code. The essential points of the record has Hywel summoning an assembly, consisting of the chief ecclesiastics together with six men from each local subdivision of the country, that discusses the laws for forty days. The result of the deliberations caused various changes and amendments to be made and then the revised laws were set down in writing and embodied in an authoritative book. This was done under the chairmanship of Blegwywrd, archdeacon of Llandaff, and thirteen scholars.

The laws survive in some seventy manuscripts, of which half date prior to the sixteenth century, the period when the law was actually practised. Two of the best studies on the laws are Aneurin Owen's *Ancient Laws and Institutes of Wales,* London, 1841 (two volumes), and *The Laws of Hywel Dda (The Book of Blegwywrd),* Melville Richards, Liverpool, 1954.

I

Ialonus. Gaulish god of cultivated fields.

Iarbanel. [I] One of the three sons of Nemed who escaped after the defeat and death of their father. His son was Béothach. Iarbanel is said to be the ancestor of the Tuatha Dé Danaan, while his brother Starn was the ancestor of the Firbolg.

Ibath. [I] Son of Béothach. A Nemedian who fled to Boeotia after the Fomorii had defeated them. He is said to be one of the ancestors of the Tuatha Dé Danaan.

Ibcan. [I] A son of Béothach.

Iberia. Spain and Portugal. The Iberian peninsula was extensively settled by the Celts, perhaps as early as 900 B.C. Louis Siret [*Questions de chronologie et d'ethnographie ibérique,* Paris, 1913], a founding father of prehistoric archaeology, suggests that the Celts introduced the working of bronze into Spain at the start of the Bronze Age. The first wave of settlers appears to have been Goidelic-speaking. According to Irish mythological traditions, it was from Spain that the Gaels (Goidelic speakers) invaded and colonized Ireland.

The story of Míle Easpain (the Spanish soldier) is recounted in the *Leabhar Gabhála* (Book of Invasions). It would seem that the Goidelic-speaking settlers in Iberia were replaced in the middle of the first millennium by a fresh wave of Brythonic (Gaulish) speakers, for by the time Greek mariners were establishing their trading posts there the Celtic population had switched languages.

Herodotus (ca. 490–425 B.C.) is the first Greek historian to give a detailed account of the Celts of Iberia, and Aristotle gives the name "Celtica" to the mass of the country. Indeed, Ephoros of Cyme, in the fourth century B.C., indicates that the Celts stretched from the Pyrenees to Gades (Cadiz) in the south.

The end of an independent Celtic Iberia had its roots in the war between Carthage and Rome. In 237 B.C. the Carthaginian general

Hamilcar Barca arrived in Iberia and began a systematic reduction of the southwest and southeast coasts. It was from Iberia that Hannibal, son of Hamilcar, decided to launch his attack on Rome through Celtic territory. Without the Celts he would have had little success. With the defeat of Carthage in 197 B.C., to which alliance the Celts firmly clung, Rome began to conquer and colonise the Celts of Spain. Rome's war against the Iberian Celts was marked by an extreme savagery. But actions like those of Servius Sulpicius Galba in 151 B.C., who massacred the Celts after they had surrendered, caused criticism even in Rome, and Galba was charged with "war crimes" before the Senate. However, the Senate approved of Galba's actions.

It was not until 49 B.C., after a century and a half of continued uprisings and warfare, that peace came to the Celts of Spain. Under more liberal governors, schools had been established for the sons of Celtic chieftains, and the old remnants of Celtic civilisation and tradition were swept away before Latin learning. Soon the Celtiberians were contributing to Latin literature such figures as Marcus Valerius Martialis (Martial) (ca. A.D. 40–103/4), who made a frank assertion of his Celtic identity, and Marcus Fabius Quintilanus (b. A.D. 35), who was the first rhetorician to receive an official salary from the Roman state. Egantius, the poet, was another Celtiberian whose work was ridiculed in Rome for its Celtic "provincialness." There are many other writers from Spain whose work needs careful analysis, such as the Senecas, Lucan, and Pomponius Mela (whose work on the Celts, especially the druids, preserves information not found elsewhere). According to Publius Tacitus (A.D. 56/57–ca. 117), a Celtic language was still spoken in many parts of Spain during the first century A.D., but after this there is no mention of a Celtic identity, and the Celts of the Iberian peninsula were, apparently, entirely assimilated. See also **Galicia.**

Ibor. [I] The charioteer who accompanies Cúchulainn during his adventures in "The Boyhood Deeds of Cúchulainn."

Ibor cind tráchta. [I] The spot where the goddess Fand arranges her assignation with Cúchulainn; but Emer, Cúchulainn's wife, having discovered this, arrives with 50 maidens carrying sharpened knives to destroy Fand. See **Cúchulainn, Emer,** and **Fand.**

Id. [I] Son of Ríangabur. He was the charioteer of Conall Cearnach and brother of Cúchulainn's charioteer, Laeg.

Idath. [I] A warrior from Connacht who marries the goddess Bé Fin, sister of Boann. He is the son of Fraoch, the most handsome warrior in Ireland.

Ilberg. [I] Son of the sea god Manannán Mac Lir. He ruled the sídhe of Eas Aedha Ruaidh, the mount of Mullachshee near Ballyshannon, Co. Donegal. He was also one of the five candidates for the kingship of the Tuatha Dé Danaan when the Dagda announced his intention to give up the role. During the subsequent war between the gods, Ilberg fought for Midir the Proud alongside the contingent of mortals led by Caoilte of the Fianna. Caoilte, however, slew his grandfather, Lir.

Ildánach. [I] A title bestowed on Lugh Lámhfada when he presented himself at the court of Nuada. It means "The All-Craftsman."

Imbolg. [I] Also given as Imbolc. One of the four great annual pre-Christian festivals, it was sacred to the fertility goddess, Brigid, and held on February 1. See **Brigid.** It was subsequently taken over by the Christian Church and became St. Brigid's feast day.

Immortality. The Celts were one of the first European peoples to develop a doctrine of immortality of the soul. The basic belief was that death was only a changing of place and that life went on with all it forms and goods in the Otherworld. A constant exchange of souls was always taking place between the two worlds; death in this world brought a soul to the Otherworld, and death in the Otherworld brought a soul to this world. Philostratus of Tyana (ca. A.D. 170–249) observed that the Celts celebrated birth with mourning and death with joy. Caesar, the cynical soldier, remarked that this teaching of immortality doubtless accounted for the reckless bravery of the Celts in battle. Sotion of Alexandria (ca. 200–170 B.C.) claimed that the Greeks accepted "much of their philosophy" from early contact with the Celts and that Pythagoras taught a doctrine of immortality of the soul based on the Celtic idea. Diodorus Siculus (d. ca. 21 B.C.) reverses the claim, saying the Celts developed the philosophy from Pythagoras. However, the third possibility is that the similarity between the Celtic philosophy and Pythagoras' philosophy (which is of reincarnation, not an exchange of souls between two worlds) is superficial. Transmigration of souls through all living things, as taught by Pythagoras, was not the Celtic idea. The Celtic belief was in rebirth of the soul in human bodies from one world to another. It is arguable that the Celtic and Pythagorean doctrines were mutually exclusive. See **Otherworld.**

Indech. [I] A Fomorii warrior, son of the goddess Domnu, who was killed by the god Ogma at the second Battle of Magh Tuireadh.

Ingcél Cáech. [I] The one-eyed son or grandson of the king of Britain who went in exile to Ireland. He met up with Conaire Mór's three dissident foster brothers and joined forces with them and other Irish dissidents, such as the sons of Ailill and Medb. Together they raided and plundered Ireland and Britain. In Britain they attacked the fortress and destroyed it, killing in the process Ingcél's father, mother, and seven brothers. The final raid of this band was against Da Derga's Hostel, in which the High King, Conaire Mór, was slain. Ingcél was sent to spy on Conaire before the attack.

Invasion Myths. No Celtic "creation myth" has survived. When works about creation began to be written down, the Celts had become Christian and the Hebrew myths of creation had been fully accepted. Therefore, the early myths became an uneasy combination of Hebrew and Celtic mythology, with the Irish tradition claiming descent from Japhet, son of Noah. However, the five invasions of Ireland before the arrival of Míl and his followers (the Gaels) show similarities with the invasion myths of the Indian *Rig Veda* and demonstrate a closeness to the Indo-European root of Celtic culture. See *Invasions, Book of.*

Invasions, Book of. [I] *Leabhar Gabhála.* The book survives in various ancient manuscripts, mainly in the *Book of Leinster* (twelfth century). It contains the mythical history of Ireland, its creation through the invasions of Cesair, before the Deluge; the invasions of Partholón, Nemed, the Firbolg, the Tuatha Dé Danaan, and the Milesians. It then follows the subsequent myth/history of Ireland down to the High King Malachaí Mór (A.D. 980–1002). It is regarded as the "national epic" of Ireland. Micheál Ó Cléirigh (1575–ca. 1645) compiled a version drawn from several ancient manuscripts that are now lost. It is this compilation to which people generally refer when talking about the book.

Iollan. [I] Iollan the Fair was son of Fergus Mac Roth. He accompanied his father and brother, Buinne the Ruthless, to Alba to bear Conchobhar Mac Nessa's invitation to Deirdre and the sons of Usna to return to Ulster. Conchobhar claimed he had forgiven

Naoise for eloping with his bride-to-be, Deirdre. While Iollan and Buinne were guarding them in the Red Branch Hostel in Emain Macha, Conchobhar betrayed his promise and ordered them killed. Iollan and Buinne defended them, but Buinne was bribed to stop fighting. Iollan ran out to meet the attackers and wounded Fiachra, son of Conchobhar Mac Nessa, who was leading the attack on the hostel. Fiachra was carrying Conchobhar's enchanted shield, Ochain (Moaner), which moaned when its bearer was in danger. The hero, Conall Cearnach, hearing its cry, came up and mortally wounded Iollan. Before he died, Iollan told Conall, who had been his friend, of Conchobhar's treachery. Conall, in rage, then slew Fiachra.

Ioruaidhe. [I] A kingdom whose ruler possessed a hound whelp called Fáil Inis, who was irresistible in battle. Any water it bathed in was turned to wine and it caught every wild beast it encountered. In reparation for killing Cian, Lugh's father, the sons of Tuireann had to bring it back to Ireland. They fought the king of Ioruaidhe, took him captive, and demanded the hound in return for his life and freedom.

Ir. [I] A son of Milesius. He was killed by a storm conjured by the Dé Danaan to prevent the Milesian landing in Ireland.

Ireland. Éire in Irish. Unlike its neighbouring Celtic island, Britain, it did not become part of the Roman Empire, although the Romans, particularly Agricola, did plan to invade. Converted to Christianity in the fifth century, Ireland also escaped the sweep of the Huns, Goths, Vandals, and other Germanic peoples through Europe, which also destroyed Celtic Britain and established a number of Anglo-Saxon kingdoms there that eventually became England.

While this was known as the Dark Ages in Europe, it was for Ireland a "Golden Age" of learning and literacy. Irish Christian monks left Ireland to establish churches and monasteries as far east as Kiev, in the Ukraine, as far north as Iceland and the Faroes, and as far south as Taranto, in Italy. Ironically, in view of Ireland's later history, they brought literacy and Christianity to the English kingdoms.

In the eighth century Ireland felt the brunt of attacks from the Vikings, and the Norse made settlements in the coastal regions. During this period, great Irish libraries, the *Tech Screpta,* were destroyed in the raids. These Norse settlers tended to merge into the native culture, especially after the High King, Brían Bóromha, defeated the Norse at Clontarf in A.D. 1014, turning the tide of the attempted Norse domination of the area.

However, in 1167 the first of the Anglo-Norman attempts at conquest began. In 1175 the High King Ruraidh Ó Conchobhar signed the Treaty of Windsor, in which he recognised the emperor of the Angevin Empire, Henry II, as suzerain lord of Ireland. Ruraidh was to be the last High King, for the Normans began to carve out their own petty kingdoms and fiefdoms. These original conquerors also merged into the Irish nation so well that when Henry VIII sent an emissary to address the Anglo-Norman barons of Ireland, his speech had to be translated into Irish for them to understand.

From the time of Mary Tudor, however, new colonisation programmes were devised that led to full-scale warfare with the native population, including the early colonists, which resulted in the Irish defeat at Kinsale in 1601. English common law was now enforced throughout the country, and a new colonisation was attempted in Ulster.

In 1641 the Irish rose up and were initially successful establishing a Confederate Parliament in Kilkenny. In 1649 Oliver Cromwell began his campaign on behalf of the English Parliament to reconquer Ireland, and the Irish armies were eventually defeated. Then began the most notorious of the English colonisation programmes. By May 1, 1654, all the native Irish population were ordered to remove west of the River Shannon into a reservation consisting of Co. Clare and the province of Connacht, on pain of death. Any natives found east of the Shannon from that date on could be killed immediately. Their lands were to be taken over by English colonists. Thousands of Irish were massacred, thousands more rounded up and sent mainly to Barbados. Yet the scheme to eradicate the Irish nation failed.

The Williamite Conquest of Ireland saw another colonisation scheme and the introduction of the Penal Laws, in which only members of the Anglican Church were given any form of civil rights. This caused a mass migration to the American colonies of Ulster Presbyterians, who played a leading role in the American War of Independence. Many returned, introducing into Ireland the new philosophy of "The Rights of Man." They played a prominent role in the establishment of the Irish Republican movement and in the first major uprising in one hundred years against the English administration in 1798.

The English administration's answer to the demand for freedom was to curtail the Irish nation even more. On January 1, 1801, the colonial parliament (a body elected by the colonists in Ireland) was merged into the English parliament and the state of the United Kingdom of Great Britain and Ireland came into being. Even the colonists had to be heavily bribed to vote for the abolition of their Dublin parliament.

Abortive uprisings against the English administration also took place in 1803, 1848, and 1867. In the period 1844–1848, Ireland lost 2.5 million of its inhabitants, by death and migration, due to an artificially induced famine caused when absentee English landlords insisted on the exportation of grain, cattle, and sheep out of the country at a time when the potato crops had failed. This feudal system of landlordism was overthrown by the "Land War" of 1879–1882.

With the failure of the uprising of 1867, the Irish people turned to the "constitutional path" opened for them by the gradual repeal of the Penal Laws, by the Catholic Emancipation Act of 1829, and by the Parliamentary Reform Act. An Irish Party was established to achieve self-government. From 1870 for the next forty years they held four-fifths of all Irish seats within the British Parliament. Yet the majority of English representatives refused to accept the democratically expressed wish of the Irish people. In 1910 the Irish Party held 84 seats out of the 105 seats, but attempts to secure self-government were thwarted and shelved by the start of World War I.

On April 24, 1916, the Irish rose again and declared an independent republic. This was militarily suppressed by England. In December 1918, the last all-Ireland general election ever held, of the 105 seats, 73 went to Sinn Féin, the Irish Republican party, 6 to the old Irish Party, and 26 to the Unionists. In January 1919, Ireland issued a Declaration of Independence. English troops were sent in and the elected Republican representatives were arrested when found. Thus began the War of Independence 1919–1921. The British government finally entered into negotiations and succeeded in coercing Irish delegates into accepting the Partition of Ireland and establishment of a Free State.

Of the nine counties of Ulster, Unionists had a clear majority in four counties. In spite of the ethical questions over democracy, Britain enforced Partition by taking two counties with Republican majorities and putting them with the four Unionist counties. The area was given a local parliament within the United Kingdom structure. To ensure a permanent Unionist rule, the state was set up on sectarian lines and the Unionist/Protestant majority was reinforced by the disenfranchisement of groups of Nationalists/ Catholics. A blind eye was turned by the British government to continued state-endorsed civil rights violations. Born out of blood-shed and violence, the statelet was never at peace, and violence was endemic every decade until the advent of the Northern Ireland Civil Rights Association in the 1960s. Protest marches demanding "one man, one vote" were met by a sectarian Unionist/Protestant backlash.

British troops were once more sent into Northern Ireland to "keep the peace" but could not save the Unionist government, and the Stormont Parliament was abolished in 1972. But this did not stop the long campaign to reunify the country, which continues today. The reunification of Ireland is a cherished aspiration for the majority of Irish people.

The Irish Free State became the Irish Republic on April 18, 1949.

Irgalach. [I] Son of Lách. He commanded "three fifties" of elderly veteran warriors of Ulster. They volunteered to accompany Conchobhar Mac Nessa in the war against Ailill and Medb in order to give advice to the younger warriors.

Irish. The language of Ireland. It is now the first official language of the Irish Republic, spoken, at the last census of 1981, by 31.6 percent (1,018,312) of the population. It is estimated that there are a further 60,000 speakers in the Partitioned northeast of the country and maybe as many as a further 500,000 in other parts of the world. While it is an official language of the European Economic Community, it is not one of the seven working languages. It has no official standing, and is openly discouraged, in the Partitioned northeast, which remains part of the United Kingdom. There have been no census figures for the language taken there since Partition, although the British government, bowing to pressure from Europe and civil rights groups, has promised to include it in the 1991 census. In the Partitioned area it is recorded that an annual average of 2,000 children pass GCE (now GCSE) in "O" and "A" levels.

Apart from early inscriptions, Irish literary survivals begin in the sixth century A.D. Calvert Watkins, Professor of Linguistics at Harvard University, has stated: "Irish has the oldest vernacular literature of Europe." He argues that both Greek and Latin were used as a *lingua franca* among diverse peoples, while Irish was a *lingua materna*. However, Irish is certainly, with the exception of Greek and Latin, possessed of a literature that is far older than any other European people.

In spite of some attempts at destruction by conquerors, a wealth of manuscript books survive. In fact, Irish contains the world's most extensive medical manuscript literature written in any one language prior to 1800. Historical works, poetry, mythological sagas, scientific discourses, musical manuscripts, as well as the complete codification of the native Irish law system (Brehon Laws) have survived.

The first printed works in Irish occur in the sixteenth century. Ironically it was Elizabeth I of England who is credited with having the first fount of "Gaelic" type struck in order that she might have a phrase-book in Irish. A Protestant Catechism in Irish was printed in 1571. The New Testament became available in 1603, although the Old Testament (translated during the 1640s) was not printed until 1681.

During this period, with the attempts to eradicate the Irish language on the part of the English administration, the Irish in exile established centres for the publication of Irish books in Antwerp, Brussels, Paris, and especially Louvain. A number of books were published abroad throughout the seventeenth and eighteenth centuries to be smuggled into Ireland. The first Irish dictionary (*Foclóir no Sanasan Nua*) was printed in Louvain in 1643.

A thriving literature continued in spite of the Penal Laws designed to destroy the language. The worst blow to the language was the artificial famine of 1844–1848. Prior to the famine it was estimated that the major part of the Irish population were bilingual, while, according to Dr. Daniel Dewar at the time, two million did not understand English. The first census following the famine, which savagely depleted the Irish-speaking population, showed only 1,524,286 Irish speakers (then 23 percent of the population), of which only 319,602 were monoglots.

Throughout the nineteenth century attempts were made to restore the language and force the English administration to recognise it. Under this administration it was presumed that no such thing as an Irish language existed. Only in 1878 was it allowed to be taught as an optional subject in intermediate schools. Campaigns were fought and concessions were won, so that by 1909 Irish was accepted as a subject for matriculation in the education system.

When the Irish Free State came into being, it was accepted as an official language of the state. There has been a flourishing of Irish literature during this century and some of the works have been widely translated. Brendan Behan's play *An Giall* (The Hostage) was written and originally performed in Irish at the Damer Hall Theatre, Dublin, in 1956, before it was translated into English. Another of his plays, "The Quare Fellow," was originally written as *Casadh Sugáin Eile* (The Twisting of Another Rope). Irish now possesses a rich and versatile modern literature as well as being the heir to one of the oldest and richest literatures in Europe, which includes a mythology that ranks second to none.

Irnan. [I] One of the three sorceress daughters of Conaran the Dé Danaan who dwelt at Dún Conaran. With her sisters she was sent to capture some members of the Fianna. This was accomplished by spinning a magic web with which to capture the warriors. But Goll Mac Morna, coming along later, saw what the three hags had done and killed two of them. When Irnan begged for mercy and promised to release the warriors, he spared her. Fionn Mac Cumhail arrived when they were being released, and Irnan changed into a monster and laid a geis on Fionn or his warriors to accept single combat. Oisín, Oscar, and Celta all refused to fight the monster. Fionn accepted but Goll said it was not seemly for Fionn to fight the hag even if she was in the shape of a monster. Goll then fought and killed Irnan, and for this Fionn gave his daughter Cebha to him in marriage.

Iron. Appears frequently in myths as a valuable and magical property. At the start of the first millennium B.C. the Celts were possessed of great skill in metalwork, especially in the use of iron, a metal only then becoming known to craftsmen of the classical world. By the sixth century B.C. their formidable armaments of spears, swords,

axes, and agricultural implements rendered the Celts militarily
superior to their neighbours, and they were able to open roadways
through the previously impenetrable forests of Europe. An ancient
Irish word for road, still in use today, is *slighe,* from the word *sligim,*
"I hew." The very word *iron* is derived from the Celtic *iarn,*
spreading from that source into most European languages via Latin.
Iron bars of certain weight were sometimes used in ancient Celtic
society as currency. In the story of the *Táin,* Ailill and Medb,
counting their treasures, list *iarn-lestair,* or "iron vessels." Sliabh an
Iairinn (Mountain of Iron), east of Lough Allen, Co. Leitrim, was
where Gobhniu, the smith god, worked. In the story of
Matholwch's attempt to obtain the magic cauldron from Llassar
Llaesgyfnewid and Cymidei Cymeinfoll, Matholwch builds a house
of iron in which to destroy these two, who are obviously deities of
death and battle.

Irusan. [I] A monstrous cat that dwelt in a cave near Knowth on the
Boyne. It is said to have seized the chief bard of Ireland, Seanchán
Torpéist, in its jaws and to have run off with him.

Ith. [I] Son of Bregon. He is said to have dwelt in a great tower that
his father had built in Spain (the Irish synonym of the "Land of the
Dead"). From this tower, Ith saw Ireland and embarked with 90
followers. They landed at Corca Duibhne (Corkaguiny, Co. Kerry).
The Dé Danaan had just defeated the Fomorii at the second Battle
of Magh Tuireadh and Nuada had been killed. Mac Cécht, Mac
Cuill, and Mac Gréine were attempting to divide Ireland between
them. Ith was asked to make a judgment on how this should be
done. His panegyric was interpreted as an indication he wanted to
rule Ireland himself. The Dé Danaan killed him. His body was
taken back to Spain, where his children resolved to take vengeance
by conquering Ireland; thus began the Milesian invasion.

Iubdan. [I] King of the Faylinn, a kingdom of diminutive people. His
wife was Bebo. Iubdan was a constant boaster and to quell the
boasting his poet Eisirt told him that Ulster was a land of giants. To
prove it he went there and returned with Aedh, dwarf of the Ulster
king Fergus Mac Léide. Eisirt then placed a geis on Iubdan to go to
Ulster and be the first to taste the porridge of the king on the next
morning. Iubdan and Bebo go to Ulster, but they fall in the porridge and are made prisoners. Fergus falls in love with Bebo and has
an affair with her. After a year and a day, Fergus offers to free them

both if Iubdan gives up his most treasured possession, his enchanted shoes. Whoever wore them could travel over or under water as freely as on dry land. Iubdan gives them to Fergus, and Iubdan and Bebo are released back to the land of the Faylinn.

The story stands a close comparison to the Jonathan Swift (1667–1745) story *Travels of Lemuel Gulliver into Several Remote Regions of the World* (1726). The story, popularly known as *Gulliver's Travels,* consists of four voyages in the tradition of the Irish *immrama,* or "voyage tale." "A Voyage to Lilliput" is similar to *Eachtra Fhergus Mac Léide.* Swift therefore had some access to this tale, either in the original Irish or through a translation.

Iuchar. [I] The second son of Tuireann. Brían is the first son. See **Brían** and **Tuireann.**

Iucharba. [I] The third son of Tuireann.

Iunsa. [I] Father of Eibhir, wife of Oisín.

J

Jowan Chy an Hor. John of Chyanhor. The only folktale surviving in the Cornish language; originally set down by Nicholas Boson of Newlyn in the seventeenth century. For some time it was thought to have been a composition by his son John Boson. Considered to be a medieval tale, Jowan Chy an Hor is similar to a tale recorded from oral transmission in *Popular Tales of the West Highlands* by John F. Campbell (1860–1862) and reprinted as *Na Tri Chomhairlean* (The Three Counsels) in *More Tales of the West Highlands* in 1940. There is also a Breton version of the tale published by Roparz Hermon in *Gwalarn no 20*. The Celtic scholar Professor Ludwig Muelhausen published a study of the tale in *Die Kornishe Geshichte von der drei guten ratschwägen.*

K

K. The letter "K" has been adopted in Breton and Cornish but not by the other Celtic languages. The letter "C" (always a hard "C") is the form used. However, in some renditions, Anglicisers tend to use "K" for easier pronunciation.

Kae Hir. [W] See **Cae Hir.**

Kay. [W] See **Kei.**

Kei. [W] Appears in Arthurian legend as Sir Kay.

Kenverchyn. [W] See **Cenferchyn.**

Kernow. [W] See **Cornwall.** In Welsh, this is given as Cernyw.

Kigva. [W] See **Cigfa.**

Kilydd. [W] See **Cildydd.**

Knights. While the tales of Arthurian knights and their code of chivalry clearly belong to the medieval concept of an armed and mounted warrior of the nobility or landholding class, with knight-hood only being conferred by the king, the basis for the "Knights of the Round Table" does have a foundation in Celtic culture. It is argued that the tales of Arthur and his knights have more parallels with Fionn Mac Cumhail and his Fianna, the Fianna being the élite bodyguard of the High Kings. Irish myths not only have the Fianna but the warriors of the Red Branch, the Ulster military élite. Similarly, in Connacht, there were the Gamhanrhide, while we find the Degad as the élite warriors of Munster. So the idea of élite bands of warriors was well established in Celtic myth when the medieval Round Table knights began to adorn the tales of Arthur. Among the ancient Celts, Polybius refers to what he thinks was a tribe called the Gaesetae, who threw themselves naked into battle against the Romans at the Battle of Telamon in 225 B.C., a major defeat of the Celts under Concolitanos and Aneroestos. Polybius did not realise that the word meant "spearmen," and the fact that they fought naked, for religious reasons, and were thus marked out from the rest of the Celtic warriors, would indicate they were a military élite—a band of "knights" in the same manner as the Red Branch or Fianna.

Kulhwch. [W] See **Culhwch.**

Kymideu Kymeinvoll. [W] See **Cymidei Cymeinfoll.**

Kymon. [W] See **Cymon.**

Kynddelig. [W] See **Cynddelig.**

L

Labraid Loinseach. [I] See **Móen.**

Labraid Luathlam ar Cleb. [I] "Labra Swift Hand on the Sword." Ruler of Magh Mell and husband of Lí Ban, whom he sent to Cúchulainn with a promise to send the goddess Fand to him in exchange for one day's fighting against three champions whom he could not overcome himself.

Ladra. [I] Pilot of Cesair's ship on its voyage to Ireland. When they landed, he argued about the fairness of the division of the country by Cesair and went off to form his own kingdom where he died "of an excess of women."

Laeg. [I] Sometimes Loeg. A son of Ríangabur, he was charioteer to Cúchulainn. His brother Id was charioteer to Conall Cearnach. He accompanied Cúchulainn on many of his adventures, and during the champion's last combat at the Pillar Stone he threw himself in front of Cúchulainn and caught the spear cast by Laoghaire.

Laighin. [I] Leinster. Anciently called Galian, there are two stories of how it was renamed. The first is that it took its name from Liath, son of Laigne Lethan-glas, a Nemedian; secondly, that it was named the province of "spearmen," after the Gauls who accompanied Móen to Ireland to help him overthrow his evil uncle Cobhthach. The termination *ster* added to Laighin was made at the time of the Norse settlement.

Lairgnen. [I] Son of a Connacht chieftain who was asked to capture the four singing swans as a bridal present by Deoca of Munster. These swans were, in fact, the children of Lir.

Laoghaire. [I] There were several persons of this name in Irish mythology; perhaps the most famous was Laoghaire Mac Crimthann of Connacht, who assisted Fiachna Mac Retach regain his wife and daughter, who were abducted by Goll of Magh Mell. He slew Goll and married Fiachna's daughter, Der Gréine.

Leabhar Gabhála. [I] See *Invasions, Book of.*

Leprechaun. [I] See **Lugh.**

Lí. [I] Son of Dedad (sometimes Degad), who founded the Degad or military caste of Munster.

Lia. [I] Lord of Luachtar, treasurer of Clan Morna and father of Conan Maol. He became treasurer of the Fianna when Goll Mac Morna slew Cumal, the father of Fionn. Lia was slain by Fionn Mac Cumhail, who took the treasure bag and subsequently had to fight Lia's son for several years.

Liadin. [I] A poetess with whom the poet Cuirithir fell in love. It is a tale of sorrowful love that survives from a ninth century A.D. text and remains one of the tragic stories of the period, with marked similarities to the later historical tragedy of Héloise and Abélard of Brittany. While the story is not technically part of Irish mythology, it is generally accepted as such. Liadin capriciously spurns Cuirithir and becomes a nun. In despair, Cuirithir also takes holy orders. Both then regret their actions. Religion prevents a happy outcome, and Cuirithir, for attempting to break his vows, is exiled. Liadin dies of grief at the stone at which Cuirithir used to pray.

Lia Fáil. [I] "The Stone of Destiny." There seems to be two separate stones. The first was in use at Temuir (Tara) and roared with joy at the touch of a rightful monarch's foot. The second, which had similar properties, was used at the coronations of the Dál Riada kings of Alba and subsequently by all Scottish monarchs until it was stolen by Edward I of England (A.D. 1272–1307) and taken to London. There is a confusion of stories. One is that the Scottish Lia Fáil was the same as the Irish stone and that Fergus Mac Erc of the Scottish Dál Riada requested from his brother, Murtagh Mac Erc (High King of Ireland A.D. 512–533), that he be allowed to borrow the stone for his coronation. Fergus then refused to return it. However, scholars claim that the six-foot-high pillar stone that still stands at Tara is the Irish Lia Fáil.

The tradition of the Scottish stone is that this was Jacob's Pillow, taken out of Egypt by Goidel, son of Scota, daughter of the pharaoh Cingris. Colmcille crowned Aidan on it and it was kept at the Dál Riada capital, now Dunstaffnage, Argyll, until the unification of the kingdom with that of the Tuatha Cruithne to form Alba. In A.D. 848 the High King of Alba, Kenneth Mac Alpin, took it to Sgàin

(Scone), which became capital of the country until the overthrow of Macbeth (1040–1057).

After Edward I stole it and took it to England, it was placed under the English throne at Westminster Abbey, where every English monarch since Edward has been crowned on it. A new legend grew up, this time among the English, which says that the end of the English monarchy would be marked if the stone was ever taken from the Abbey. In 1951 four Scottish patriots succeeded in removing it, to the delight of Scottish public opinion, which had long felt that the ancient relic should be returned to the country from which it had been plundered. Some months later, after intensive searching, the Lia Fáil was found wrapped in a Scottish flag in Arbroath Abbey, site of the Scottish Declaration of Independence in 1320. A second attempt was made to remove it to Scotland in 1967.

Liagin. [I] The most powerful runner of the Fianna.

Liath. [I] A son of the Nemedian Laigne Lethan-glas who cultivated the lands of Tara, which were first called Druimm Leith after him. The province of Leinster is also said to have been named for him.

Liath Macha. [I] See **Grey of Macha.**

Lí Ban. [I] Beauty of women. Wife to Labraid, ruler of Magh Mell. She was sister to Fand, Pearl of Beauty. She invited Cúchulainn to Magh Mell, where, if he helped to slay three evil Fomorii warriors, he would be given Fand as his lover. Cúchulainn sent Laeg, his charioteer, with her, and on his report he followed and became the lover of Fand.

Linné. [I] A friend of Oscar's who was accidentally slain by him while he was in a battle fever.

Lir. [I] The ocean god, cognate with Llyr in Welsh myth. His greatest son was Manannán, who took over the role as god of the seas. Lir married Aobh and had three sons and a daughter, who were changed into swans by his second wife, Aoife, who was Aobh's sister but jealous of the children. See **Llyr.**

Lir, Children of. [I] See **Aobh** and **Aoife.**

Llacheu. [W] A son of Arthur. He was murdered by Kei.

Llassar Llaesgyfnewid. [W] A god of death who owns a magic cauldron into which warriors who are slain are cast but who come forth alive. His wife, Cymidei Cymeinfoll, gives birth to a fully armed warrior every six weeks.

Llefelys. [W] Son of Beli, brother of Lludd (Nudd). He ruled in Gaul while Lludd ruled in Britain. Lludd sought his brother's aid to stop three plagues that were devastating the land. Together they were able to rid the island of the plagues. See **Lludd Llaw Ereint.**

Lleu Llaw Gyffes. [W] Son of Aranrhod. His mother swears that he will never be named, but her brother, Gwydion, who has concealed the child at birth, tricks Aranrhod into naming him "Bright One of the Skilful Hand." Aranrhod swears that Lleu will never bears arms unless she equips him. Again, she is tricked. Finally, she swears Lleu will never have a human wife. Gwydion and Math conjure a wife from the flowers of an oak, broom, and meadowsweet and call her Blodeuwedd, "Flower aspect." She is very beautiful but soon is discontented with Lleu and takes a lover, Gronw Pebyr. They try to murder him. But it has been said that Lleu can never be killed within a house or outside it, neither on horseback nor on foot, and moreover he could then only be slain by a spear crafted for a whole year only during the time when people attended Sunday Mass. His unfaithful wife relays this to her lover and the conditions are fulfilled. But Lleu escapes, only wounded, in the form of an eagle. Gwydion seeks him out and restores him to health and human form. Lleu slays Gronw Pebyr in combat and Blodeuwedd is turned into an owl, outcast among even the birds. Lleu Llaw Gyffes appears to be the counterpart of the Irish Lugh.

Lloegyr. [W] "The lost territory." The name by which the British Celts referred to that territory which the Anglo-Saxons had invaded and conquered. Today, Lloegyr is the Welsh name for England.

Lludd. [W] In the tale "Lludd and Llefelys" three plagues fall on Britain. See **Coraniaid** and **Lludd Llaw Ereint.**

Lludd Llaw Ereint. [W] The son of Beli, god of death. He appears in the tale of Culhwch and Olwen, and the name is the equivalent of Nuada Airegetlámh. He is also referred to as Nudd. According to Geoffrey, he built London. There was, according to Geoffrey, a temple to Lludd on the site of St. Paul's, and nearby the entrance to it was gained through Parth Lludd, or "Lludd's Gate" (Ludgate). Also, it is interesting to note, a gate named after Lludd's father, Beli, opened onto the river Tamesis (the sluggish river)—Beli's gate (Billingsgate). He ruled Britain while his brother Llefelys ruled Gaul. Three plagues pester Britain. A demoniac race called the Corianiad, could hear every whisper in the land if the winds caught it (a feat also attributed to Math son of Mathonwy). The second plague was the scream of two dragons fighting. The third was a giant wizard. The two brothers slew the Corianiad with insects to which ordinary people were immune. The dragons were slain while intoxicated with mead, and the giant was overcome in combat by Lludd.

Llwyd. [W] Son of Cil Coed. The friend of Gwawl who tries to avenge him by placing a curse on the Dyfed and taking Rhiannon and her son Pryderi prisoner. However, Manawydan rescues them and forces him to promise never again to curse the Dyfed.

Llwyr. [W] Son of Llwrion, who owns a magic vessel in the tale of Culhwch and Olwen.

Llychlyn. [W] Country of the Norsemen, "land of lochs." Cognate to the Irish *Lochlann*. It could well be a synonym for the Otherworld, but some have also chosen to interpret it as a name for Alba. However, Norway is the more common interpretation.

Llyn y Fan. [W] A tale in which an a beautiful Otherworld maiden, dwelling in a lake, appears. The hero offers her bread but she disappears; on her second appearance he offers her dough. On the third appearance, when he offers half-baked bread, the gulf between their two worlds is bridged. But she warns the mortal that if he strikes her three careless blows he will lose her straightaway forever.

They lived at Esgair Llaethy, six miles from the lake out of which she came. They had three sons and a prosperous farm with good livestock. Of course, eventually the husband strikes the three careless blows and she gathers up all the livestock and disappears into the moonlit lake. However, she leaves behind her three sons, and when they grow she appears to them and hands them a satchel of medical recipes and prescriptions, so the three bothers become known as Meddygon Meddfai, the most skilled physicians in all Wales. The story has an echo of the Irish tale of Ó Laoidhigh (O'Lee), in which a book full of medical recipes and prescriptions was brought from Hy-Breasal. On finding it Ó Laoidhigh read it and became the greatest physician in Ireland. The *Book of the O'Lees* (Royal Irish Academy) was written in 1443, partly in Latin and partly in Irish. The pages of writing form patterns resembling astrological symbols. It is a complete system of medicine, treating everything from wounds to hydrophobia.

Llyr. [W] The equivalent of the Irish Lir. Llyr seems to have two
wives. The first was Iweriadd (Ireland), by which he fathered Bran
and Branwen. Branwen seems to fill the role of a goddess of love.
By Penardun, daughter of the mother goddess Don, he gave birth
to Manawydan, god of the sea. Penardun then appears to have
married Euroswydd and given birth to Nisien and Efnisien. Geoffrey of Monmouth's mention of him as a king, King Leir, caused
him to eventually be immortalised as Shakespeare's "King Lear."
Llyr was widely venerated in Britain. It is argued that Leicester was
Llyr (leir) ceastar, the Old English addition for a fort. Manchester
is also argued to contain the name *Manawydan* with the addition of
ceastar.

Llyr, Children of. [W] The second branch of the Mabinogi features
Bran the Blessed, his sister Branwen, and Manawydan, the children
of Llyr. They have two half-brothers, Efnisien and Nisien, but it is
not clear whether they belong to the same father.

Loch. [I] Son of Mofebais and champion of Connacht who wounds
Cúchulainn at the combat at the ford. Cúchulainn, however, slays
him with the fabulous Gae-Bolg.

Lochlann. [I] The country of the Norsemen, "land of lochs." This is
cognate with the Welsh Llychlyn.

Lodan. [I] Son of Lir and father of the goddess Sinend.

Lot. [I] A Fomorii who is wife of Goll and mother of Cichol
Grucenchos. She had bloated lips in her breast and four eyes in her
back and led the Fomorii into battle against Partholón.

Luchtar. [I] God of carpentry, brother of Goibhniu and Credne.

Lugaid. [I] There were several characters bearing this name. One was
the son of Ailill Mac Máta, who, at his father's behest, killed the
champion Fergus Mac Roth while he was swimming. Another was
the son of Cú Roí and killed Cúchulainn's charioteer, Laeg. Others
give this name as Laoghaire. Another was Lugaid Riab nDerg ("of
the Red Stripes"), whose body was divided into three sections by
red stripes, each section resembling part of each of the three men
who sired him by Clothra.

Lugh. [I] One of the most important of the Irish gods. The son of
Cian and Ethlinn, daughter of Balor of the Evil Eye. Renowned for
the splendour of his countenance, he is clearly a solar deity and
cognate with Lugus in Gaul and Lleu in Wales. He is god of all arts
and crafts. Rescued from death as a baby when Balor tried to thwart

a prophecy that he would be killed by his grandson, he was fostered by Manannán Mac Lir. In other versions it is Goibhniu, the smith god, who fosters him. He fulfils the prophecy by killing Balor and becomes ruler of the gods when Nuada is killed. He was the father of Cúchulainn by the mortal woman Dechtíre. Lugh fought alongside Cúchulainn during the Táin war when Cúchulainn began to weaken. He was last seen in his godlike guise when Conn of the Hundred Battles (High King A.D. 177–212) saw him emerge from a magical mist and foretell the length of his reign and the number of his children. However, when the old gods were driven underground, Lugh diminished in people's minds, becoming a fairy craftsman named Lugh-chromain, "little stooping Lugh." Now all that is left of the potent patron of arts and crafts is the Anglicised version of Lugh-chromain—leprechaun.

Lughnasadh. The feast of the god Lugh, which was introduced by him to commemorate his foster mother, Tailtu. It was one of the four major pre-Christian festivals and was basically an agrarian feast in honour of the harvesting of the crops. Christianity took this feast over as Lammas. The name survives in modern Irish as *Lúnasa* (August), in Manx as *Luanistyn* (August), and in Scottish Gaelic as *Lúnasad,* for the Lammas festival. In Wales the festival is marked as *Calan Awst.*

Lugoves. Plural of "Lugus," which occurs on an inscription at Osma, in Spain, and at Avenches, in Switzerland, and is most likely a reference to the triune godhead of Lugos, cognate with the god Lugh (Irish) and Lleu (Welsh).

Lugus. The name of a god that occurs in place-names in Britain and Gaul, cognate with the Irish Lugh and the Welsh Lleu. His inscriptions and monuments are more numerous than any other Celtic god, and it is generally accepted that when Caesar spoke of the Gaulish "Mercury" he was speaking of Lugus. Lugdunum (Lyon) was chosen by Augustus Caesar as the capital of Roman Gaul. It is significant that he ordered the inauguration of a festival in his commemoration to be held on August 1, which obviously continued the older Celtic festival of Lugus. Today in modern Irish, August is still the month of Lunasa, while the feast of Lughnasadh is still celebrated July 31/August 1. The name appears in many lands: Lyons, Léon, Loudan, and Laon in France; Leiden in Holland; Liegnitz in Silesia; and Carlisle (Luguvalum in Roman times) in

England, as well as, it is argued, in the capital city of England itself, whose name is thought to be derived from Lugdunum—hence the Latin "Londinium." There is some argument on this as to whether the name London actually derived from the Celtic root *londo*, signifying "the wild place."

Lúin. [I] The enchanted spear of the Red Branch hero Celtchair, which was left abandoned after the second battle of Magh Tuireadh by one of the Dé Danaan. When it smelt the blood of an enemy it twisted and writhed in the hands of its owner, and if blood was not spilt, a cauldron of venom was the only means of quenching it before it turned on its holder.

Luned. [W] A maiden who rescues Owain from imprisonment and gives him a ring to make him invisible. She then brings about his marriage to the Lady of the Fountain. Some time later Owain rescues her from being burnt alive.

Lycanthropy. Shape-changing is a frequent occurrence in Celt myths. Gods and even mortals can change their shapes into many forms, mostly animals. Often a druid can change the shape of his or her victim, hence the Dark Druid of Irish myth changes the goddess Sadb into a fawn. In Welsh myth the treacherous Blodeuwedd, who betrays her husband, Lleu, is changed into an owl and bidden to shun the light of day. Often death comes to the victim while in animal shape. Aoife, changed into a crane for daring to love the son of the sea god Manannán Mac Lir, is killed and her skin made into the famous "crane bag." Often wizards and sorceresses can change themselves into fearsome monsters. The whole idea of lycanthropy is very much in keeping with the old Celtic belief that everything, even inanimate objects such as stones, are possessed of indwelling spirits and that the human spirit, which is immortal, can dwell within other creatures and objects just as well as within human form.

M

Mabinogi. [W] "The Four Branches of the Mabinogion" is a collection of medieval Welsh tales that form the mainstream of Welsh mythology. The tales are preserved in two Welsh sources: *The White Book of Rhydderch* (1300–1325) and the *Red Book of Hergest* (1375–1425). The evidence is that these tales originated far earlier than the surviving forms. The style used in the story of "Culhwch and Olwen," for example, shows forms of eleventh century style, vocabulary, and custom. This is, incidentally, the earliest surviving Arthurian tale in Welsh. Archaism in language and custom reflect that the tales belonged to an ancient time and had been handed down by oral tradition until being written down.

The term *mabinogi* has been variously explained. Sir John Rhys [Preface to the *Red Book of Hergest*, I, vii (1887)] interpreted it as "the collection of things that formed the literary training of the *mabinog,*" who was "a young man who had not yet acquired the art of making verse but one who received instruction from a qualified bard." The word *maban,* the diminutive of *mab,* meant a son or youth. Cecile O'Rahilly favours a theory put forward by Professors T. Gwynn Jones and J. Lloyd Jones that the word *mabinogi* is identical with the Irish *mac ind óc,* the name applied to Aengus (Aonghus), son of the Dagda, the "son of the ever young." In Welsh tradition Pryderi is the *mac ind óc.* O'Rahilly points out:

> Nowhere is the essential kinship of Welsh and Irish literature more marked than in the Welsh prose tales popularly known as the *Mabinogion. The Four Branches of the Mabinogi,* in particular, dealing as they do with the adventures of the Children of Don, the Welsh counterpart of the Irish Tuatha Dé Danann, exhibit this kinship in a marked degree.

These tales were first translated into English by Lady Charlotte Elizabeth Guest (1812–1895), being published from 1838 to 1849. Of the eleven prose tales she chose, some fall into the "Four Branches of the Mabinogion," others are classed as "Independent Native Tales," while the third group consists of three late Arthurian romances, such as "The Lady of the Fountain."

One of the most powerful retellings of the *Mabinogi* in English is by the American writer Evangeline Walton, who wrote her first volume, *The Virgin and the Swine,* in 1936. This was the "Fourth Branch" and was retitled *The Island of the Mighty* in 1970. This republication, 34 years after its first appearance, was highly successful and Miss Walton, still alive, was persuaded to finish the saga with *The Children of Llyr* (1971), *The Song of Rhiannon* (1972), and *The Prince of Annwn* (1974).

Mabon. [W] Son of Modron. A warrior and hunter among Arthur's champions. Culhwch rescued him from captivity at Caer Loyw, used in the tale as a synonym for the Otherworld. In return, Mabon helps Culhwch seek out Olwen and fulfil the tasks required to win her hand in marriage. He hunts the magic boar Twrch Trwyth and takes a razor from between its ears. Mabon obviously equates with the cult of Maponos, "The Divine Youth," which existed among the pre-Christian Celts, a cult found in the north of Britain and in Gaul. The Romans equated him with Apollo, for he was credited with skill in music. In Ireland the obvious parallel is Mac ind Óg, also known as Aonghus. His mother, Madron, is Matrona, "The Divine Mother," eponymous goddess of the Marne in France. The Cymric tradition has him stolen from his mother three days after his birth. He also survives in Continental Arthurian tradition as Mabon, Mabuz, and Mabonagrain.

Mac an Lùin. [I] "Son of the Spear," the sword of Fionn Mac Cumhail.

Mac Cécht. [I] A son of Ogma, god of eloquence. He was the husband of Fótla, one of the three goddess, with Banb and Éire, who asked that their name be given to Ireland. He was slain by Eremon, the son of Milesius. The same name also attaches itself to a son of Snade Teched, who was a champion of Conaire Mór, who accompanied the High King to Da Derga's Hostel. He slew the warrior who had killed the High King and then gave the severed head of Conaire a last drink.

Mac Da Thó. [I] A king of Leinster with two possessions coveted by others—a hound and a boar. To prevent an attack on his kingdom he agrees to sell the hound, but both to Connacht and Ulster. Ailill and Medb of Connacht and Conchobhar Mac Ness of Ulster arrive to feast and take possession of the hound. They find Mac Da Thó has slaughtered his boar for the feast. An argument then breaks out as to how the boar should be divided, with the point of contention being the hero's portion. Finally, the Ulstermen and Connachtmen engaged in battle. Mac Da Thó loses his boar and his hound, but he is able to keep his kingdom by setting his enemies against each other.

Mac Gréine. [I] A son of Ogma. He was the husband of the goddess Éire, who gave her name to Ireland. He was slain by the Milesian druid Amairgen.

Macha. [I] A triune goddess of war. As the wife of Nemed, she makes her first appearance. Then, as the wife of Nuada, she is killed by Balor of the Evil Eye at the second battle of Magh Tuireadh. Thirdly, as the wife of Crunniuc Mac Agnomain of Ulster, she utters a curse that the men of Ulster would suffer the pangs of childbirth for five days and four nights in times of Ulster's greatest difficulty. The curse would last for nine times nine generations. Mac Mong Ruadh, or Macha of the Red Tresses, is not a war goddess, though her traditions seem to have inherited those of the triune goddess. She is listed as the seventy-sixth monarch of Ireland, reigning in 377 B.C. She built Ard Macha (Macha's Height = Armagh), established Emain Macha (Navan) as the capital of Ulster, and is credited with building the first hospital in Ireland, called Bron-Bherg (House of Sorrow), which was in use until its destruction by fire in A.D. 22.

Mac Moincanta. [I] He succeeded the Dagda as father of the gods. In folklore, however, he became a short-lived "king of the fairies," succeeded by Fionnbharr.

MacPherson's *Ossian*. James MacPherson of Kingussie, Scotland (1736–1796), published *Fragments of Ancient Poetry Collected in the Highlands* (1760), which he maintained was a translation of authentic Scottish Gaelic poetry, written by Ossian (Oisín), constituting the Fenian sagas. MacPherson extended this with *Fingal* (1762) and *Temora* (1763), the three volumes constituting *Ossian*. It made a tremendous impact in European literature and reawoke an interest in Celtic mythology. Dr. Samuel Johnson denounced the work as a forgery in 1770. Goethe praised it and it also left a deep impression on Blake, Byron, and Tennyson. Napoleon Bonaparte is known to have carried a copy with him on his campaigns, and he took it with him into his exile on St. Helena.

Mac Roth. [I] Medb's steward, not to be confused with the champion Fergus Mac Roth, who was asked to get Medb details about the fabulous Brown Bull of Cuailgne.

Macsen Wledig. [W] Magnus Maximus, a Roman from Spain who arrived in Britain about A.D. 368. He married a Celt named Elen Lwddog, sometimes referred to as Helen, and was declared emperor of Rome by the Legions stationed in Britain. He crossed to Gaul and made himself "western emperor" in A.D. 383. He marched on Rome, and Valentinian II fled from the city. However, Theodosius, the eastern emperor, fought against him and defeated him in several battles. He was put to death on July 28, A.D. 388. It is argued that the Welsh red dragon banner had its origin with the standard of Maximus. Ammianus Marcellinus describes how the emperor's imperial standard showed a dragon on a purple background. His widow, Elen, then returned with her children to Britain, settling in the area that was to become Wales, where she devoted herself to Christian works and her children became the ancestors of several royal dynasties. Her daughter, Severa, is supposed to have married Vortigern. Macsen Wledig (*gwledig* means ruler) is the subject of several stories in Welsh myth. In one, "The Dream of Macsen Wledig," he is accompanied in a hunt by 32 crowned kings and has a vision. This is similar to the story of the Irish "Bricriu's Feast," in which 32 heroes accompany Conchobar Mac Nessa to Bricriu's Hall.

Mael Dúin. [I] Sometimes given as Maeldun. One of the major heroes of Irish myth whose fabulous voyage, the oldest voyage tale so far identified, is thought to have been the inspiration of the later Christian epic *Navigatio Brendani* (The Voyage of Brendan). Alfred Tennyson made the hero popular with nineteenth century readers in his epic poem "The Voyage of Maeldune." The oldest manuscript is *Immram Curaig Maile Dúin,* in a tenth century version, although the orthography and style places the composition to the eighth century.

Mael Dúin, son of Ailill, "Edge of Battle," of the sept of the Eoghanachta of Aran, was born after his father had raped a nun. The nun died in childbirth and Ailill went on to meet his own death at the hands of raiders from overseas. The boy was fostered by the nun's sister, who eventually tells him the story of his birth. Mael Dúin then sets out in a quest to avenge his father's death. He takes sixty warriors with him, and his subsequent voyage and adventures have been considered the "Irish *Odyssey.*"

Mael Fhothartaig. [I] Son of Ronán of Leinster who rejected his stepmother's advances but was falsely accused by her. His father, believing his wife, had his son slain. Mael Fhothartaig's sons later avenged him.

Maen Tyriawc. [W] The burial place of Pryderi, lord of Dyfed.

Maer. [I] A married woman, she fell in love with Fionn Mac Cumhail and sent him nine charm nuts to make him reciprocate her sentiments. Suspecting their purpose, Fionn refused to eat them.

Maga. [I] Daughter of the love god Aonghus Óg, she wed Ross the Red, and their son Fachtna wed Nessa, the mother of Conchobhar Mac Nessa.

Magh. [I] Sometimes Anglicised as Mag or Moy, the word indicates a plain. Plains frequently occur in the myths and sagas as euphemism for the Otherworld: for example, Magh Da Cheo (Plain of the Two Mists), Magh Mell (The Pleasant Plain), and others.

Magh Indoc. [I] The Plain of Indoc features in a Christian embellishment to the myths in which Cúchulainn appears when St. Patrick is walking with Laoghaire Mac Néill (High King A.D. 428–463) on the plain. Cúchulainn appeals to Laoghaire to be converted to Christianity and asks St. Patrick to intercede so that he might be released from Hell and go to the Christian Heaven.

Magh Slecht. [I] Sometimes given as Moyslaught. The Plain of Adoration, said to be located in north Co. Cavan, where the idol Crom Cruach was erected.

Magh Tuireadh. [I] Sometimes given as Moytura. The Plain of Towers. This is the site of two famous battles in mythology. The first battle was fought when the Dé Danaan led by Nuada clashed with the Firbolgs led by Erc. The Dé Danaan won but Nuada's hand was struck off and the god of medicine, Dian Cécht, replaced it with a silver one. The second battle was between the Dé Danaan and the Fomorii. Nuada was slain in this battle by Balor of the Evil Eye, who was in turn slain by Lugh Lámhfada.

Maine. [I] There are several people called Maine in Irish myth, but they are usually minor characters. The seven sons of Ailill and Medb of Connacht are all called Maine. The most prominent, however, is a Norse prince who, in one version of the tragic tale of Deirdre and the sons of Usna, is the person who kills Naoise and his brothers.

Manannan Beg/Mac y Leirr. Manx equivalent of Manannán Mac Lir/Manawydan Fab Llyr.

Manannán Mac Lir. [I] The major sea god, son of Lir. He ruled from Emain Ablach (Emain of the Apple Trees) in Tír Tairnigiri (Land of Promise). His wife was Fand, the Pearl of Beauty. His appearance is always as a noble and handsome warrior, but he is a shape-changer and can drive his chariot over the waves as if they were a plain. Although he sired children among the gods, such as Gaiar, whose affair with Bécuma caused her expulsion from the Land of Promise, Manannán also sired human children like Mongán. In one version of Mongán's begetting, Manannán is said to have appeared to Fachtna, the king, who was being worsted in a battle, and offered to help him if he could go, disguised as Fachtna, and sleep with his wife. To this Fachtna agrees. The child of this union became a great king and mighty warrior. This tale is remarkably similar to that of the conception and birth of Arthur in Brythonic Celtic myth.

Manannán appears more frequently than most gods, creating storms or wrecking Milesian ships, appearing to Bran at the start of his epic voyage, and conducting Cormac Mac Art around Tír Tairnigiri. When the Dagda resigns the leadership of the gods, it is Manannán who refuses to accept the succession of the Bodb Dearg and retreats into seclusion.

Manawydan fab Llyr. [W] See **Manannán Mac Lir.** Manawydan, son of Llyr, the counterpart of the Irish sea god Manannán, son of Lir, forms a close though not exact parallel. However, we can assume that they were a single deity known and venerated among both linguistic Celtic groupings. In the Third Branch of the *Mabinogion,* Manawydan is represented as a wise and patient counsellor, but there is no indication that he is thought of as the god of the sea. It seems that the traditions had been reshaped at a later date, with Manawydan changed into a mortal rather than an immortal. There was a similar tendency in Ireland, to appease the sensibilities of the Christian scribes, to change the status of the ancient gods. There are close parallels in the tales of Bran of Ireland and Bran of Wales, in which Manannán and Manawydan feature. Manawydan is depicted as brother of Benedigeid Vran, or Bran the Blessed, king of the Isle of the Mighty (Britain).

In the story of Pryderi and Manawydan, Manawydan appears as the husband of Rhiannon. Manawydan and Rhiannon, with Pryderi and his wife, Cigva, are living at their palace at Arbeth, in the kingdom of Dyfed, when a peal of thunder is heard and a mist falls. When it clears, the land is desolate. None of the people remain except the four of them. There are no cattle herds nor crops. After two years, existing on wild honey and what little they could kill, they decided to seek their fortune in Lloegyr (England). After several adventures, Pryderi, despite the wise counsel of Manawydan, follows a magic boar into a castle where he finds a fountain with a golden bowl on a marble slab. (See **Cauldron, Magic,** and **Grail**). He tries to take hold of it, is struck dumb, and is unable to let go. Manawydan tells Rhiannon, who tries to rescue him but suffers a similar fate. A mist causes them to disappear.

Manawydan and Cigva have more adventures until an encounter with Llwyd, son of Cilcoed, who reveals that all the enchanted happenings have been placed on Dyfed by him as an act of revenge for his friend, Gwawal, son of Clud, whom Pryderi's father and warriors had ill-used. Thus the tale takes us back to the story of Rhiannon's wedding in the first *Mabinogi*. Pryderi and Rhiannon are released from the spell, as are all the people and animals of Dyfed.

Mannin. The Isle of Man or, in Manx, Ellan Vannin. Said to have been named after Manannán Mac Lir, it is often referred to as the "Island of the Ocean God." The island is mentioned several times in the myths and sagas. Little is known about the island before the fourth century A.D. It was originally thought to have been Brythonic Celtic–speaking. Goidelic, or Gaelic-speaking, settlers began to arrive from Ireland at this time, effecting a language change. Several Ogham inscriptions have been found on the island.

The Kingdom of Man and the Isles included the Hebridean Islands as well as Man. It was not until 1263 that the Manx lost the Western Islands to Scotland following the battle of Largs. The last independent king of the island, Magnus, died in 1266. He ceded the kingship to Alexander III of Scotland. But the English also coveted the island, and there began a series of conflicts and occupations through which the Manx still managed to govern their own domestic affairs through their ancient parliament, Tynwald (Thing-völlr), which has the longest continuous history of any legislature in the world. If one accepts the English claim that Westminster is "the mother of parliaments," then Tynwald is surely the great-grandmother! The elected house in the Tynwald is the House of Keys (from Manx *kiares-es-feed*—twenty-four—the number of elected members). In 1346 the English finally drove out the Scots and set up permanent rule on the island. Edward III appointed William de Montecute as "King of Mann" on the condition that de Montecute acknowledge him as his suzerain.

In 1504 the title was changed to "Lord of Mann." In 1736 this lordship was inherited by the duke of Atholl, who sold it to the English government to pay his debts. In May 1866, after threatening to annex the island, the English government recognised the Tynwald as a popularly elected parliament and the island became a Crown dependency outside the territory of the United Kingdom.

Manx. The language of the Isle of Man, closely related to Irish and Scottish Gaelic and descending from a Common Gaelic (Old Irish) form. Manx emerged as a identifiable written language in 1610, the date of the Manx translation of *The Book of Common Prayer.* Manx shared a common Old Irish literature and, indeed, Aodh De Blacam has observed: "Manxmen were among writers of scholastic verse that survives in the corpus of Irish letters" [*Gaelic Literature Surveyed,* Talbot Press, Dublin, 1929, p. 366]. It has become hard to discern what writing in Old and Middle Irish is of Manx provenance and what is Irish or Scottish. That the same literary heritage was shared in this early period is illustrated by an account of a visit to the Isle of Man by the chief bard of Ireland, Seanchán Torpéist (ca. A.D. 570–647). It is recorded that he arrived on the island with 50 of his followers and entered into a literary contest there.

That stories from mythology, cognate with the early Irish tales, survived on the island in oral tradition is attested. However, the first written evidence does not occur until the eighteenth century. For example, the ballad *Manannan Beg, Mac y Leirr, ny slane coontey jeh Ellan Vannin* (Little Manannan, son of Leirr, an account of the Isle of Man) dates from 1770, when two versions were copied down by John Kelly from oral tradition [Manx Museum mss. 519 and 5072]. From the wording it would appear that the oral composition was composed, or added to, during the time of Thomas III of Man (1504–1521), whose landing on the island in 1507 is described. It is also clear from the wording that Thomas III was still alive when it was composed. There are fourteen examples of obsolete Manx grammatical forms in the poem, which places it to an early period.

Another example is the ballad *Fin as Oshin* (Fin and Oshin). This was copied by the Manx scholar Reverend Philip Moore, one of the supervisors of the translation of the Bible into Manx. The ballad concerns the heroes Fin and his son Oshin, Fionn Mac Cumhail and Oisín (Fingal and Ossian in Scots form). This Manx version adds a unique contribution to the myths known in Irish literature as the Fenian Cycle. It entwines "King Orry" (Godred Crovan) into the story. Moore copied the verses down from the recitation of an old Manx woman and gave a copy to Deemster Peter Heywood. In 1789 Heywood presented the manuscript to Professor Thorkelin of Copenhagen, who, in turn, presented it to the British Museum.

Maol. [I] The bald. A druid of Laoghaire who, with his brother Calpait, taught Laoghaire's daughters Ethné and Fedelma.

Maponos. Gaulish, "The Divine Youth." See **Mabon.**

Marbán. [I] A swineherd who became the chief poet of Ireland after contesting with Dael Duiled, the *ollamh* of Leinster.

March ap Meirchion. Welsh version of Mark of Cornwall.

Mark of Cornwall. Mark features in the medieval tales of Tristan and Iseult as the husband of Iseult and uncle of Tristan. He is generally depicted as an unsympathetic person, becoming a base figure in Malory's *Morte d'Arthur* (ca. 1469). There is enough evidence to show that a historical King Mark existed in Cornwall in the sixth century A.D. The name Mark comes not from the Roman *praenomen*, "Marcus," but from the Celtic word for "horse"

[Cornish—*margh*; Breton—*marc'h;* and Welsh—*march*]. Significantly, in Beroul's twelfth century rendering of Tristan and Iseult's story, the poet actually states that Mark has ears like a horse.

Reference to Mark of Cornwall comes into the medieval "Lives" of several Celtic saints. In the "Life of St. Pol de Léon," written about A.D. 880 by Urmonek, a monk of Landévennec in Brittany, we are told that St. Pol (who gave his name to Paul, near Penzance) was Mark's chaplain. Mark had a beautiful set of hand bells. When Pol left Cornwall to take his mission to Brittany, he asked Mark for one of the bells. Mark refused. When Pol was on the Ile de Baz, near Roscoff, a fisherman caught a large fish, and on cutting it open one of Mark's bells was found inside and it was given to the saint. A sixth century hand bell is preserved with St. Pol's relics in the cathedral of St. Pol de Léon in Brittany.

In this same "Life" the author tells us that Mark had another name "*quem alio nomine Quonomorium vocant*" (whose other name was Quonomorius). This would be the Celtic name Cunomor or "hound of the sea." Urmonek further says that he was a powerful monarch under whose rule lived peoples speaking four different languages. We hear of him as usurping the rule of King Judal of Dumnonia and being defeated by the diplomacy of St. Samson (ca. A.D. 490–ca. 565), whose "Life," written within fifty years of his death, is by far the earliest biography extant of a British Celtic saint. Marcus Cunomorus also comes down in Breton tradition, as well as Cornish, as the ruler of Carhaix in Cornouaille. There is also a Carhays in Cornwall associated with Mark. In Breton tradition, Mark is an unscrupulous tyrant.

See **Tristan and Iseult** for reference to the "Cunomorus Stone" near Castle Dore.

Math, Son of Mathonwy. [W] Lord of Gwynedd. Regarded as a god of increasing wealth. He can live only if his feet are held in a maiden's lap, unless the turmoil of war prevents this. He loses the services of his foot holder through the intrigues of his sister's sons, Gwydion and Gilfaethwy. This is the intrigue that results in the death of Pryderi. It is Gwydion who advises Math to take Aranrhod, his sister, as his new foot holder. But Aranrhod, after a test, turns out not to be a maiden. Math could be cognate with the Irish

Mathu, one of three gods, the others being Nuada and Goibhniu, who appear as three heathen prophets in an early account of St. Patrick. There is also Mathgen, a druid of the Tuatha Dé Danann in "The Second Battle of Mag Tuired."

Matholwch. [W] King of Ireland who marries Branwen, daughter of Llyr. He is slighted by her half-brother Efnisien and in revenge mistreats Branwen, forcing her to do menial tasks in his kitchens despite the birth of their son Gwern. This leads to an invasion of Ireland by Bran, Branwen's brother, and a destructive battle in which Matholwch is killed. Only five pregnant women are left alive in all Ireland to repopulate the country.

Mathonwy. [W] Ancestor of the house of Don. His children were Don, the mother-goddess, and Math, god of increasing wealth.

Matrona. Divine Mother, a Gaulish goddess. See **Mabon.**

Meargach. [I] "Of the Green Spears." Husband of Áille who is killed by Oscar.

Mechi. [I] Son of the Mórrígán, goddess of death and battles, who is slain by Mac Cécht, son of Ogma, because it is prophesied that he will bring disaster to Ireland. He had three hearts in which grew three serpents that, when full grown, would break out and devastate the land.

Medb. [I] Sometimes Anglicised as Maeve. It has been argued that she was another triune goddess representing sovranty. She is most famous for her appearance in the epic of the *Táin Bó Cuailgne.*

Meddygon Meddfai. [W] Three sons of a mortal and an Otherworld spirit who, through her knowledge, became the greatest physicians in Wales. See **Llyn y Fan.**

Medicine. Much is made of the skills of ancient Celtic physicians, especially the Irish. During the Dark Ages (the Golden Age of Learning for Ireland) the Irish medical schools were famous throughout Europe. The premier medical school of Europe was at Tuaim Brecain (Tomregan, Co. Cavan) in the fifth century A.D. Both the Brehon Laws and the Laws of Hywel Dda are very explicit on medical practices. The oldest surviving medical books in Irish date from the early fourteenth century and constitute the largest collection of medical manuscript literature, prior to 1800, surviving in any one language.

Dian Cécht was the main Irish god of medicine, but he became jealous of the abilities of his children, such as Miach, who gave Nuada a flesh and blood hand while he could only give him one of silver. The *Book of the O'Lees,* written in 1443, is written in forms resembling the pattern of astrological figures. It is said that the book was given to O'Lee by Otherworld folk from Hy-Brasil. This tale is remarkably similar to the story of the Meddygon Meddfai, who are also given an Otherworld book of medical knowledge and become the greatest physicians in Wales.

Medrawd. [W] See **Melwas.**

Meilge. [I] A High King who slew Aige when in the form of a deer. Her brother Fafne composed a satire about him that caused a blemish to form three blotches on his face. For this Fafne was put to death.

Melwas. [W] King of the Summer Land, Somerset, who kidnaps Arthur's queen Gwenhwyfar. Gildas intervenes and persuades him to return the queen. He appears as Meleagant in *Le Chevalier de la Charrette* by Chrétien de Troyes, and as Mellyagraunce in Malory's *Morte d'Arthur.*

Menw. [W] A warrior who accompanies Culhwch.

Merlin. [W] A magician, or druid, who plays an important role in the Arthurian sagas. He is of distinctly Celtic origin and figures prominently in early Welsh writings. The first known fully developed treatment of him is in *Libellus Merline* (Little Book of Merlin), ca. A.D. 1135, a Latin tract written by Geoffrey of Monmouth, which was incorporated into his *Historia.* See **Myrddin.**

Mermaids/Mermen. As in other cultures, mermaids and mermen (*muirgen* = sea child) abound in the sagas and tales of Celtic myth. From Brittany to Ireland and from Scotland to Cornwall, such tales survive in folkloric tradition. Half human, half fish, they dwell in the sea. While the mermaids are always enticing and beautiful, the mermen usually have pig's eyes, red noses, and green hair. They are both benevolent and malevolent.

Cornwall is especially replete in mermaid traditions. There are tales of mermaids at Padstow, at Seaton, of the mermaid's rock off Lamorna, and of voices from the sea. Most famous of all is the story of the Zennor mermaid who fell in love with the squire's son and spirited him away to sea. In the church at Zennor one of the bench ends has a carving of the mermaid. The story inspired the film

Miranda (1947) with Glynis Johns and its sequel, *Mad About Men* (1955). These films were translated to America in 1988 as *Splash!*

Mess Buachalla. [I] Daughter of Étain Oig and Cormac, king of Ulster, her father ordered her to be killed because he wanted a son. The two men who undertook the task left the child in the barn of the cowherd of the High King Eterscél. It was prophesied that a woman of an unknown race would bear a son who would be famous, so when her beauty becomes known, Eterscél plans to marry her. On the night before the wedding she is visited by Nemglan, the bird god, and the result of their union is Conaire Mór, although Mess Buachalla is wedded to the High King, who brings him up as his own child.

Miach. [I] A son of Dian Cécht, god of medicine, who proved a better physician than his father, who grew jealous at his accomplishments and murdered him. Herbs grew from his grave that were gathered by his sister Airmid, who laid them out on a cloak in order of their curative values. But her father shook the cloak and so jumbled them that their secrets vanished forever.

Mide. [I] Eponym of Meath, the Middle Province. In the days of the Ulster cycle, Ireland consisted of only four provinces. The fifth province, Mide, was established by the High King Tuathal Teachmhair, A.D. 130–160, so that the High Kings might be independent of the politics of the four provinces. Hence the term "Royal Meath," which still survives.

Midir the Proud. [I] Son of the Dagda and a powerful god himself. He dwelt at the *sídhe* of Bri Leith, Slieve Callory, west of Ardagh, Co. Longford. When the Dagda resigned the leadership of the gods, he refused to accept the choice of the Bodb Dearg and made war on him. This "civil war" among the gods seemed inconclusive, but it meant the end of the power of the gods and they retreated into their underground palaces and became fairies in the minds of the people.

Milesians. [I] The followers of Milesius, the ancestors of the Gaels.

Milesius. [I] Sometimes given as Míl. His original name is Golamh, but he became popular under the Latin form Milesius, signifying a soldier. Míle Easpain, a soldier of Spain, is one epithet. On hearing of the death of his nephew Ith in Ireland, slain by the Dé Danaan, Milesius sets out to conquer Ireland. He does not reach it, but his wife Scota does. She is killed in Kerry. It is their sons who carry out the conquest.

Miodchaoin. [I] A fierce warrior who dwelt on a hill with his three sons. He and his sons were slain by the children of Tuireann.

Mòd. Assembly. An annual gathering organised by An Comunn Gàidhealach (the Scottish Gaelic association, which, in English, refers to itself as "The Highland Association," formed in 1891). This is like the Welsh Eisteddfod.

Modred. [W] The nephew of Arthur who attempts to usurp his crown and marry his wife Guinevere. His historical progenitor, Modreuant, is recorded as being killed with Arthur at the battle of Camluan.

Modron. [W] Mother of Mabon, one of Arthur's champions. The name seems to be a form of Matrona and therefore a mother-goddess.

Móen. [I] The word signifies dumb. Son of a king of Leinster who was poisoned by his uncle, Cobhthach, and made to eat his father's heart, the boy was struck dumb in disgust. He is taken out of Ireland to save him from a worst fate. In the Gaulish kingdom of the Fir Orca, he falls in love with the beautiful Moriath. She teaches him how to regain his speech. Then her father gives him an army with which he sets out and regains his kingdom and destroys the evil Cobhthach. It is interesting to find that Móen is said to have horse's ears, like Mark of Cornwall. Lest the blemish preclude him from kingship, everyone who cut his hair was put to death. Having spared one man on oath that he would hold his tongue, the man told a tree. The tree was cut down and made into a harp for Craftine his bard. When the harp played, Móen's secret was revealed.

Mongán. [I] Son of Manannán Mac Lir by the queen of the Dál nAraidi. He was born in circumstances that so closely resemble those in which Arthur of Britain was born that the Arthur legend was doubtless crafted from the Irish tale. Mongán is also said to have been a reincarnation of Fionn Mac Cumhail, whose story also gives a lot to the Arthurian legends. Because his father was the sea god he, too, was possessed of supernatural gifts. He married Dubh Lacha, and one of the tales associated with him is how he outwits Brandubh, king of Leinster, who secretly desires Dubh Lacha and tricks Mongán into giving him her. A historical Mongán is recorded as ruling Ulster in A.D. 625. See **Manannán Mac Lir.**

Mongfhinn. [I] She was the hostile and bitter stepmother of Niall of the Nine Hostages who tried several times to kill the boy. She died by mistakenly taking poison that she had prepared for him. The deed was said to have been done on Samhain, and in later tradition Samhain (Hallowe'en) was called the Festival of the Mongfhinn. In Munster women used to address prayers to her to ward off her evil presence.

Morann. [I] Chief judge and druid of Ulster during the Red Branch Cycle. He was born with a caul on his head. His father ordered him to be drowned but he was rescued and raised by a smith. His most famous judgment was on who should foster Cúchulainn.

Morca. [I] Son of Dela and a king of the Fomorii. He defeated the Nemedians and forced the 30 survivors to flee from Ireland.

Morda. [W] A blind man ordered by Ceridwen to keep a fire lit under her magic cauldron.

Morfan. [W] Son of Tegid, who was so ugly that no man opposed him at the battle of Camluan because they thought him a devil. A warrior of Arthur.

Morgan. [I] King of the Land of Wonder and husband of the monstrous warrior woman Coinchend. He is father of the beautiful Delbchaem. He is slain by Art.

Moriath. [I] Daughter of Scoriath, king of the Fir Morca of Gaul. She became the lover and wife of Móen.

Mórrígán. [I] Sometimes given as Mórrígú. The major triune goddess of war, death, and slaughter. The name signified "great queen," and she is interchangeable with Macha, Badb, and Nemain. Her favourite shape is that of a crow or raven. She helped the Dé Danaan at the battles of Magh Tuireadh. Having first tried to incite Cúchulainn to make love to her, she fought with him and he managed to wound her. For this his fate is sealed and he is eventually killed. In triumph, she settled on his shoulder in the form of a crow and watched while a beaver drank his blood.

Mug's Half. [I] The southern half of Ireland.

Muinremuir. [I] Son of Ferrgend and one of the three greatest heroes of Ulster who features in the tales of Mac Da Thó's boar and Bricriu's feast. He is the first to accept the challenge when a churl appears and invites the warriors to cut off his head if he, on the next day, can return the stroke. "Bricriu's Feast" is, in fact, an early version of the Green Knight story that became part of the medieval sagas of Arthur.

Muirthemne, Plain of. [I] Cúchulainn dwelt there in his fortress of Dún Dealgan (Dundalk). Lady Gregory's retelling of the Cúchulainn saga was entitled *Cuchulain of Muirthemne* [John Murray, London, 1902].

Munster. [I] The southwest province of Ireland, originally called Mumham, with the addition of the *ster* during the Norse settlement. Like Dyfed in Wales, it is associated with the Otherworld. Tech Duinn, the gathering place of the dead, lies just off its coast, as Annwn lies off the coast of Dyfed. Munster is associated with more female gods than any other place, and it appears in the ancient stories as a primeval world, a place of origin.

Murias. [I] One of the four great cities of the Dé Danaan. It was from Murias that the magic cauldron of the Dagda, a gift from Lugh, came.

Murna of the White Neck. [I] A descendent of Nuada and Ethlinn, the daughter of Balor of the Evil Eye. She elopes with Cumal, son of Trenmor of the Clan Mascna. Her father, a druid, incites Goll Mac Morna to kill Cumal. Murna flees to the forests and gives birth to Cumal's son, Demna. But the boy grows up to be called "The Fair One"—Fionn. He goes on to seek vengeance for his father's death.

Mur y Castell. [W] Lleu Llaw Gyffes' fortress at Bala Lake.

Music. Music always plays its part in the myths. Heroes and heroines, even the deities, all seemed to be accomplished. Various instruments—harps, stringed instruments, bagpipes, and timpani—are mentioned by name. In Ireland, the earliest surviving example of Irish musical notation and composition is contained in an eleventh century manuscript. Irish musicians were celebrated from earliest times.

Mynwy. [W] St. David's. The principal shrine of Dewi Sant, patron saint of Wales. One of four bishoprics—the others being Llandaff, Bangor, and St. Asaph.

Mynyddawn Mwynfawr. Lord of Dineiddyn (Edinburgh) who led the Gododdin (the Votadini of the Roman occupation) to recapture Catraeth (Catterick) from the Anglo-Saxons in the sixth century. The event is recorded in a sixth century poem by Aneurin.

Myrddin. [W] The original form of Merlin. One of the Welsh Triads tells us that Britain was called Clas Myrddin, "Myrddin's enclosure," before it was populated. Professor John Rhys argues that Myrddin was a deity specially worshipped at Stonehenge, which, according to a tradition recorded by Geoffrey of Monmouth, was erected by him. As Christianity replaced the old religion, it is said that he took nine attendant bards and the "thirteen treasures of Britain" and went to Bardsey Island, off the Lleyn peninsula, Gwynedd. In his Hibbert Lectures [English Text Society, p. 693] Rhys says that a Greek traveller in the first century A.D. mentioned an island where Kronos was supposed to be imprisoned with his attendants. Kronos slept, for that was the bond forged for him. This is a Hellenised account, for Kronos (Cronos) was one of the Titans and father of Zeus. He is believed to be an ancient pre-Hellenic god of fertility. The Romans identified him as Saturn. Rhys also believes that the Greek was referring to Myrddin and that Myrddin was therefore a sun god who made the descent into the western sea and was imprisoned there by the powers of darkness. See **Merlin.**

Myrddin Wyllt. [W] The Welsh equivalent of Suibhne Geilt, who took himself into the wood and there grew feathers and could leap from tree to tree.

N

Naas. [I] Wife of Lugh Lámhfada who died at the site of Nass, Co. Kildare, which bears her name.

Náir. [I] "Modesty." A goddess who took the High King Crebhán to the Otherworld and gave him fabulous treasures.

Naisii. [I] See **Naoise.**

Naked Warriors. There are many references to the Celtic custom of stripping naked to do battle or to engage in single combat. They did so from their religious concepts. Naked and at one with the world around them, the "aura" and life force of the warriors was increased. Polybius recorded, in his account of the Battle of Telamon in 225 B.C., that a Celtic tribe he designates as the Gaesatae hurled themselves naked into battle against the Romans. He did not realise that the word meant "spearmen" (Irish *gae,* Welsh *gwayw* = spear) and that they were probably a group of élite warriors like the Fianna, the Red Branch warriors, or Gamhanrhide. See **Knights.**

Nantsovelta. Gaulish goddess probably connected with water (Welsh *nant* = a brook).

Naoise. [I] Also given as Noisiu, Noise, and Naisii. The eldest son of Usna and his wife, Elbha, daughter of Cathbad the druid. With his brothers Ainlé and Ardan, he was a champion of the Red Branch. When Deirdre came to wed the king, Conchobhar Mac Nessa, Naoise fell in love with her and she with him. They eloped and fled to Alba accompanied by Naoise's brothers. After some years, Fergus Mac Roth arrived in Alba to say that Conchobhar had forgiven them and invited them to return to Ulster. In spite of Deirdre's forebodings, they did so. Fergus, in fact, had been tricked by Conchobhar. They journeyed to Emain Macha under the protection of Fergus' sons, Buinne and Iollan, and spent the night in the Red Branch Hostel. Conchobhar then ordered the hostel to be attacked. While Buinne was bribed to stop fighting to protect his charges, his brother Iollan was killed, as were Ainlé and Ardan. Naoise was killed by Eoghan Mac Durthacht, who slew him by seizing the magic sword Manannán Mac Lir had once given Naoise. Another version says a Norse prince named Maine killed him. See **Deirdre.**

Narberth. [W] More popularly given as Arberth, court of the lords of Dyfed.

Nár Thúathcaech. [I] The name means "shame." He was a swineherd of the Bodb Dearg and rival of the swineherd of Ochall Ochne of Connacht. The two swineherds fought through many reincarnations until Nár was born as Donn, the Brown Bull of Cuailgne.

Natchrantal. [I] A Connacht champion in Medb's army who found the Brown Bull of Cuailgne and drove it to the Connacht army. In another version, this adventure falls to Buic.

Navan. [I] See **Emain Macha.**

Nechtan. [I] A water god and husband of Boann.

Nechtan Scéne. [I] Mother of three supernatural sons, Foill, Fannell, and Tuachell, who were slain by Cúchulainn.

Nectanebus. [I] Pharaoh of Egypt who emerges in Irish myth because his daughter Scota married Milesius. She is not to be confused with Scota the daughter of the pharaoh Cingris and mother of Goidel, the progenitor of the Gaels. There were, in fact, two pharaohs named Nectanebus in the Thirtieth Dynasty; the first ruled from 380–363 B.C. and the second from 360–343 B.C. The name Nechtan, derived from Nectanebus, was apparently popular in Ireland, and several historical personages, as well as mythical characters, bore it.

Neide. [I] A Red Branch poet who fought a contest with Fer Cherdne for the honour of being chief poet of Ireland.

Neimed. [I] See **Nemeton.**

Néit. [I] Sometimes Net. A god of war. His wife appears as Nemain, part of the triune goddess Mórrígán. It may well be that the name is merely a synonym for Nuada, for Nemain is often confused with Nuada's wife, Macha.

Nemain. [I] A war goddess and wife of Néit. She is listed as one of the five goddesses who hover over battlefields, inspiring battle madness:

Dea (Hateful), Badb (Fury), Nemain (Venomous), Macha (Personification of Battle), and the Mórrígán (Great Queen or supreme war
goddess).

Nemed. [I] Leader of an invasion of Ireland. A descendent of Magog
and Japhet whose people spent half a year on the sea in their travels.
Only Nemed and four women survive to land on Ireland. Their
numbers increased from this, and Nemed was able to defeat the
Fomorii three times in battle.

Nemedians. [I] The followers of Nemed. After his death they were
subjugated by the Fomorii, but under their king, Fergus, they rose
up. Fergus killed the Fomorii king Conann during an attack on his
stronghold on Tory Island. However, only thirty Nemedians were
left alive and these left Ireland in despair, searching for a new
homeland.

Nemeton. A sanctuary or sacred grove. The name is found in Celtic
place-names as far afield as Turkey, where the Celtic state of Galatia
existed. Drunemeton, the sacred oak grove near Ankara, was recorded as the capital of Galatia. Nemetacum (northeast Gaul),
Nemetobrigia (Galicia, Spain), Nemetodurum (Nanterre),
Nemeton (Vaucluse), Vernemeton (Nottingham, England), and
Medionemeton (Scotland) are just some of the many places using
this name. Neimed was the Old Irish for "sanctuary," and the word
is probably cognate with Nemed, the leader of the Nemedians.

Nemetona. Regarded as a Gaulish war god, the name contains the
word "nemeton" (sanctuary). There could be a connection to the
Irish Nemhain (frenzy), goddess of war, or Nemed, who led the
third invasion of Ireland and fought the Fomorii. Nementona was
worshipped as the goddess of the sacred grove at Aquae Sulis (Bath,
England).

Nemglan. [I] A bird god who appeared to Mess Buachalla and made
love to her. Their son was Conaire Mór. He placed a *geis* on
Conaire, telling him that he must walk naked along the road to
Tara, armed only with a sling and one stone. If he did so, he would
become High King. Conaire Mór obeyed and the prophecy was
fulfilled.

Nennius. (ca. A.D. 800) An early Welsh historian who is important in
connection with the origins of Arthurian literature and specifically
mentions Arthur, crediting him with twelve victories over the

Anglo-Saxons. In a manuscript dated A.D. 817, now in the Bodleian
Library, Oxford, it is written that Nennius was once attacked by an
Englishman who sneered that the Welsh had no native alphabet and
had to use the Latin characters. This was a rather curious attack as
not only did English use the *Latin* alphabet for writing, but it was
the Celts, predominantly the Irish, who taught literacy to the
English. However, the manuscript records that, as a response,
Nennius invented an alphabet to confound his critic.

Nera. [I] A servant of Ailill of Connacht who went on an adventure to
the Otherworld, where he lived, became a lover of a woman of the
sídhe, and had a son. Nera escaped from the *sídhe* with his wife and
child and warned Ailill and Medb that people of the sídhe were
planning to destroy their city. Ailill sent Fergus Mac Roth to
destroy the *sídhe,* but not before a great deal of plunder was taken.

Nessa. [I] Daughter of Eochaidh Sálbuidhe of Ulster. She married
Fachtna, king of Ulster. In one version of the tale she slept with
Cathbad the druid and bore him a son who became Conchobhar
Mac Nessa. Her husband Fachtna died and his half-brother, Fergus
Mac Roth, fell in love with her. She agreed to become his wife if
he let her son Conchobhar rule as king for one year. She was an
ambitious and powerful woman and, after the year was up,
Conchobhar refused to give up the throne and Fergus was chased
into exile.

Niall Noíghiallach. [I] Niall of the Nine Hostages, youngest son of
Eochaidh Muigl Mheadoin, High King of Ireland, A.D. 358–366.
Niall was High King from A.D. 379–405 and was the progenitor of
the Uí Néill dynasty. He is recorded as raiding Britain and Gaul
during the time of Theodosius the Great. But myth and history are
fused in the story of his rise to kingship whereby he has to overcome
his wicked stepmother, Mongfhinn, who abandons him as a baby
naked on a hill. He is raised by a wandering bard, Torna Éices.
Sithchenn the smith foretells he will be High King. Then he comes
across an old hag who demands that he and his companions give her
a kiss. Only Niall has courage to do so, and she turns into a
beautiful woman named Flaithius (Royalty), the personification of
sovranty. She foretells he will be the greatest of Ireland's High Kings.

Niamh. [I] There are three characters called Niamh in the sagas. One,
the daughter of Manannán Mac Lir, becomes the lover of Oisín,

dwells with him in Tír Tairnigiri (Land of Promise), and bears him
a daughter named Plur na mBan (Flower of Women). Another
Niamh, the wife of Conall Cearnach, becomes the mistress of
Cúchulainn during the last period of his life. The third Niamh, the
daughter of Celtchair, married Conganchas Mac Daire, a warrior
whom no one could slay. She learns the secret of his invulnerability
and tells her father, who slays Conganchas. Niamh then marries the
son of Conchobhar Mac Nessa, Cormac Cond Longes.

Nisien. [W] Brother to Efnisien and half-brother to Bran, Branwen,
and Manawydan, children of Llyr. He is the "peace-maker," as
opposed to his strife-inducing brother. He is the son of Penardun,
wife of Llyr, who marries Eurosswyd.

Niul. [I] Son of Feinius Farsaidh, a famous wise teacher invited by the
pharaoh Cingris to settle in Egypt. He marries Cingris' daughter
Scota; their son is Goidel. Niul befriends Aaron, and Moses heals
Goidel from the bite of a serpent, it being foretold that no serpent
would live in the land of the Gaels.

Nodens. See **Nudd.**

Noidhiu. [I] Son of Fingel. His father was a mysterious god who slept
with Fingel. She gave birth after nine years and nine months. She
wanted to destroy the child, but the baby uttered nine judgments
and obtained the right to live.

Noinden. [I] The curse put on the men of Ulster by Macha, sometimes called "The Birth Pangs of Ulster."

Nos Galan-Gaeof. [W] The Welsh winter festival, equivalent to the
Samhain Feis.

Nuada. [I] Chief druid of Cahir Mór, a king and ancestor of Fionn
Mac Cumhail who built the fortress on the Hill of Allen. More
famous, however, is Nuada Argetlámh, Nuada of the Silver Hand.
He appears as the supreme leader of the gods, possessed of a sword
from which none could escape. He was the first ruler of the Dé
Danaan on their arrival in Ireland but lost his hand at the first battle
of Magh Tuireadh fighting against the Firbolg. The god of medicine, Dian Cécht, made him a silver hand, but later Dian Cécht's
son, Miach, made him a new hand of flesh and blood with which
he regained his position, displacing the half-Fomorii, Bres. Nuada
set off the events that led to the second battle of Magh Tuireadh
against the Fomorii. In this battle Nuada and his wife, Macha, are
slain by Balor of the Evil Eye. Nuada is cognate with the Welsh

Nudd of the Silver Hand. The name also appears in the form of Nodens. There is a third Nuada, Nuada Necht. He is a king who directly preceded Conaire Mór as the High King.

Nudd. [W] Nudd is cognate with Lludd and in this form is clearly identified with Nuada of the Silver Hand. See **Lludd Llaw Ereint.** A temple to Nodens, by which Roman soldiers in Britain came to know him, was founded at Lydney by the Severn. He is referred to in triad fashion (with Mordaf and Rhydderch) as one of the three generous ones of Britain.

Numbers. Numerology plays a significant and symbolic part in all Celtic myth. Some numbers can be particularly noted. Five, for example. There are five great roads in Ireland, five provinces (*cuigi,* the word for a province, means, literally, a fifth), five celebrated hostels, five paths of law, five prohibitions for provincial kings. Fionn Cumhail counts in fives, as do the people of the *sídhe.* There are five masters to each art, Cúchulainn has five wheels painted on his shield, and a medieval tract on language teaches that five words are adjudged to be a breath of the poet.

There is the number nine. It is argued that the Celts had a nine-day week; Medb rides off to Ulster with nine chariots; Cúchulainn has nine weapons; the curse on Ulster is for nine times nine generations; there are the nine judgments of Noidhiu and there is Niall of the Nine Hostages. In Welsh law the ninth day of the month marks the end of the beginning of a period, and a house was considered to have nine components (indeed, in Ireland, Bricriu's Hall has nine rooms). Three nines, twenty-seven, also becomes significant.

Twelve, too, is important, for kings usually have twelve companions. Seventeen also occurs. Events are listed as taking place after periods of seventeen days or seventeen years; a youth becomes a man on his seventeenth birthday; a druid suggests to Mael Dúin that he take seventeen men on his voyage, and on the fabulous Island of Women they are greeted by seventeen maidens. Lastly, the number thirty-three occurs as a frequent numerical symbol.

Nuts of Knowledge. [I] Nine hazelnuts of wisdom grew over Segais' Well (sometimes Conlaí's Well). The nuts dropped into the well, causing bubbles of mystic inspiration. The Well of Segais is said to have formed the Boyne River. The salmon Fintan had eaten of the Nuts of Knowledge and settled in a pool, where the druid Finegas caught it and gave it to his pupil Fion Mac Cumhail to cook. Fionn's thumb brushed against the salmon and he sucked the spot where it was burnt, thus obtaining knowledge. The tale has a remarkable similarity to that of Gwion Bach, who also burnt his thumb while preparing a magic dish for his mistress. By sucking the spot, he, too, obtains wisdom, but is chased through many reincarnations until he emerges as Taliesin.

Nynniaw. [W] A son of Beli and brother of Peibaw. Nynniaw and Peibaw were two kings of Britain. They had a quarrel over the meaning of the stars in the sky and went to war with one another. Their armies were destroyed and the lands laid waste. Finally they were turned into oxen as a punishment for their stupidity.

O

Oak. Of all the trees, it is the oak that has been most associated with the druids as their sacred tree. Some scholars argue that the very word "druid" derives from the word "oak-knowledge" (dru-vid), mainly because Pliny the Elder associated it with being cognate with the Greek word for oak. Certainly veneration of the oak was widespread among the Celts wherever they were. In Galatia, the state set up by the Celts on the central plain of Turkey, the capital was recorded by Strabo as Drunemeton—the oak sanctuary. Maximum Tyrius went further and claimed that the Celts saw the father of the gods (Zeus) in the image of a lofty oak. However, in Irish mythology the yew, hazel, and rowan trees are more frequently referred to than the oak. Certainly sacred trees were common and used as totems. Each clan had its sacred tree, and the most demoralising thing a hostile clan could do to another was to invade and fell the sacred tree. These were regarded as the *crann bethadh*, or "tree of life." In early Christian tradition we find many churches significantly sited by druidic oaks in Ireland: Cill Daire (Kildare), the "Church of the Oak," founded by Brigid; the great monastic school of Daire Maugh (Durrow), "Plain of the Oaks," in Wexford; and Daire Calgaich (Derry), Colmcille's favourite spot, which was the "Oak Grove of Calgaich." Mistletoe, associated with the Continental Celts, is not a native Irish plant and was only transported to Ireland in the eighteenth century.

Ocean-sweeper. [I] *Aigéan scuabadóir.* A magical ship that knew a man's thoughts and was propelled without sails or oars wherever he willed it. Lugh Lámhfada brought it from the Otherworld. It was given as a gift to Manannán Mac Lir.

Ochain. [I] The "Moaner." Enchanted shield of Conchobhar Mac Nessa that moaned whenever its owner was in danger.

Ochall Ochne. [I] King of the sídhe of Connacht, whose swineherd was Friuch, who was in perpetual rivalry with Nár, the swineherd of Bodb Dearg of Munster.

Octriallach. [I] Son of Indech of the Fomorii, killed by Ogma at the second battle of Magh Tuireadh. He had been able to discover how Dian Cécht, the Dé Danaan god of medicine, was able to bring back the slain Dé Danaan to life by the use of a magical "Spring of Health." Octriallach led the Fomorii in filling in the spring by placing great rocks over it.

Odras. [I] Daughter of Odarnatan, keeper of the hostel of Buchat Buasach. The Mórrígán turned her into a pool of water.

Ogham. [I] Sometimes Ogam. The earliest form of Irish writing, frequently referred to in Irish myths and sagas. Its invention is ascribed to Ogma, god of eloquence and literature. The sagas contain many references to great libraries of bark and wands carved with the Ogham script. However, the bulk of surviving Ogham scripts, dating from the fifth and sixth centuries A.D., are recorded on stones. There are 369 such inscriptions, some found in Wales, Scotland, and Ireland, but the bulk are in Ireland, and of these the highest density is in southern Ireland, with 121 of them in Co. Kerry alone. Mairtín Ó Murchu [*The Irish Language,* Dublin, 1985] suggests that Ogham originated in southwest Ireland. A text from the fourteen century, *Book of Ballymote,* is devoted to Ogham and gives an explanation of the characters. The most easterly Ogham inscription is recorded on stone at the site of Silchester. This was the tribal capital of the Celtic Atrebates (Calleva Atrebatum, according to the Romans), which, during the Roman occupation, became a walled town. After the occupation it would appear that Irish settlers, or early Christian missionaries, settled and put up an Ogham inscription. Then, with the invasion of the Anglo-Saxons, the Celts abandoned the town.

Ogma. [I] God of eloquence and literature. A son of the Dagda. He was skilled in dialects and poetry as well as being a warrior. He also had a role in conveying souls to the Otherworld. He was called Ogma *Grian-aineach* (of the Sunny Countenance) and Ogma *Cermait* (of the Honeyed Mouth). He is credited with the invention of the Ogham script. He is also credited with various children, of which his daughter Étain married the god of medicine, Dian Cécht. He ruled from the *sídhe* of Airceltrai.

Ogmia. The name found on a piece of pottery at Richborough, in England, depicting a figure with long curly hair and sun rays emanating from his head. He also holds the whip of the *Sol Invictus*. This is obviously the British equivalent of Ogma and Ogmios.

Ogmios. The Gaulish god cognate with Ogma in Irish mythology. Lucian identified him as a Celtic Heracles. Ogmios was thought to transport the dead to the Otherworld, although Bíle also had this role.

Oillipheist. [I] A fabulous beast whose passage westward caused the River Shannon to be formed.

Oílmelc. [I] The alternative name for Imbolg, meaning "sheep's milk."

Oirbsen. [I] An alternative name for Manannán Mac Lir. Loch Oirbsen was an ancient name for Loch Corrib, Co. Galway, where the ocean god is said to have met his death by drowning.

Oireachtas. [I] An assembly. An annual gathering organised by Conradh na Gaeilge, founded in 1893, and similar to the Welsh Eisteddfod.

Oisín. [I] Ossian in Scotland and Oshin in the Isle of Man. Son of Fionn Mac Cumhail and the goddess Sadb, daughter of the Bodb Dearg. He was acknowledged as the greatest warrior in Ireland and a great warrior of the Fianna. He was found by his father, who was searching for Sadb, who had been turned into a deer. Fionn called him Oisín, or "fawn." He grew up to be one of the leading champions of the Fianna. He married a yellow-haired stranger from a sunny country named Eibhir. His most famous son was the warrior Oscar. Oisín took part in many of the adventures of the Fianna but refused to help Fionn exact vengeance on the lovers Diarmuid and Gráinne. He consorted with Niamh, a goddess from the Otherworld, and dwelt there with her for three hundred years—a period that seemed like only three weeks to him. The Fenian Cycle is often referred to as the Ossianic Cycle. The tales were made famous by the Scot James MacPherson, whose rendering of them under the general title *Ossian* became a European classic and started the Romantic Movement.

Ol. [W] The best tracker in Britain at Arthur's fortress.

Ollamh. [I] Sometimes given as Ollave. Of the seven grades of poets, it was the highest grade. It took candidates nine to twelve years of study, for they had to memorise 250 prime stories and 100 secondary stories to claim the title. Ollamh Fódhla was the eighteenth

High King of Ireland, reigning in 714 B.C., and is traditionally recognised as founding rule by legislature and giving the country the first codified law system. He is said to have been buried at Tailltinn (Teltown, Co. Westmeath).

Olwen. [W] "She of the white track," so named because four white trefoils sprang up wherever she trod. The beautiful daughter of Yspaddaden Pencawr, "chief giant," who lived with her father in a fortress. Culhwch overcomes many difficulties to make her his wife. She has similarities to Étain in Irish myth.

Oonagh. [I] Wife of Fionnbharr, relegated from an ancient goddess of the Dé Danaan in popular folklore to "queen of all the fairies in Ireland." Oonagh and Fionnbharr dwelt at the *sídhe* of Meadhna, five miles west of Tuam.

Oral Tradition. It was not until the early Christian period that the Celts began to write extensively in their own languages. For hundreds of years prior to that time, Celtic law, poetry, philosophy, science, history, genealogy, and literature were passed down in oral form. Julius Caesar commented of the Celts: "They commit to memory immense amounts of poetry. And some of them continue their studies for twenty years. They consider it improper to commit their studies to writing." It is clear that this was a religious prohibition rather than an inability to write, for we find that the Celts could and did leave inscriptions on occasion, mainly funerary inscriptions in Greek and Latin characters. Such Celtic inscriptions have been found in northern Italy and northern Spain. A find in 1983 of a lead tablet written in Latin cursive has provided us with the longest known Gaulish text to date (*Études celtique,* Paris, CNRS, Vol. XXII, 1985). Prior to this, the most extensive text in Gaulish was the Coligny calender, dated to the first century B.C., now in the Musée Des Arts, Lyons, France.

It is argued that when the Greeks first recorded the name *Keltoi* as a name for the Celts, they were recording a name by which the Celts referred to themselves—"the secret people." The word *ceillt* still means "hidden" in modern Irish, and this is also thought to be the etymology of the word "kilt," for obvious reasons.

It is accepted that many of the stories of Celtic myth were ancient even at the time when Christianity had replaced the ancient Celtic religion, which had placed such a prohibition on writing. And when the Christian scribes came to write down the stories, such as the Red Branch Cycle, they might have already been passed down orally for a thousand years. In the myths we learn that the Irish literati had a secret literary language, *bérla na filied* (the language of the poets), which only the initiated could understand.

Orc-Triath. [I] See **Torc Triath.**

Oriel. [I] The Irish form for Airgialla, signifying "subject people." The kingdom of Oriel consisted of the modern countries of Armagh, Monaghan, Tyrone, and most of Fermanagh and Derry.

Orlam. [I] A son of Ailill and Medb slain by Cúchulainn.

Orna. [I] The sword of Tethra, the Fomorii king, which could speak and recount its deeds. Having killed Tethra at the second battle of Magh Tuireadh, Ogma claimed the sword.

Oscar. [I] Son of Oisín and Eibhir and grandson of Fionn Mac Cumhail and Sadb. The name—*Os* (deer) and *car* (lover)—reflects that of his father, whose mother was the goddess Sadb, who had been turned into a deer by the Dark Druid. Oscar was the mightiest warrior of the Fianna, a man of hard strength with a heart "like a twisted horn sheathed in steel." He was given command of a battalion of the Fianna that was called "The Terrible Broom" because it would not retreat an inch but swept its enemies from the field. He married Aidín. When Cairbre the High King sought to curb the power of the Fianna, which Oscar now commanded, Oscar led them in the battle at Gabhra (Garristown, Co. Dublin). The battle saw the destruction of the Fianna. Oscar, however, killed Cairbre in single combat but was himself mortally wounded. His wife, Aidín, died of grief. Fionn Mac Cumhail returns from the Otherworld to lament him, and his father, Oisín, comes to carry his bier with the hero Celta.

Oshin. Manx equivalent of Oisín, son of Fionn Mac Cumhail.

Ossar. [I] The hound of Mac Da Thó that was coveted by Ailill and Medb and also by Conchobhar Mac Nessa. In another version, the hound is called Ailbe. At the end of the story of "Mac Da Thó's Boar," the dog chases Ailill's chariot and is killed by his charioteer.

Ossian. Scottish equivalent of Oisín, son of Fionn Mac Cumhail.

Otherworld. A general term for the various lands of the gods, both good and evil, and for the place where one was reborn after death. The Celts were one of the first European peoples to evolve a doctrine of immortality of the soul. The basic belief was that death was only a changing of place and that life went on with all its forms and foods in another world, a world of the dead that gave up living souls to this world. An exchange of souls was always taking place between the two worlds; death in this world brought a soul to the Otherworld, and death in the Otherworld brought a soul to this world. Because of this, Philostratus of Tyana (ca. A.D. 170–249) observed that the Celts celebrated birth with mourning and death with joy. They mourned birth because it meant someone had died in the Otherworld and celebrated death because it meant a rebirth in the Otherworld.

It was believed that on one night of the year the Otherworld became visible to mankind. This was the Feast of Samhain (October 31/November 1). On this night all the gates to the Otherworld were opened and the inhabitants could set out to wreak vengeance on those living in this world who had wronged them. This ancient belief survived into Christianity as Hallowe'en, the evening of All Hallows, or All Saints' Day on November 1. The modern Christian idea is that it is the night when witches and demons and spirits from Hell set out to ensnare unsuspecting souls.

The forms of Otherworlds range from dark, brooding purgatories of the Fomorii islands to the sunny lands of the Land of Youth or Land of Promise. The Otherworlds of both the Irish and Welsh are similar, and mortal humans could adventure and live in the Otherworld. Pwyll can journey to Annwn, while Cúchulainn can adventure in Hy-Falga. Most of the renditions of the Otherworld are generally as islands to the southwest of Ireland or Wales. The most famous sojourn in the Otherworld was that of Oisín, who rode off on a magical horse with Niamh, the daughter of the sea god Manannán Mac Lir, and stayed there for three hundred years.

Owain. [W] Son of Urien. He is a warrior of Arthur's, and in the tale of "The Dream of Rhonabwy" he plays a chess game with Arthur. When Cymon is defeated by the Black Knight, Owain sets out to find and defeat him. Having done so, he finds the Castle of the Fountain and is rescued from imprisonment by a maiden called Luned, who gives him a ring to make him invisible. She then helps him win the hand of the Lady of the Fountain. After three years Arthur and his companions come looking for him. He returns to Arthur's court and forgets his Lady. She comes after him and calls him a deceiver, a traitor, and faithless. He is ashamed and flees into a desolate country where he becomes a recluse. Near death, he is restored to strength by the magic of a noblewoman and her hand-maidens. He has to slay a lion and a serpent. Finally he finds Luned imprisoned and about to face death by burning. He rescues her, defeats a black giant and releases 24 maidens from his imprison-ment, and then returns to the Lady of the Fountain. The saga therefore ends happily. One mysterious point of the tale is that Cenferchyn, according to "The Dream of Rhonabwy," gave Owain 300 ravens, which formed his army, and wherever Owain went with them he was victorious in battle. How this happened or why has been lost to tradition.

Owl of Cwm Cawlwyd. [W] One of the oldest creatures, who is unable to help Culhwch in his hunt for Olwen.

P

Palug's Cat. [W] A speckled feline who swam ashore on Ynys Mon and ate 180 warriors. Cei fought with it and killed it.

Paris. [W] King Paris of France, "from whom Paris takes its name," appears in the story of Culhwch and Olwen as a friend of Arthur's who helps in the quest. The claim is not so far-out, for there was a Belgae tribe called the Parisi who settled, or had a branch who settled, north of the Humber (Yorkshire). The area has produced some of the most spectacular Celtic chariot burials (designated the "Arras culture" by archaeologists). [See *The Parisi,* Herman Ramm, Duckworth, London, 1978.] The Parisi, or their Gaulish branch, gave their name to Paris.

Parthanán. [I] It is suspected that Parthanán may be a folk memory of Partholón. He is a mischievous spirit who, at the end of the harvest, would thresh any corn left standing.

Partholón. [I] Partholón was the leader of the third mythical invasion of Ireland. He murdered his father, Sera, and his mother, hoping to inherit their kingdom. When he failed he led his followers to Ireland and landed in Munster. Partholón discovered Ireland was inhabited by the Fomorii and their ruler Cichol Grinchenghos (the footless) and did battle with them. He went on a journey, leaving his wife, Dealgnaid, alone with his servant Togda. They had an affair in his absence. Discovering this on his return, he accepted the blame, saying it was his fault for leaving his wife alone. Varying accounts credit him with three sons and "a hireling" or with four sons. His eldest son appears as Eber, the same name as a son of Míl, the others being Rudraidhe and Laighlinne. The Partholónians are said to have introduced agriculture into Ireland, cleared the plains, and established hostels. They were killed by a plague.

Peibaw. [W] The brother of Nynniaw and a king of Britain. See **Nynniaw.**

Penardun. [W] Daughter of the mother-goddess Don who weds Llyr. She is the mother of Bran, Branwen, and Manawydan, although in some traditions Iweriadd is given as mother of Bran and Branwen. She later weds Eurosswyd and has two sons, Nisien and Efnisien, the first a youth of gentle nature and lover of peace, the second who loved nothing so much as strife and conflict.

Pendaran Dyfed. [W] A swineherd, one of the three most renowned in Britain, and foster father of Pryderi.

Percival. His first appearance in literature is in *Perceval, ou le conte du Graal,* written ca. A.D. 1175 by Chrétien de Troyes. The Celtic model seems to be Peredur, and a medieval Welsh tale entitled "Peredur, son of Efrawg," included in the *Mabinogi,* is parallel to the tale. He becomes Parzifal in the German version of the story. From the time of Malory's *Morte d'Arthur* he is Sir Percival, the virgin knight, whose quest for the Grail is the main thrust of all the stories about him.

Peredur. [W] The Celtic model for the later Percival and Parzifal. His father was Efrawc and he was a seventh son. The syllable *Per* occurs in all forms of this hero's name and, interestingly enough—because Peredur is the figure around whom the first Grail legends revolve— the word means a bowl or vessel in Brythonic Celtic. The earliest Peredur tale is simply one of vengeance for the slaying of a kinsman, although setting out for magical treasure is included. See **Percival.**

Perilous Plain, The. A plain of devouring wild beasts that Cúchulainn had to cross to reach the fortress of Scáthach.

Picts. Sometimes given as the Pictii. In Irish saga they appear as the *Tuatha Cruithne.* They are also mentioned in Welsh saga as *Priteni.* The Picts were British Celts, a confederation of some of the northern tribes, such as the Caledonii and the Maecatae. The term "Pict" was first recorded in a Latin poem of A.D. 297, and it was simply a nickname given by the Roman soldiers garrisoned on Hadrian's Wall to the northern Celtic warriors, who, in order to give themselves a more fearsome appearance in war, painted or tattooed their bodies: *pictii* is the past participle of the Latin *pingere,* "to paint." There is a general misconception that the Picts were a new ethnic element in Britain. This would be the equivalent of seeing national groupings in the United States called "Yanks" or "Rebs," or, indeed, "Limeys" or "Pommies" in England.

Professor Kenneth Jackson points out that there are no texts extant in a "Pictish language," but that both the Latin king-lists and place-names are unquestionably Celtic: moreover, they are P-Celtic (i.e., Brythonic). However, within a few centuries after the Roman period, a switch to Goidelic (Gaelic) language had been made. The king-lists of the Picts actually show both Goidelic and Brythonic forms, but Joseph Loth and Kuno Myer have pointed to the predominance of Brythonic names. There is an intriguing reference to eighth century Pictish literacy in chronicles that cite quotations *in veterimus Pictorium libris* (in old books of the Picts). By this period the Picts would have been fully absorbed into a Gaelic culture. The *Annals of Ulster* record Picts living in the midlands of Ireland as late as A.D. 809.

A Pictish warrior named Cruithne is said to have settled in Alba with his seven children and divided the country between them: hence Tuatha Cruithne. Cat ruled Caithness, then came Cé (Marr and Buchan), Círech (Angus and Mearns), Fiobh (Fife), Moireabh (Moray), Fótla (Ath-fhótla = Atholl), and Fortriu (Strathearn).

Pigs. Pigs have a special place in Celtic myth and are magical animals with certain properties of enchantment. The pigskin of Tuis, which the sons of Tuireann were asked to bring back to Ireland, cured all wounds and sickness and, if dipped into a stream, would turn the water into wine for three days. The seven pigs of Easal of the Golden Pillars provided an inexhaustible feast—if eaten on one night, they would appear the next day ready to be slaughtered for another feast. Pigs were highly prized. Gwydion was successful in stealing Pryderi's pigs, but Arthur was unable to capture the swine of March ap Meirchion. A Gaulish god, whom the Romans equated with Mercury, had the epithet Moccus (pig).

Plant Rhys Ddwfn. [W] A land supposedly lying off the coast of Dyfed, probably corrupted from *Pant yr Is-ddwfn* or *Plant Rhi Is-dwfn*—"The Children of (the King of) the Netherworld." They were said to be an Otherworld people who had the power to make their country invisible except from one small patch of ground to be found in Dyfed.

Plur na mBan. [I] "The Flower of Women." Daughter of Oisín and the goddess Niamh, daughter of Manannán Mac Lir.

Polyandry/Polygamy. Plurality of marriages was permitted in ancient society and enshrined in the Brehon Laws and Laws of Hywel Dda. The practice continued well into the Christian era. Men and women enjoyed equal rights, and nowhere is this more carefully demonstrated than in the laws relating to marriage. Divorce could be had by mutual consent as well as for numerous "offences." Rights that were carefully listed in the laws gave protection to both sides.

Pooka. See **Púca.**

Powys. [W] The ancient kingdom of mid-Wales, which has now been reestablished in the new county boundary system.

Pryderi. [W] Son of Pwyll and Rhiannon and the only person to figure in all the branches of the Mabinogi. When a babe, he is kidnapped by malignant forces, and those who were supposed to be looking after him, to protect themselves, accuse his mother of killing him. He is found by Teyrnon of Gwent Is-Coed who, with his wife, names him Gwri, "golden hair," and raises him. But they eventually find out his true identity and return him to Rhiannon and Pwyll. Rhiannon then names him Pryderi, "Care," for the care she has suffered during his absence. Pryderi is fostered by Teyrnon who, with his wife, befriends Pwyll and Rhiannon.

It is in the third branch that Pryderi is seen as lord of Dyfed, having succeeded his father. He now gives his mother Rhiannon in marriage to Manawydan. At Arbeth, they are feasting when there is a peal of thunder and a mist falls. When it rises, all human life has vanished, as have all the buildings, leaving the countryside desolate. Thus begins a series of adventures (see **Manawydan fab Llyr**). Rhiannon is abducted, and Pryderi, who is depicted as an impulsive character, is enticed into a magic fortress and made prisoner by the author of the magic curse, Llwyd. Pryderi and Rhiannon are rescued by Manawydan, who forces Llwyd to promise that no further spells shall ever again be cast on Dyfed. Llwyd, by the way, is the friend of Gwawl, the suitor for the hand of Rhiannon who had been bested by Pwyll, Pryderi's father.

Prydwen. [W] The name of Arthur's ship.

Púca. [I] Anglicised as Pooka. A mischievous spirit who led travellers astray or performed other devilment. It occurs in later legend and seems to have no basis in myth. It could well be an import through the Danish settlements in Ireland, taken from the Norse *pukí*. It also went into Welsh as *pwca* and into English as Puck.

Pursuit. In Irish, *toruidheacht*. A class of tales that were popular with audiences. The most famous is *Toruidheacht Dhiarmuda is Ghráinne* (The Pursuit of Diarmuid and Gráinne).

Pwyll. [W] Lord of Dyfed whose chief court is at Arberth. He has to repay Arawn, king of Annwn, for a discourtesy by taking his form for a year and meeting Arawn's enemy Hafgan in combat. During the year he is in Arawn's image he is invoked not to make love with Arawn's wife even though he shares her bed. Pwyll carries out his task, slaying Hafgan, and becomes head of Annwn. He wins the hand of Rhiannon, although she is taken by a rival suitor, Gwawl, by a trick. Using a similar trick, Pwyll gets her back. In the third year of marriage, Rhiannon bears his son Pryderi. The child is stolen and Rhiannon's maids cause her to be suspected of killing the child. Pwyll treats her badly but eventually the child is found.

R

Ragallach. [I] A king of Connacht whose death at the hands of his own child is foretold. Ragallach attempts to avoid his fate by destroying his only child, a daughter. The child is saved and raised by a swineherd. She grows into a beautiful maiden and Ragallach makes her his concubine. She fulfils the prophecy.

Raighne. [I] A son of Fionn Mac Cumhail.

Rann. [I] Also *rannaigecht*. A stanza of four heptasyllabic lines often appearing in Old Irish texts.

Rath. [I] He was lulled to sleep by a mermaid and then torn to pieces by her and her companions, a fate that occurs to many unwary mariners in the Irish tales.

Ráth. [I] A fortress or earthwork, generally circular.

Red Branch. [I] The body of warriors who were guardians of Ulster during the days of Conchobhar Mac Nessa. Cúchulainn was their greatest champion. As far back as Irish tradition goes there is an institute of "knighthood." The Red Branch were the Ulster equivalent of the Fianna, the bodyguard of the High King. Out of this concept came the later medieval Christian idea of Arthur's "Knights of the Round Table." The Red Branch were founded by Ross the Red of Ulster, who wed Maga, daughter of the love god Aonghus Óg. Their banner was a yellow lion on a green field of silk.

Red Branch Cycle. [I] Also known as the Ulster Cycle, this is the great heroic cycle of Irish mythology. The main stories comprise the famous epic of the *Táin Bó Cuailgne*. Scholars accept that the cycle must have been transmitted orally for nearly a thousand years before it was transcribed. The basic text of the epic survives in the *Leabhar na hUidre* (twelfth century Book of the Dun Cow) and in the *Leabhar Laigneach* (twelfth century Book of Leinster).

Redynvre, Red Stag of. [W] One of the oldest creatures in the world in the story of Culhwch and Olwen.

Reincarnation. The reincarnation, or transmigration, of souls theme frequently occurs in Celtic mythology. Not only the gods could be born again (sometimes entering the womb of a woman as a fly or ear of corn) or pass through different stages of existence, but mortals could also participate in this complex process. In Irish mythology one of the most interesting reincarnation cycles is that of the swineherds Friuch and Nár, who go through various changes to emerge, in their final forms, as Finnbhenach and Donn, the two massive bulls who have their final clash in the closing stages of the *Táin Bó Cuailgne*. In Welsh myth, perhaps the most fascinating transmigration tale is that of Gwion Bach, who changes from youth into hare, fish, bird, and grain of wheat and, finally, is reborn from the womb of his enemy as the great poet Taliesin.

Retaliator. [I] Díoltach. One of the three swords of Manannán Mac Lir, it never failed to slay.

Rheged. [W] The ancient British Celtic kingdom before it split into Strath-Clóta and Cumbria.

Rhiannon. [W] "Great Queen." Pwyll, lord of Dyfed, is seated at Arberth when he sees a beautiful maiden riding by on a majestic white horse. It is Rhiannon. Rhiannon and Pwyll arrange their marriage, but at the wedding feast Pwyll, by thoughtlessly granting a boon to a suppliant, has to give Rhiannon to Gwawl (Light), son of the goddess Clud, who is his rival for the hand of the girl. However, at Gwawl's wedding feast, by means of a ruse, Gwawl has to give her back to Pwyll. Pwyll, having entered the feast in disguise, tricks Gwawl into entering a magic bag provided by Rhiannon. Then Pwyll's men gather around to kick and beat the unfortunate man. There is a similarity here to the Irish tale of Brandubh, king of Leinster, who wins Mongán's wife from him by a similar trick and in which Mongán then recovers her in like fashion.

In the fourth year of marriage Rhiannon bears Pwyll a son, but on the night he is born the women in attendance fall asleep. The child is carried off in mysterious circumstances. Finding the child gone, the women, to save themselves, kill some dog pups and smear the blood on Rhiannon and accuse her of killing her own child. Years later, having suffered an unjust punishment, Rhiannon hears that her child is safe and has been raised by Teyrnon, lord of Gwent

Is-Coed, and his wife. "I should be delivered of my care if that were true," says Rhiannon. The boy takes the name Pryderi (Care).

In the story of Culhwch and Olwen, Culhwch has to obtain Rhiannon's birds to give entertainment to the giant Yspaddaden in order to obtain Olwen's hand.

Manawydan, son of Llyr, becomes Rhiannon's second husband after the death of Pwyll. A curse falls on Dyfed and she is abducted by Llwyd, the friend of her former suitor Gwawl. Pryderi is also captured, but they are rescued by Manawydan.

Rhinnon Rhin Branawd. [W] The possessor of a magic bottle needed in the story of Culhwch and Olwen.

Rhitta. [W] A giant who is king of Gwynedd and who takes a hand in the argument between Nynniaw and Peibaw.

Rhonabwy. [W] A warrior under Madawc, son of Maredudd. Madawc's brother, Iorwerth, rose against him. Rhonabwy takes Madawc's troops to quell the rebellion. He goes to rest one night in a hut and lies on a yellow calfskin by the fire. Here he sleeps for three nights and has a wonderful dream in which he sees Arthur and his warriors as they prepare for the battle at Mount Badon. The chief incident narrated is that of the game of chess between Arthur and Owain.

Rhun. [W] He was sent by Arthur to seduce Elphin's wife.

Riada. [I] The ancestor of the Dál Riada (of both Ulster and Alba). In the fourth century A.D. there was a famine in Munster and its ruler, Conaire, allowed his son, Riada, to go north with some of the people. He settled first in Co. Antrim and then crossed the sea into Alba (Scotland), where he formed a second kingdom of Dál Riada on Airer Ghàidheal (Argyll), the seaboard of the Gael.

Ríangabur. [I] Father of the two most famous charioteers of Ulster: Laeg, charioteer to Cúchulainn, and Id, charioteer to Conall Cearnach.

Ríastarthae. [I] The name given to Cúchulainn's battle fury.

Roc. [I] The steward of the love god Aonghus Óg. Roc had a son by the wife of Donn, father of Diarmuid Ua Duibhne. Donn killed Roc's child by crushing it. Roc smote his child with a magic wand and revived it as a huge boar without ears or tail. Roc charged this boar to encompass the death of Donn's own son, Diarmuid. It went off to Ben Bulben to await its destiny. See **Diarmuid** and **Gráinne.**

Rómit Rígoinmít. [I] The jester of Conchobhar Mac Nessa.

Ronán. [I] King of Leinster and father of Mael Fhothartaig. After his wife Ethné died, Ronán married the daughter of Eochaidh of Dunsverick. She was young and lusted after Ronán's son. Mael Fhothartaig rejected her advances, and in a jealous rage she persuaded Ronán that he had attempted to rape her. Ronán ordered his son killed, but when he later learned the truth, he died of grief and his wife took poison.

Ron Cerr. [I] A young champion of Brandubh of Leinster. He managed to enter the camp of the High King Aedh, with whom Brandubh was at war, and slew him.

Rosualt. [I] A mighty and fabulous sea monster that was cast ashore on the plain of Murrish under Croagh Phádraig (Co. Mayo). Rosualt is said to have vomited three times in three successive years before its death. By its vomiting it destroyed all the fish and sea creatures, all the birds of the air, and all the men and four-footed creatures on the land.

Round Table, The. According to Malory, there were 150 knights who sat at Arthur's round table, which had been made by Merlin at Carduel for Arthur's father, Uthr Bendragon. The first reference does not occur until Wace's *Roman de Brut,* but the most complete details of this later addition to the Arthurian saga occur in Malory's *Morte d'Arthur.*

Ruadán. [I] A son of Bres, the half-Fomorii ruler of the Dé Danaan, and the goddess Brigid. Ruadán wounded the smith god Goibhniu at the second battle of Magh Tuireadh. He was slain in the combat and his mother, the goddess Brigid, came to the battlefield to bewail her son; this is recorded as the first keening (*caoine,* "lament") to be heard in Ireland. There is also a Ruadán of Lorrhaa, also known as Ronán, Rodán, and Ruadhan, one of the "Twelve Apostles of Ireland." He occurs in the myths for—having sheltered a kinsman accused of murder and being arrested by the High King's men—cursing the High King (Diarmuid) and Tara, the seat of the High Kings. According to the myths, Tara became desolate from that time onwards.

Ruadh. [I] A son of Rigdonn who voyaged with three ships off the north of Ireland. He was becalmed and so, with his crew weak for want of food and water, he set off to swim in search of assistance. He came on a mysterious island under the sea on which dwelt nine beautiful women. He spent nine nights with them and one of them bore him a son. A second Ruadh may well be the same character as the first. He too was on a voyage when his ship was stopped by three goddesses who took him to the seabed, where he slept with them. They told him that they would collectively bear him a son and entreated him to return to them when his voyage was done. When he did not return, they pursued him and cut off his son's head, throwing it after him.

Rudraidhe. [I] One of the sons of Partholón who is acclaimed as founder of the royal house of Ulster. The men of Ulster became known as the Clan Rudraidhe or, sometimes, Rudricans.

S

Sacra. A name anciently applied to Ireland, mentioned by Rufus Festus Avienius (ca. fourth century A.D.) in an account of the voyage of Himilco the Phoenician in 510 B.C.

Sacrifices. In Celtic literature there is little evidence of human sacrifice being practised except in a story in the *Dinnsenchas* tract (Book of Leinster), which speaks of children being sacrificed to Cromm Cruach, an idol set up by Tighernmas on Magh Slécht. The story is put forward as an aberration rather than a norm. Cromm Cruach was quickly overthrown.

Sadb. [I] Daughter of Bodb Dearg. She was turned into a fawn by the "Dark Druid." One day, hunting near the Hill of Allen, Fionn Mac Cumhaill came across a fawn and his two hounds refused to kill it. Another version has Fionn crushing his hound to death between his legs to prevent it from killing the fawn. That night the fawn takes on Sadb's mortal form and becomes Fionn's mistress. They live happily for a while until the Dark Druid discovers them and turns Sadb back into a fawn. She vanishes and Fionn searches Ireland until, near Ben Bulben, he finds a naked boy who has been raised by a fawn. Fionn recognises in him his son by Sadb and calls him Oisín (Little Fawn).

Saidhthe Suaraigne. [I] "Bitch of evil," one of the hounds of Cromm Dubh.

Sainnth. [I] Son of Imbath and father of Macha who cursed the men of Ulster.

Sál Fhada. [I] Son of a king of Greece who, when his father died, was sent into exile in Ireland and then joined the Fianna. The Fianna restored him to his kingdom but not before he had been mortally wounded and restored to life by a magic cup.

Salmon of Knowledge. [I] See **Fintan.**

Salmon of Llyn Llyw. [W] The oldest and wisest of living things, who eventually tells Culhwch where Mabon is being held prisoner.

Samaliliath. [I] A Partholón who introduced ale into Ireland according to the myths.

Samhain. [I] One of the gods, a brother of Cian and Goibhniu. He was looking after a magical cow, Glas Gaibhnenn, which belonged to his brother Cian. Balor of the Evil Eye, disguised as a little red-haired boy, tricked him into parting with it. Samhain's role as a god is not clearly defined, although one of the four major Celtic festivals was named after him. The *Feis na Samhna,* or the Samhain Festival, was held on the evening of October 31 into the following day, November 1. It marked the end of one pastoral year and the beginning of the next. It was an intensely spiritual time, for it was the one period when the Otherworld became visible to mankind and when spiritual forces were let loose on the human world. Christianity took this pagan festival over as a harvest festival. The feast became St. Martin's Mass (Martinmas). The festival also became All Saints' Day or All Hallows, and the evening prior was Hallowe'en, still celebrated as the night when spirits and ghosts set out to wreak vengeance on the living and when evil marched unbridled across the world. In all the Celtic countries, fires were extinguished and could only be rekindled from a ceremonial fire lit by the druids. Significant events happened on Samhain or its equivalent. It was the time when the Fomorii oppressed the people of Nemed and when the Dé Danaan defeated the Fomorii at the second battle of Magh Tuireadh.

Samhair. [I] Daughter of Fionn Mac Cumhail who marries Cormac Cas, son of Ailill Olom of Munster. Cormac Cas is recorded as ruling in the third century A.D. He built a palace for his bride and their bed was supported by three pillar stones. Hence, the palace was called Dún-tri-lag, the fortress of the three pillar stones, which is now Duntryleague, Co. Limerick. It is recorded that Cormac Cas received a terrible wound on his head but recovered.

Sandda. [W] "Angel Face." A warrior at Arthur's fortress who was so fair no man dared attack him during the Battle of Camluan for fear he was an angel. He is asked to help Culhwch in his quest.

Scáthach nUanaind. [I] Also known as Scáthach Buanand (Victorious). Daughter of Ard-Greimne of Lethra. She is the most famous of female warriors. Living on Scáthach's Island (*scáthach,* "shadow"), which is thought to be Skye, she ran a military academy at which the heroes of Ireland received their training in the martial arts from her. Her most famous pupil was Cúchulainn, to whom she taught his famous battle leap and also gave the Gae-Bolg, the terrible spear. Cúchulainn trained with her for a year and a day, during which time her daughter, Uathach, was his mistress. Later he joined Scáthach in her battle against her sister Aoife, reputed to be the strongest of female warriors. Cúchulainn defeated Aoife in combat and she became his lover and bore him a son, Connlaí.

Sceanb. [I] Wife of the harpist Craiftine. She became lover of Cormac Cond Longes, who her husband then had killed in a jealous fury.

Scena. [I] Wife of Amairgen, son of Milesius. She died on the voyage to Ireland and was buried at Inbhirscena, said to be an ancient name for the mouth of the Kenmare River in Co. Kerry.

Scenmed. [I] Sister of Forgall Manach. Following his death, when Cúchulainn eloped with Forgall's daughter, Emer, Scenmed raised an army and followed the Ulster champion to exact vengeance. Cúchulainn defeated and slew her.

Sceolan. [I] A hound of Fionn Mac Cumhail but also his nephew. With its brother Bran it was born to Fionn's sister (sometimes referred to as sister-in-law and even aunt), Tuireann, while she was transformed into a bitch-dog by magic practised by the jealous mistress of her husband, Ullan. See **Tuireann.**

Sciathbhreag. [I] "Speckled shield." A member of the Fianna.

Scoriath. [I] King of the Fir Morca in Gaul and father of the beautiful Moriath. He welcomed Móen to his court, allowed him to marry his daughter, and supplied him with an army of Gauls to help him establish himself as king of Leinster and exact vengeance on his evil great-uncle Cobhthach.

Scota. [I] Daughter of the Egyptian pharaoh Cingris. She became wife of Niul and mother of Goidel, the progenitor of the Gaels. There is a second Scota who was daughter of the Egyptian pharaoh Nectanebus and wife of Milesius. She was killed fighting the Dé Danaan and was buried in Scotia's Glen, three miles from Tralee in Co. Kerry.

Scotland. See **Alba.** Scotland was never part of the Roman province of Britain, although the Romans, having conquered the Celts of the south, tried several times to exert their military domination in the north. During the spring or summer of A.D. 79, the Roman governor Agricola turned north. His campaigns lasted six years, during which the tribes of the north made a fierce resistance under Calgacos (the name means "swordsman"). But try as he would, Agricola could not conquer the northern tribes, the major one of which was the Caledonii. By A.D. 105, the Romans gave up any pretence of establishing their rule and, following a visit by the emperor Hadrian in 122, built a wall stretching for 117 kilometers, dividing the north from the Roman-occupied south. It was called Hadrian's Wall and can still be seen today. In 138 a new emperor, Antoninus Pius, made a determined attempt to extend his rule north, and the governor, Lollius Urbicus, pushed as far as the Forth-Clyde isthmus and constructed another wall, the Antonine Wall, stretching only 60 kilometres in length. In 180, however, the Celts swept across the Antonine Wall and pushed the Romans back to Hadrian's Wall, which remained a border for a while.

At this time the Celts of what was to become Scotland spoke a Brythonic or P-Celtic language. They had a custom of using war paint, much like the American Indians or many other peoples in recent times. Because of this the Roman soldiers, stationed on Hadrian's Wall, called them "the painted ones." The term "Pict" was first recorded in a Latin poem of A.D. 297, and it was simply a nickname given to these northern Celtic warriors. Pictii is the past participle of the Latin *pingere*, "to paint." The Picts were not a new element among the Celtic tribes of Scotland. They were from many tribes, such as the Caledonii and Maecatae. They called themselves Preteni, which in Gaelic, because of the famous substitute of the "q" for "p," became Cruithin. Professor Kenneth Jackson has pointed out that when the Picts emerged into recorded record they were already Gaelic-speaking. Yet their king-lists show names that are unquestionably Brythonic or British Celtic in form. This, of course, is not surprising.

However, in recent times, a new myth about the Picts has sprung up in which it is claimed that they were not Celtic. Gaelic was introduced, or reintroduced if you accept the argument that it was the earliest form of Celtic spoken and that the first Celts in Britain spoke the Goidelic form, in the fourth century A.D. with the establishment of the kingdom of Dál Riada on the western seaboard. By the sixth century three main kingdoms had emerged in Scotland: Dál Riada, the kingdoms of the northern and southern Picts in the northeast, and the kingdom of Strath-Clóta (Strathclyde). In A.D. 730 Aonghus Mac Feargus, king of the Picts, was recognised as High King of all three kingdoms. The next century, Coinneach Mac Alpín became king of both Picts and Scots and united the two kingdoms. It was obvious that at this time Gaelic was spoken throughout the north of Scotland. In A.D. 945, the former independent kingdom of Cumbria, conquered by Edmund of England, became a province of Scotland. Lastly, in A.D. 1018, following the battle of Carham, the small kingdom of the Angles, around the mouth of the Tweed, became part of Scotland, or Alba, as it then was known. This was the greatest territorial expansion of the kingdom. However, in A.D. 1157 Maol Callum a' chinn mhòir, High King of Alba, gave up Cumbria. In the next century, the monarchy, followed by the southern gentry and traders, began to Anglicise themselves, and the Gaelic language was on the defensive.

The next centuries saw England ever trying to advance her domination over Scotland and a continual defensive war by the Scots against incursions from England. In 1603 the Anglicised James VI of Scotland was invited to become monarch of England on the death of Elizabeth I. He became James I of England. James made several attempts to unite his two kingdoms, one of which was rejected by the English Parliament in 1607. Exactly one hundred years later, in 1707, at a time when it became economically advantageous for England to do so, the union was carried out. It was achieved by bribes, both of finance and of position and title. "We're bought and sold for English gold," lamented the poet Robbie Burns.

In the years following the union, in which both England and Scotland were supposed to disappear and a new state of co-equal partners called Great Britain was supposed to emerge, the Scots, realising how they had been duped, made several efforts to sever the union. The first parliamentary effort was made in 1714, while insurrections and attempted insurrections occurred throughout the eighteenth century. The last major one was in 1820.

The constitutional position of Scotland is curious indeed. The English broke the Treaty of Union, the written constitution of Great Britain, almost as soon as the ink was dry. "Have we not bought the Scots and the right to tax them?" demanded the Speaker of the House of Commons in 1714. "We have catch'd the Scots and will hold them fast." The latest clear breaking of the Treaty of Union was by Margaret Thatcher in her imposition of her notorious Poll Tax (called Community Charge by her Government) in Scotland a year before its imposition in England. Yet the British Parliament still pretends the Treaty of Union runs in Scotland, allowing Scotland its own judicial system and, until recently, its own educational system. But the Westminster Parliament breaks the terms of the treaty with apparent impunity. The legal position of Scotland within the state of the United Kingdom of Great Britain and Northern Ireland is no longer clear.

Scots. In early medieval Latin, the term *Scottus* was applied to the Irish. This created confusion when, in the thirteenth and fourteenth centuries, the kingdom of Alba began to be referred to as "Scotland." The confusion is demonstrated by the story of the Würzburg Schottenklöster, which was an Irish Benedictine foundation until 1497. By that time the linguistic change had been made and the terms "Scottus," "Scotia," and "Scot" applied to Alba. Scottish clerics demanded that the pope expel the Irish from Würzburg on the grounds that it was, by name, a *Scottish* foundation. The pope did so and Würzburg became a Scottish monastery until as late as 1803. However, Johannes Scottus Eriugena, Sedulius Scottus, Marianus Scottus, and Clemens Scottus were all Irish and not from Scotland.

Scottish Gaelic. The language of Alba. It began to diverge from Old Irish before the ninth century. The first written differences between Old Irish and Scottish Gaelic (Gàidhlig) occurs in the ninth century *Book of Deer,* now in Cambridge. Scottish Gaelic achieved its greatest territorial expansion around 1018 when Alba annexed most of the tiny kingdom of the Angles established at the mouth of the Tweed. According to Dr. John Watson, "in consequence of this the whole of Scotland became for a time Gaelic in speech." The language did not begin to recede from the "Lowlands" until the fourteenth century. The last native speakers of Galloway did not die out until the late eighteenth century. Today only 1.6 percent of the people of Scotland speak Gaelic as a first language (according to the

1981 census, 79,303 persons), mostly in the western islands. The census only applies to Scotland, but many thousands of Gaelic speakers are to be found elsewhere. The 1971 Canadian census gave 18,420 "mother tongue" speakers of Scottish Gaelic. The language survived in the Cape Breton Island of Nova Scotia after settlement during the notorious "Highland Clearances." The language has been considered one of Europe's most persecuted tongues.

Literary remains date from the eleventh century, but they are sparse though indicative of a greater lost literature. The Reformation certainly destroyed many Gaelic libraries. The first printed book in Gaelic was *Form na hOrdaigh,* a book of common prayer, in 1567. Scottish Gaelic is heir to a common mythological tradition with Irish.

Scuab Uasáfach. [I] "Terrible Broom." The name of the battalion of the Fianna commanded by Oscar. It swept the enemy from the battlefield, never giving an inch of ground. Its banner was a broom.

Seanchaidhe. [I] *Seanchaí* in modern Irish. A storyteller and historian. The word has now been adopted into English in such varying forms as seannachie, seannachy, and sennchie.

Seang. [I] Daughter of the king of Scythia and wife to Milesius. She died, and he left Scythia for Egypt, where he remarried Scota. See **Scota.**

Searbhán. [I] "The surly." A one-eyed Fomorii who guarded a magic tree, squatting at its foot all day and sleeping in its branches all night. So terrible was his appearance that none of the Fianna would go near him. During the pursuit of Diarmuid and Gráinne, Diarmuid made friends with him so that the couple was able to hide in the tree, safe from the pursuing Fianna. All went well until Gráinne grew restless and wanted to eat the magic berries from the tree. Searbhán refused to allow her to do this and Diarmuid slew him.

Sechnasach. [I] Son of Fingen Mac Aedha, whose wife was Mór of Munster. She fled before his birth under the influence of voices prophesying evil.

Segais, Well of. [I] See **Nuts of Knowledge.**

Ségda Saerlabraid. [I] Son of the king and queen of Tír Tairnigiri, "sinless people," according to medieval scribes, who never slept together except at his conception. This Christian embellishment forgets that the rulers of Tír Tairnigiri were Manannán Mac Lir and his wife Fand.

Semion. [I] Son of Stariat from whom all the Firbolg were descended.

Senach Síaborthe. [I] A warrior with whom it was suggested that Cúchulainn fight. If he won, Fand, the wife of Manannán Mac Lir, would be his reward.

Senboth. [I] Partholón's eldest chieftain and adviser.

Sencha Mac Ailella. [I] Chief judge and poet of Ulster in the days of Conchobhar Mac Nessa. He acts as a foil to Bricriu, the creator of discord, and it was he who taught Cúchulainn how to speak.

Sequena. Gaulish goddess of the source of the Seine. In her sanctuary were found many votive offerings.

Sera. [I] Father of Partholón and Starn. In some accounts it was Sera who was husband of Dealgnaid and not Partholón.

Sétanta. [I] Cúchulainn's original name. It is interesting to note that, according to Ptolemy, there was a Celtic tribe called the Setantii who inhabited an area in northwest England (Fylde) that was part of the confederation of tribes known as the Brigante (or High Ones).

Seth. [I] In the Christian adaptation of Irish myth, this Biblical character, son of Adam and Eve, and the three daughters of Cain are the first people to see Ireland.

Sgeimh Solais. [I] "Light of Beauty." Daughter of Cairbre, the High King, whose marriage to the son of the chieftain of the Dési started the war between Cairbre and the Fianna that resulted in the eventual destruction of the Fianna.

Sgilti. [W] "Lightfoot." He was the greatest runner in Arthur's entourage and never needed a road to run, for he could run across the treetops.

Shape-changing. A very common motif in Celtic myths and tales. Gods often changed their shapes (as did druids and druidesses) and were able to curse those who displeased them.

Sídhe. [I] A mound or hill, the dwelling place of the Dé Danaan after their defeat by the Milesians. The ancient gods, driven underground below the hills, were relegated in folk memories to fairies, *aes sídhe,* the people of the hills. Thus the word became the word for "fairies." Most popular is the banshee (*bean sídhe*), the woman of the fairies. Each of the gods was allotted a sídhe by the Dagda before he gave up leadership of them.

Simon Breac. [I] Son of Starn. After the Nemedians' defeat by the Fomorii, he and his followers fled from Ireland. Upon arriving in Thrace, they were enslaved and became ancestors of the Firbolg. An interesting choice of country, for Thrace was invaded and settled by Celts in the third century B.C., and the kings of Thrace bore Celtic names for several centuries.

Simon Magus. [I] The New Testament character makes a surprising appearance in the myths when his sons are said to have raped the goddess Tlachtga.

Sionan. [I] Daughter of Lir's son Lodan. She went to the Well of Knowledge at the source of the Shannon, even though it was forbidden. The water of the well rose up and chased her westward and drowned her. The path of the water became the River Shannon, named after her. The story is parallel to that of Boann and the formation of the Boyne.

Sirona. Gaulish goddess whose name means "star." She is usually paired with Grannos.

Sithchenn. [I] A druid, seer, and smith to whom Niall of the Nine Hostages and his four brothers were sent by Mongfhinn to see what their futures were. Sithchenn enticed them into his forge and set fire to it to see what items they would rescue. When Niall emerged with the anvil, Sithchenn prophesied he would be the greatest High King of Ireland.

Sláine. [I] Sometimes Slainge. "Health." He was a son of Partholón and the first physician in Ireland. Another Sláine was the son of Dela the Firbolg who ruled Leinster. He was an enemy of Nemed.

Slemuin. [I] A bull that belonged to the Mórrígán. See **Odras.**

Sliabh Mos. [I] Anglicised as Sleemish. A mountain situated in Corco Duibhne (Co. Kerry) that was the site of the fabulous fort of Cú Roí. The entrance could never be found after sunset. The fortress was able to revolve like a millstone when Cú Roí uttered the word. It is not to be confused with the mountain in Co. Antrim where St. Patrick passed his youth herding swine.

Slieve. [I] In Irish *sliabh*, "mountain." Mountains, naturally, feature prominently in the myths, especially in Irish mythology, for they are the dwelling places of the gods. Lir dwelt at Slieve Fuad, near Newtonhamilton, Co. Armagh, where the hero Fuad was slain.

Smirgat. [I] A wife of Fionn Mac Cumhail. She prophesied that if he drank from a horn he would die. He was always careful to drink from a goblet or bowl.

Snedgus. [I] A cleric in the service of Colmcille who enters into the myths in a tale of a fabulous voyage—"The Voyage of Snedgus and Mac Riagla"—in the fourteenth century *Yellow Book of Lecan.* Scholars date the tale to the seventeenth century. Snedgus and Mac Riagla visit many marvellous lands, see strange beasts, and come upon a land where they dwell in a form of immortality.

Socht's Sword. [I] It would cut a man in two "so that neither half knew what had befallen the other."

Somhlth. [I] A supernatural without shape.

Sovranty of Ireland. [I] The form of "sovranty" appears in various myths as a female figure. Invariably she starts off as an ugly crone but turns into a beautiful maiden who bestows kingship on the man deemed "rightful."

Spain. [I] In Irish myth "Spain" is frequently mentioned as a synonym for "The Land of the Dead." It was probably introduced by Christian monks who objected to pre-Christian terminology. See **Iberia.**

Sreng. [I] A Firbolg who was sent as ambassador to the Dé Danaan when they landed in Ireland. He met with Bres, who suggested that Ireland be divided between them. Sreng was impressed with the weapons of the Dé Danaans; they were light and sharply pointed compared with the Firbolg's heavier and more blunt weaponry. But the Firbolg rejected the Dé Danaan's offer and fought the first battle of Magh Tuireadh. Sreng and Nuada fought in single combat and he was able to cut Nuada's shield in two and sever his hand. The god Dian Cécht gave Nuada a silver hand in replacement.

Starn. [I] A son of Sera and brother of Partholón. However, the name also occurs for the son of Nemed and father of Tuan, the ancestor of the Firbolg.

Stone Worship. Reverence for stones was common among the ancient Celts. They dwelt in firm communication with nature, believing in the consciousness of all things. Trees, fountains, even weapons and implements were but a fragment of one cosmic whole. Stones particularly, being "old beyond time," were possessed of an indwelling spirit; thus could the Lia Fáil (Stone of Destiny) roar with joy when it felt the touch of a righteous ruler's foot. Another stone could tell if a man lied. See **Lia Fáil.**

Strath-Clóta. The British kingdom of southwestern Scotland—Strathclyde. The Clyde were named after Clud, a British goddess. The capital of the kingdom was Alcluyd, which became known to the Gaelic-speaking Scots as Dún Breatann (Dumbarton), the fortress of the Britons, while the form Cluaidh replaced Clóta or Clud. A province of Alba after the unification of the kingdoms, Strathclyde, separated from Cumbria to the south, eventually moved from being Brythonic Celtic to being Goidelic, or Gaelic, in speech. Part of it became known as the land of the foreign Gaels, Gall-Gháidheal, or Galloway, where Gaelic remained a spoken language until the mid-eighteenth century.

Sualtam Mac Roth. [I] Also Sualdaim. The brother of Fergus Mac Roth. He was the "mortal father" of Cúchulainn. The night before his wedding to Dechtiré, the god Lugh took her off and slept with her. She gave birth to Sétanta, who was later known as Cúchulainn. When Ailill and Medb invaded Ulster, Sualtam attempted to raise the warriors of Conchobhar Mac Nessa. Unable to awake the men of Ulster, he turned his horse, the spirited Grey of Macha, so angrily that the sharp rim of his shield sliced off his head. The severed head continued to cry its warning until the curse of Macha was lifted and the warriors were roused to the danger.

Súantrade. [I] One of the harpists of Uaithne who made such sad music that men died listening to it.

Sucellus. Gaulish god. "The good striker" who appears with Nantosvelta. He carries a mallet, appears with a cask or drinking vessel, and is often accompanied by a dog. Some scholars have claimed he is identical to the Dis Pater.

Sugyn. [W] "The Thirsty." He once drank a whole ocean and left 300 ships stranded on the sand.

Suibhne Geilt. [I] A king cursed by St. Ronán so that, in spite of his human form, he assumed the characteristics of a bird, leaping from tree to tree. The Welsh counterpart of Suibhne is Myrddin Wyllt.

Sulevia. (pl. Suleviae) Gaulish goddess/goddesses that Caesar seems to associate with Minerva. Patroness of the art of healing, she was honoured at the thermal springs in Bath (Aquae Sulis). Her counterpart in Ireland would be Brigid, daughter of the Dagda.

Sulis. See **Sulevia.**

Sun. Heliolatry, or sun worship, was a common practice among the Celts, judging by the abundance of solar motifs, although there is little direct evidence of a sun cult in the myths and sagas. There are references to obvious sun deities such as Mac Gréine (son of the sun), who was the husband of Éire, who gave her name to Ireland. The god Belenos (Irish Bilé) was known as "the shining one," and his feast on Beltaine (May 1) was obviously connected with a sun cult. On Mount Callan (near Ennis) there stands a sun altar where the Beltaine festival was celebrated on midsummer's day down to 1895. Near Macroom is a standing stone called "stone of the sun," while Seathrún Céitinn claimed that many of the dolmens associated with Gráinne were, in fact, originally connected with Gréine (the sun). Among the various sun references in Irish, we have Giolla Gréine, whose mother was a sunbeam.

Swans. A favourite form among shape-changers. The children of Lir were turned into swans. Cáer, of whom the love god Aonghus Óg dreamt and went in search, was a human who lived in the form of a swan.

Syfwlch. [W] With Bwlch and Cyfwlch, they were three of Arthur's warriors who possessed the brightest and sharpest weapons.

T

Tabhfheis. [I] The Bull Feast. A ceremony associated with the choos-
ing of the High Kings of Ireland. A druid would eat the flesh of a
bull and drink its blood. He was then put to sleep by four other
druids. The person that he dreamed of was the one chosen to
become High King. If he lied about his vision, the gods would
destroy him.

Taboo. Celtic society, and therefore mythology, abounds in prohibitions, taboos, or bonds that, when placed on a person or persons,
compel them to obey instructions. From the sagas, as well as the
Celtic law systems, the taboos come down primarily as a *modus
operandi* put at the disposal of the druids to ensure their authority
and the efficacy of their edicts. In Ireland they had two particular
powers: the *geis* and the *glam dicín*. The *geis* tended to be more
complex. It was primarily a prohibition imposed on a particular
person and, since it influenced the whole fate of that person, it
could not be cast or imposed lightly. Anyone transgressing a *geis*
was exposed to the rejection of his society and placed outside the
social order. Transgression, in addition to bringing shame and
outlawry, usually meant a painful death. The power of the *geis* was
above human and divine jurisdiction and brushed aside all previous
rulings, establishing a new order through the wishes of the person
controlling it.

The *glam dicín* was a satirical incantation directed against a
particular person and having the strength of obligation—in other
words it is a curse that can be pronounced for such valid reasons as
an infringement of divine or human laws, treason, breaking a
contract, or murder.

In Welsh myth, the same taboos (*ysgymunbeth*) exist. Several
characters have "a destiny laid upon them," such as Lleu Llaw
Gyffes, who has a series of taboos placed on him by his mother,

Aranrhod, and Culhwch, whose step-mother places a taboo on him that causes his famous quest for Olwen.

Even until recent times the Celts were keenly observant of taboos. None has been more interesting than their perception of the stars and planets. The power of the word was always uppermost in Celtic perception, and Dr. Tomás De Bhaldraithe, compiler of the modern *Irish Dictionary,* has argued that the names given to planets were forbidden druidic words so that the ordinary people could only refer to them by euphemisms. In Irish, for example, *gealach* (brightness) is the popularly used word for the moon. Other words exist as well. Old Irish contains *ésca* (*aesca*), and this word still survives in the Manx form as *eayst* but nowhere else. Another Irish word for moon was *ré,* and this, too, survives in Manx used as a combined word with that for light, *shollys,* in the word *rehollys* (moonlight). And yet another Irish word for moon, *lúan,* is now used as *An Lúan* as the name of the moon-day, or Monday. This word is thought to derive from the native Irish word for "radiance" rather than being a loan-word from the Latin *luna.* So here are four distinct words for moon, all being euphemisms rather than a proper name.

We can turn to Manx for a practical example of taboo names with this regard. In the nineteenth century, when Manx fishermen set foot on shipboard they were under a taboo (a superstition imposed by folklore) not to use the word *eayst* for moon until they returned to land. Until then they would refer to the moon as *ben-reine ny hoie* (queen of the night). Likewise, the sun was only referred to as *gloyr na laa* (glory of the day) and not as *grian.* In Old and Middle Irish we find several words for the sun also: as well as the modern word *grian,* we have *ló-chrann* (head of the day), still in use in Scottish Gaelic. The same word in modern Irish becomes the word for bright, brilliance, gleaming, guiding light, and leader. We also have *ré-an-lá* (light of the day), which is also used as *ree yn lá.*

It is interesting to note that while the ancient Celts (who were renowned for their ability in astronomy) must have had their own native names for the planets and stars, it is the Arabic, Greek, and Latin names that have been adopted into their languages. This supports the argument that there was initially a druidic proscription that continued into the period of early Christianity. Therefore, the native names by which the planets were known, the names of the stars that played so central a part in people's lives, continued as a taboo on the population. Therefore, when scribes began to write in Irish and Welsh, they eagerly accepted the foreign loan-words as euphemisms for their own proscribed names, and thus these names have been lost. Or have they?

Only in Manx Gaelic do we have the survival of the native names of two planets. In Manx, which developed away from Old Irish from the fifth and sixth centuries but did not emerge as its own developed written language until the seventeenth century, words for Mercury and Venus occur. There are two names for Mercury— *Yn Curain* and *Yn Crean*. Likewise, there are two names for Venus—*Yn Vadlag* and *Yn Vaytnag*. These survivals confirm the existence of earlier native names for the planets, which have now been lost because of the proscription against their use.

Tadhg. [I] Son of Cian of Munster. Cormac Mac Art promised to reward Tadhg's alliance against Ulster with any land that he could circumnavigate in his chariot after the battle. Cormac knew that Tadhg wanted Temuir (Tara) and the High Kingship itself, so he bribed Tadhg's charioteer to make a circumnavigation in the shape of an "L," which excluded Temuir. The story of "The Adventures of Tadhg, son of Cian, son of Ailill Olum" is thought to date back to the third century A.D., and in this voyage tale the goddess Cliodhna appears to him.

There is a second Tadhg who appears, the son of Nuada. He was a druid and father of Murna of the White Neck, mother of Fionn Mac Cumhail. He opposed the marriage of his daughter to Cumal and persuaded Conn, the High King, to send warriors after them when they eloped. Cumal was killed, but not before Murna became pregnant with Fionn.

Tailltinn, Battle of. [I] A great battle between the Dé Danaan and the Milesians in which three kings and three queens of the Dé Danaan were slain.

Tailtu. [I] Daughter of the Firbolg king of the Great Plain, she became foster mother to Lugh Lámhfada and gave her name to Tailltinn (Anglicised as Teltown). She cleared the forest of Breg and died as a result of her labours. Lugh decreed a feast in her honour, which became known as Lughnasadh (August 1). At the feast, official games that correspond to the Olympics of ancient Greece were held. The last games were held on August 1, 1169, under the jurisdiction of the last High King, Ruraidh Ó Conchobhar.

Táin. [I] A cattle raid. There are several of these tales in Irish mythology, but the two most famous ones are the *Táin Bó Cuailgne* and the *Táin Bó Fraoch*. The *Táin Bó Cuailgne* is the most famous epic in Irish mythology, comparable to the *Iliad*. The basic texts are found in *Leabhar na h-Uidhre* (eleventh century Book of the Dun Cow) and *Leabhar Laighnech* (twelfth century Book of Leinster). Both versions are incomplete and additions are found in the *Yellow Book of Lecan*. The saga popularly describes the campaign by Medb of Connacht to capture the famous Brown Bill of Cuailgne in Ulster. The Ulster warriors are prevented from defending themselves against her army by a strange debility placed on them by Macha, goddess of war. Only Cúchulainn is able to carry on a defence until the Ulster warriors recover. It is the longest, most elaborate and powerful of all the Irish myths, and is the central theme of the Red Branch cycle.

The *Táin Bó Fraoch* is the second most popular cattle raid tale. Professor C. W. von Sydow [*Beowulfskalden och nordisk tradition*, Arsbok, 1923] suggests that the story provided the model for the later English saga of *Beowulf*. There are many points of similarity between the two sagas. The story concerns Fraoch, the most handsome warrior in Ireland, who sets out to woo Findbhair, daughter of Ailill and Medb.

Taliesin. [W] "Shining Brow." A quasi-mythical figure, said to be the greatest of the bards, living during the sixth century A.D. He is claimed as the first bard to acquire the secret of prophetic poetry. He could divine the future and strike less gifted poets dumb. In the myths he is Gwion Bach reborn and his mother is the magician Ceridwen, who swallowed Gwion Bach in the form of a grain of wheat. Taliesin is rescued from the sea by Elffin and, at the age of thirteen, is able to dumbfound Arthur's bards. "I am old, I am new . . . I have been dead, I have been alive . . . I am Taliesin." [*Chwedl Taliesin*, vol. I, Williams, Cardiff, 1957.] His song is rather similar in style and import to that of the druid Amairgin.

Taliesin, Book of. [*The Book of Taliesin*, ed. J. G. Evans, Llanbedrog, 1910.] A collection of poetic tradition associated with Taliesin.

Tanáiste. [I] The successor to a king or professional man elected during his predecessor's lifetime.

Tara. [I] Temuir and Temair in Old Irish. The site in County Meath that was the main royal residence of the High Kings and was regarded as the Irish capital. The name derives from the goddess Tea, wife of Eremon, the first Milesian High King. The ancient site dates back to 2000 B.C. and includes an intricate complex of fortifications. Five roads anciently led to provinces, three of which are still discernible. It is said that St. Ruadán (Ronán) of Lorrha pronounced a curse against Tara in A.D. 560 and this led to its abandonment as the seat of the High Kings. However, the annals show that as late as A.D. 786 Tara was neither cursed nor neglected.

Taranus. According to Caesar, the Gaulish god who "held the empire of the skies" and whom he likened to the Roman Jupiter. The name means "thunderer." A Taran occurs in Welsh myth as the father of Gluneu.

Tarvos Trigaranus. Gaulish. "The Bull with Three Cranes." A relief found on a pillar in 1711 in Notre Dame along with a relief showing the Gaulish god Esus. The Divine Bull with a triad of Otherworld birds is a familiar feature of insular Celtic tradition. The scenes shown on these two reliefs are obviously an episode from some myth. We would not be making a too wild guess to see some connection with the Brown Bull of Cuailgne (see **Táin**).

Tea. [I] See **Tara**.

Tech Duinn. [I] The House of Donn, the gathering place of the dead, said to be an island lying to the southwest of Ireland presided over by Donn, god of the dead. There is an obvious parallel with Welsh mythology, for Annwn (the Otherworld and place of the dead) is perceived as an island lying off southwest Wales (Dyfed), sometimes as Lundy Island.

Tech Screpta. Sometimes Teach Screpta. The libraries of ancient Ireland presided over by *leabhar-coimdaech*. Many of these libraries were destroyed during the Viking raids.

Tegid Foel. [W] Husband of Ceridwen at Penllyn. He is the father of Afagddu, the ugliest man in the world, and of Morfan, a warrior so ugly that no man would fight him at Camlann, fearing he was a devil.

Teirnyon. [W] See **Teyrnon**.

Tethra. [I] A Fomorii who seemed to be a sea god. He owned the sword Orna, formed by Ogma, which was, significantly, picked up by Manannán Mac Lir at the second battle of Magh Tuireadh.

Teutates. Gaulish god likened to Mercury by Caesar. The root of the name is retained in Irish, Welsh, and Breton and signifies "the people." It is argued that it was the Celts who designated the Germanic people crowding on their eastern borders as "the people," or Teutons, which name has survived as a designation for any speaker of a Germanic language. Teutates was therefore thought to be a "tribal god." The Gauls, says Caesar, "regard him as the inventor of all the arts, the god who directs men upon their journeys and their most powerful helper in trading and getting money."

Teyrnon. [W] Lord of Gwent Is-Coed. He always releases the colt that his mare foals on Beltaine, May Eve. Keeping watch, he sees a great claw come through the stable window and seize the newborn colt. He strikes off the claw with his sword and then rushes out. He fails to see anything, but on his return to the stable he finds that a child, in swaddling clothes, has been left at the door. He and his wife bring up the child as their own son. Later they learn the child is the son of Pwyll and Rhiannon and return it. The boy is named Pryderi.

The name Teyrnon is also given as Ternan but refers to a sixth century Christian missionary to the Picts and is thought to be one and the same with the Cornish St. Erney, whose name is remembered at St. Erney near St. Germans and also at North Hill east of Bodmin Moor, where the name is recorded as St. Torney. Teyrnon and other early Celtic Christian saints are frequently mixed up with mythological characters.

Three, Significance of. See **Triads.**

Tigernmas. [I] "Lord of death." Son of Follach. A High King who is said to have introduced the worship of an idol called Cromm Cruach (Blood Crescent), which involved human sacrifice at the feast of Samhain. Tigernmas was slain during the frenzied worship of the idol.

Tiobraide Tireach. [I] An Ulster king who slew Conn of the Hundred Battles.

Tír. [I] The Irish word for "land" or "country."

Tlachtga. [I] A goddess who is also the daughter of the druid Mug Ruith of Munster. She produced three sons by different fathers at one birth and died in the process. She gave her name to the Hill of Tlachtga, now the Hill of Ward, Co. Meath, which is associated with the Samhain Festival.

Tobar. The Irish word for "well." See **Wells.**

Torc Triath. [W] King of Boars. Sometimes given as the Orc-Triath. This is the Irish equivalent of the Welsh Twrch Trwyth, hunted in the story of Culhwch and Olwen. The Torc Triath is listed as being among the possessions of the fertility goddess Brigid, daughter of the Dagda.

Tory Island. [I] Chief island of the Fomorii. The name derives from *torach* (tower-like), which is an apt description of the island. However, it is here that Conann built his tower, which the Nemedians attacked, and that Balor of the Evil Eye had his daughter imprisoned in a tower of crystal.

Trachmyr. [W] One of Arthur's two herdsmen. The other was Eli.

Transmigration of Souls. A basic pre-Christian belief among the ancient Celts. See **Otherworld.** Souls migrated from the Land of the Living to the Land of the Dead and vice versa. They also migrated through various births. Not only could people be reborn as other people, they could go through various changes. Fintan survived the Deluge by changing into a salmon. Gwion Bach also achieved several changes.

Treasure Bag of the Fianna. [I] It contained numerous articles with magical properties, such as the knife and shirt of Manannán Mac Lir. It was made form the skin of Aoife, who was killed while in the form of a crane. Also known as the "Crane Bag."

Triads. The concept of the trinity seems more or less universal among Indo-European cultures, although nowhere is it more prominent than in Celtic culture. Diogenes Laertius (third century B.C.) mentions that the druids taught in the form of triads. In both Irish and Welsh myths and featured on surviving Gaulish head carvings, the triune deities are noticeable. Three and three-times-three permeate Celtic philosophy and art. Hilary, who became bishop of Poitiers in A.D. 350, is regarded as the first native Celt to become an outstanding force in the Christian movement. His greatest work was *De Trinitate,* defining the concept of a Holy Trinity, which is now so integral to Christian belief. As a Celt, Hilary was imbued with the mystical traditions of the triune god, and, therefore, the trinity in Christian tradition owes its origin more to Celtic concepts than to Judaic-Greco philosophies.

Tristan and Iseult. A medieval cycle of tales featuring Tristan, nephew of King Mark of Cornwall, and Iseult, daughter of an Irish chieftain and the wife of Mark. There are hundreds of different versions of the tale, written in practically every European language, the majority reflecting individual interpretations of the language. Joseph Bédier (*Le Roman de Tristan par Thomas*, Paris, 1902) discovered that all Tristan manuscripts, medieval and modern, could be traced back to one extant manuscript written by Beroul (about whom nothing is known) in the middle of the twelfth century. Beroul, writing in French, was obviously translating from a Breton source. The saga, one of the world's greatest love stories, had evolved from Celtic sources. The core motif is the traditional Celtic "elopement tale," known in Irish as *aithedha*, in this case the elopement of the king's wife with the king's nephew. Many of the essential characteristics of the tale are to be found in other Celtic elopement tales, but more particularly in the tale of "Diarmuid and Gráinne" and "Noísu and Deirdre" [*Tristan and Isolt*, G. Schoepperle, Frankfurt, 1913].

Tristan is generally depicted as a strong warrior, skilled hunter, musician, poet, and teller of tales, and a great lover. He is sent to Ireland to escort the bride of his uncle King Mark to Cornwall. On the voyage, Tristan and Iseult accidentally drink a magic love potion and become irrevocably bound to one another. The ensuing narrative charts the perilous course of their love, banishment, and tragic death. See **Mark of Cornwall.** The story has been assimilated into the Arthurian cycle and subsequently used as one of the major literary themes of all time, from Malory's *Morte d'Arthur* to Tennyson's *Idylls of the King*. It has also been used as inspiration for major musical works, such as Wagner's *Tristan and Isolde*.

For visitors to Cornwall in search of the original settings for the legend, a visit to Castle Dore, the ancient earthwork fortress, two miles north of Fowey, is essential. Although originally constructed in the second century B.C., excavations have discovered buildings from the sixth century A.D., the age of King Mark. Castle Dore appears as Mark's capital in the legends. But most importantly, nearby, a mile or so from Fowey towards Par, near the disused entrance to Menabilly House, stands an engraved stone dated to the mid-sixth century A.D. The accepted reading is *"Drustaus [or Drustanus] hic iacit Cunomori filius"*—Here lies Drustanus son of Cunomorus. Philologically the name Drustanus equates with

Tristan, while Mark's name is Marcus Cunomorus. So the final contentious reading is "Tristan, *son* of Mark lies here." How much more powerful the tragic love story had later scribes made Tristan elope with his stepmother!

Another historical "footstep" was found by the Celtic scholar Professor Joseph Loth, who found Iseult's name associated with a site on the Lizard peninsula, Cornwall, in a charter of A.D. 967. *Hryt Eselt* (Iseult's ford) was described as a boundary for the lands of Lesmanaoc in St. Keverne. See also **Trystan.**

Trystan. Having seen from the previous entry that the oldest extant versions of the "Tristan and Iseult" romance are to be found in French and German sources and not in Celtic, we should refer to the first Celtic language version of the tale, which occurs in a sixteenth century Welsh manuscript [edited by I. Williams, *Bulletin of the Board of Celtic Studies,* vol. 115]. In this version Trystan elopes with Esyllt, wife of March ap Meirchion. They go to the woods of Kelyddon accompanied by Trystan's servant, Bach Bychan (Little Little-one), and Esyllt's maid, Golwg Hafddydd (Aspect of a Summer's Day). March complains to Arthur and sets out to fight Trystan. Trystan overcomes three armies led by March, and the news is taken by Trystan's companion, Kae Hir, to Esyllt. Kae Hir is promised the hand of Golwg if the news be true. Arthur now intervenes at March's request and mollifies Trystan, sending him Gwalchmei (Hawk of May) as a peacemaker. Trystan comes to Arthur, who offers a judgment on the problem. One of the two men shall have Esyllt when there are leaves on the trees, the other when there are no leaves on the trees. March, as husband, is given first choice and chooses the leafless period (winter) because the nights are longer during it. But Trystan points out that the yew tree always bears leaves. Therefore March cannot have Esyllt at all, for there are always leaves on the trees.

Trystan and Ysolt. The only version in Cornish, the language that gave the romance its birth, is a modern Cornish translation of the medieval Beroul and Thomas texts, as edited by J. Bédier, by A. S. D. Smith, the bard "Caradar" (1883–1950). It was published in 1951. However, Smith had not completed his translation at the time of his death, and 1,000 lines of the poem were left uncompleted. The work was finished by David Watkins, "Carer Brynow"

(1892–1969). These were not published until 1973. These two volumes now constitute the complete Beroul and Thomas texts in modern Cornish.

Tuan Mac Cairell. [I] His story typifies the Celtic belief in reincarnation. Son of Starn, brother of Partholón, he survives the plague that destroys his people by being reborn as a stag, then as an eagle, then as a salmon that is caught and eaten by the wife of Cairell. She then gives birth to him in human form, again with his memory of the whole history of Ireland from the coming of Partholón. This is strikingly similar to the birth of Taliesin.

Tuatha. [I] A people, tribe, or nation. See **Teutates.**

Tuatha Cruithne. See **Picts.**

Tuatha Dé Danaan. [I] The people of the goddess Dana. The gods of pre-Christian Ireland who inhabited the land before the coming of the Milesians. The Milesians drive them underground. When Christian monks started to write down the sagas, they were demoted into heroes and heroines, although much remained to demonstrate their godlike abilities. Under their leader Nuada, they came to Ireland from a northern country where they had four fabulous cities, Falias, Gorias, Finias, and Murias. They defeated the Firbolg and then overcame the Fomorii. They are represented as the gods of light and goodness, while the Fomorii are the more sinister gods of darkness. They are totally human in all the virtues as well as the vices.

Tuireann. [I] There are males and females who bear this name in Irish myth. Tuireanns appear as the sister, sister-in-law, and aunt of Fionn Mac Cumhail. A male Tuireann had three sons by the goddess Brigid.

Tuireann, Children of. [I] The sons of Tuireann and the goddess Brigid were Brían, Iuchar, and Iucharba, who slew Cian, father of Lugh Lámhfada. As recompense to Lugh they were forced to set out on a journey to secure various items. The saga of their travels and adventures is said to be the Irish equivalent of the voyage of Jason and his quest for the Golden Fleece.

Twrch Trwyd. [W] See **Twrch Trwyth.**

Twrch Trwyth. [W] In the story of Culhwch and Olwen, Twrch Trwyth (or Trwyd) is a king turned into a boar. Arthur features as hunting the boar with some of his notable warriors, including

Mabon, son of Modron; Gwyn, son of Nudd; and the son of Alun Dyfed. The story is cognate with that of Torc Triath in Irish mythology, and, indeed, Twrch Trwyth and Torc Triath are equivalent forms. In the Cymric tale it is Mabon who manages to retrieve a razor, lodged between the magical boar's ears, that is needed by Culhwch to fulfil the tasks set him by Yspaddaden the Giant.

Tylwyth Teg. [W] The Welsh fairies of whom Gwynn ap Nudd became king.

U

Uaithne. [I] Sometimes Uathe. The harp of the Dagda. An enchanted instrument that would only sound when summoned to do so by the Dagda. It was stolen by the Fomorii, but the Dagda traced it to their feasting house and called to it. It leapt forward, killing nine Fomorii, and began to sing a paean of praise to the Dagda. Uaithne was also the name of the Dagda's harpist, who had an affair with Boann. They had three sons, Goltrade, Gentrade, and Suantrade, who played such sad music that it was said twelve men once died listening to it and weeping for sorrow.

Uaman. [I] The name of the Connacht *sídhe* ruled by Ethal Anubhail, father of Cáer, with whom Aonghus Óg, the love god, fell in love.

Uan. [I] One of the six servers of the High King at Temuir (Tara).

Uar. [I] "The Cruel." He and his sons, "Ill-Omen," "Damage," and "Want," dwelt in Munster but appear to be Fomorii. They clashed with Fionn Mac Cumhail. Uar's three sons were described as "three foemen—lame thighed . . . left handed, of the race of wondrous evil, and from the gravelly plain of Hell below . . . venom on their weapons, and venom on their dress, and on their hands and feet and on everything they touched."

Uarad Garad. [I] Sometimes Uarán Garaid. A river in Connacht where Conall Cearnach (in some versions, Mac Cécht) fills his cup to take water back to Conaire Mór at the time of the "Destruction of Da Derga's Hostel."

Uathach. [I] Daughter of Scáthach, the female champion who ran a school of martial arts in Alba. The name means "spectre." She is usually referred to as "Uathach of the Glen." When Cúchulainn arrived at Scáthach's fortress, it was Uathach who let him in. While she was serving food to him, Cúchulainn forgot his strength and broke her finger in taking the dish from her hand. Her scream brought Cochar Crufe, her lover, to champion her. He challenged

Cúchulainn to combat and Cúchulainn slew him. In reparation
Cúchulainn had to accept Cochar Crufe's duties as guardian of Dún
Scáthach. Uathach became Cúchulainn's mistress.

Uath Mac Imoman. [I] "Horror, son of Terror." During the story of
"Bricriu's Feast," Cúchulainn, Laoghaire, and Conall are sent to
Oath's Lake, where Uath dwelt, so that he should judge which of
them was the greatest warrior in Ireland. Uath is said to have been
able to transform himself into any shape that pleased him. Uath
asked the warriors to submit to a test. They could take his axe and
cut off his head, provided that he could cut theirs off the next day
in turn. This is also the basic theme of the tale of "Sir Gawain and
the Green Knight" and may well be the source for the later Welsh
version. In the Red Branch Cycle, Cú Roí also makes the same
challenge. In the Uath tale there are two versions as to what hap-
pens. In one, both Laoghaire and Conall refuse on the grounds that
they had not the power to remain alive when Uath cut their heads
off, but they knew that Uath, being a *sirite* (elfman), had such
power. The other version says that they did cut off Uath's head,
but when he picked it up and replaced it, they refused to return the
next day to receive Uath's stroke.

In both versions only Cúchulainn agreed to the conditions.
When Uath came to cut off Cúchulainn's head, the blade of the axe
reversed, whereupon Uath hailed him as the true champion of
Ireland. Laoghaire and Conall refuse to accept the judgment. There
are other variants of the tale apart from the Uath and Cú Roí
versions, including one in which a nameless churl presents himself
at Bricriu's hall and challenges all the warriors of Ulster along the
same lines. This, of course, is much closer to the story recounted in
"Sir Gawain and the Green Knight" (ca. 1370), in which a green
giant bursts into Arthur's court on horseback and dares the knights
to chop off his head on the condition that one year later he be
allowed to return the blow. Gawain takes the role of Cúchulainn.

Ugaine Mor. [I] Sometimes given as Ugony Mór. A High King in
the sixth century B.C. His rule is reported to have included all of
Ireland and also Gaul. He married Cesair, a Gaulish princess, and
their children were Laoghaire Lorc and Cobhthach. On his death
Ireland was divided into 25 parts among his children, and that
division of Ireland lasted three hundred years. The number 25
frequently appears in the myths; there are 25 battalions of the

Fianna, and, according to Seathrún Céitinn, originally 25 dioceses in the country.

Uí Corra. [I] Lochan, Emne, and Silvester were three heroes of the Uí Corra who went on a voyage among strange and exotic islands. Scholars suggest that the composition of this story seems to date from the sixth century A.D. and it was written for Christian moral edification.

Uigreann. [I] Sometimes Uirgriu. He was slain by Fionn Mac Cumhail, and his five sons sought vengeance on Fionn, each casting a spear at him, so it was said that all five killed him. It was also significant that Fionn was one of the five masters of every art, the numeral having special significance.

Uillin. [I] A grandson of Nuada who is said to have drowned Manannán Mac Lir in Loch Corrib and given his name to Moycullin, Co. Galway.

Uisneach. [I] The name is often used as a synonym for Usna. There is also the Hill of Uisneach (formerly Balor's Hill), which was thought to be the exact centre of the country, "the navel of Ireland," where the great Stone of Divisions (Aill na Mirenn) stood, marking the joining of the five provinces of Ireland. The actual site is near Ráthconrath, Co. Westmeath. Tuathal Teachtmhair built one of his four great palaces here, and one of the three major festivals of Ireland was held here. St. Patrick was said to have cursed the stones here, while Geoffrey of Monmouth claims that Stonehenge, in Britain, was built by Merlin, who took the stones from "Mount Killarus," which is identified as Uisneach.

Ulaid. [I] Dative form Ulaidh. Ulster. The ancient province and kingdom covers approximately the same geographical boundaries as the modern province, though this province must not be confused with the political province of Northern Ireland, which includes only six out of the nine Ulster counties. These six counties (Antrim, Armagh, Down, Derry, Fermanagh, and Tyrone) were partitioned from the rest of Ulster and Ireland in 1921. Cos. Cavan, Monaghan, and Donegal also form part of the province of Ulster. Rudraidhe, son of Partholón, was said to have founded the royal house of Ulster, and the people were sometimes known as Clan Rudraidhe and as Rudricans. The capital was Emain Macha (Navan), two miles west of Armagh. The heroes of Ulster are more widely known than those of the other provinces because of the tremendous popularity of the Red Branch or Ulster Cycle. Tradition has dated the decline of this kingdom as a significant power to the time of Cormac Mac Art (A.D. 254–277). But some records show that the change in its fortunes was brought about by the northern expansion of the family of Niall of the Nine Hostages (ca. A.D. 379), which is the Uí Néill dynasty.

Ullan. [I] Husband of Tuireann, sister of Fionn Mac Cumhail. He had an affair with a druidess who became jealous of his wife and changed Tuireann into a bitch-dog. In this form she gave birth to Sceolan and Bran, who became Fionn's faithful hounds. Ullan promised the druidess that he would go with her if she turned his wife back into human shape.

Ulster. See **Ulaid.**

Ulster Cycle. See **Red Branch Cycle.**

Ultonia. Latin name for Ulster.

Uma. [I] Son of Remanfissech.

Umai. [I] One of the nine best pipers in the world.

Uman-Sruth. [I] The bronze stream. Cúchulainn possessed a spear named Cletiné with which he had slain many warriors and that Medb of Connacht coveted. She asked a bard to go to Cúchulainn and request the spear on the grounds that one must never refuse a gift demanded by a poet. The bard and Cúchulainn were standing by a stream when the bard made his request. Cúchulainn was so enraged that he flung the spear at the poet. It pierced the man's head and the force broke the bronze *(umal),* which fell into the stream, giving it its name.

Underwater. There are several stories in Celtic myth of human beings taken underwater by the gods who were then able to return to the surface unharmed. Numerous submerged cities, fortresses, towns, and even kingdoms are a peculiar part of Celtic folklore. In the *Book of the Dun Cow* there is a story of the flooding of Lough Neagh by Ecca. A woman survives the flooding and lives under the waves, in her house, with her dog, for a year. Bored by the existence, she changes into a salmon and lives for three hundred years until rescued by Congall, who names her Muirgen, "born of the sea." Ruadh and Mael Dúin also visit underwater kingdoms. The Cothulín Druith, placed on the head, enables humans to live underwater.

Underworld. See **Otherworld.**

Undry. [I] Sometimes Uinde (an act of beholding). The enchanted cauldron of the Dagda in which everyone found food in proportion to their merits and from which no worthy person went away hungry.

Urddawl Ben. [W] The Venerable Head. Also referred to as Uther Ben, "wonderful head." The head of Bran as invoked by Taliesin.

Urias. [I] "Of the Noble Nature." He dwelt in the city of Gorias, one of the four fabulous cities from which the Dé Danaan originated. He was steeped in wisdom.

Urien. [W] A sixth century A.D. king of Rheged (Cumbria or Strath-Clóta) celebrated by Taliesin. He defeated the Anglo-Saxons at Argoed Llwyfain. The Anglo-Saxon leader was called Fflanddwyn (Flame-bearer) by the Celts. Urien's son was Elffin, who discovered Taliesin in a river and thus plays his part in myth. Urien is also claimed as the father of Owain, the Arthurian warrior who features in "The Dream of Rhonabwy" and in the story of the Lady of the Fountain.

Ursceal. Old Irish *ursgeul.* A saga or romance.

Usna. [I] Variously given as Uisliu, Usnach, Uisneach, and Usnagh. He was the husband of Ebhla. Ebhla was the daughter of the druid Cathbad and of Maga, a daughter of the love god Aonghus Óg. Usna and Ebhla had three sons, the Red Branch heroes Naoise, Ainlé, and Ardan, who feature in the tragic tale "The Exile of the Sons of Usna." It is the oldest of the famous "Three Sorrows of Story-telling." See **Deirdre** and **Naoise.**

Uthechair. [I] Hornskin. Father of the Red Branch champion Celtchair.

Uthr Bendragon. [W] In Geoffrey of Monmouth's story about the conception of Arthur, Uthr Bendragon (Pendragon) is named as Arthur's father. Aided by Merlin's magic, Uthr visited Igerna, wife of Gorlois of Cornwall, in the form of her husband and made love to her. Arthur was the result of this union.

Vortigern. [W] Mentioned by Geoffrey of Monmouth, the name means "overlord" or "High King." He is also known in Welsh tradition as Gwrtheyrn, meaning "supreme leader." He is said to have been ruler of Britain in the fifth century and to have invited Jutish mercenaries under Hengist and Horsa into the island of Britain. Hengist and Horsa then turned on him and began to carve out kingdoms for themselves. This was the first appearance of the ancestors of the English in Britain. Because of this, he is regarded as the archtraitor in Celtic tradition.

W

Wales. Cymru. Separated from their fellow British Celts by the beginning of the eighth century A.D., the Celts of the western peninsula of Britain were consolidated into several kingdoms. Offa, the Anglo-Saxon king of Mercia, who attempted to annex all the Anglo-Saxon kingdoms under his rule, ordered the construction of a rampart from the River Dee to River Wye in A.D. 782, marking the western border of the English kingdoms and hemming the British Celts, called *welisc* or "foreigners" by the Anglo-Saxons, into their peninsula. It was designed on the principle of Hadrian's Wall. Any British Celts found on the English side were subject to severe penalties.

In A.D. 844 Rhodri Mawr (Rhodri the Great) became king of Gwynedd, the main north Wales kingdom, and also inherited the kingdom of Powys. Rhodri found Wales a collection of small states and left it a united country. He was still called "king of the Britons" (*Annals of Ulster,* A.D. 876). In A.D. 916 his grandson Hywel Dda (Hywel the Good) consolidated this unity. He is reported as calling the first recorded parliament, and under his direction the law system was first codified. The Welsh law system became known as the Laws of Hywel Dda. Comparison to the Irish Brehon Law system shows their common Celtic origins. [*The Latin Text of the Welsh Laws,* H. D. Emanuel, Cardiff, 1967, and *Welsh Medieval Law,* A. W. Wade-Evans, Oxford, 1909.] Hywel Dda was king when the last great Celtic alliance was defeated by Athelstan. Athelstan had united the English kingdoms and in A.D. 937, at Brunanburh, Celts from all the remaining Celtic countries united to attempt to drive the Anglo-Saxons out of Britain. A poem entitled *Armes Prydein Fawr* (The Prophecy of Great Britain) was composed in support of this attempt. But the Celts were defeated.

At the time of Hywel Dda's death in A.D. 940, Cymru as a kingdom had consolidated itself and no longer thought of itself as British. To England, however, Cymru (land of compatriots) was Wales (the land of foreigners). Both the Anglo-Saxons and later the Normans continued their policy of expansion through Britain, making continued attempts at conquest. In A.D. 1282 Llywellyn ap Gruffydd ap Llywellyn was killed by an Englishman at Cilmeri and his brother Dafydd ap Gruffydd ap Llywellyn became the last native monarch of Wales. But six months later he was captured and beheaded by the English. From 1287 until 1400 Wales was a restless country, continually engaged in insurrection against English rule. Then Owain Glyn Dwr reasserted Welsh independence. However, by 1409 the English were once more attempting a reconquest, and by 1415 Wales was back under English control.

The English parliament passed acts in 1535 and 1542 that annexed Wales to England, incorporating it fully—politically, administratively, and culturally—into England. The Welsh language and culture was to be utterly destroyed. In 1968 a Welsh Language Act relieved the cultural conquest to some extent, but administratively Wales continues to be part of England.

Wells. The veneration of water, in the form of rivers and wells, was dominant in ancient Celtic society. It has been argued by Professor Richard Bradley, of Reading University, that the Thames (*Tamesis* = the sluggish river) occupied a place with the Britons paralleled by the Ganges with the Hindus. Certainly many items, skulls, swords, shields, and other items, which have been deemed votive offerings, have been found in the Thames, especially in the London area.

Nowhere is this religious observance more clearly seen than with regard to springs and wells. Like many aspects of the landscape—with which the Celts felt at one—wells were formed by the deities. In Gaul, Grannos and Borvo were said to be especially connected with wells. But it seems from the long list made by the Romans of Celtic "well nymphs" that each well had its own indwelling spirit.

Those who did not observe the taboos connected with wells, even though they be deities themselves, could be in trouble. The Well of Segais rose up and drowned Boann, and the path it made chasing her became the Boyne. In medieval times, as reflected in certain Arthurian tales, the spirits of the wells were still there. Indeed, veneration at wells could not be stamped out by the new Christian religion. Therefore, it was adapted to it. Pope Gregory, writing in A.D. 601, told the missionaries of the church not to destroy the pre-Christian sites of worship but to bless them and convert them from "the worship of devils to the service of the true God." Therefore, throughout the Celtic lands, Holy Wells still survive that were once the sites of pagan veneration.

Welsh. The name given to the British Celts by the Anglo-Saxons, from *welisc* and *wealh,* meaning "foreigners." Many names with the prefix *Wal* in England refer to places where the British Celts last held out against the encroaching Anglo-Saxon conquest. In London there is Walbrook (brook of the Welsh); in Yorkshire, the Walburn, which is similarly derived; in Kent there is Walmer (mere of the Welsh); Walcot in Berkshire (cottage of the Welsh); Saffron Walden in Essex (valley of the Welsh); Wallasey in Cheshire (island of the Welsh); and so on. Until the tenth century the evidence is that the British Celts continued to call themselves Britons. As they were slowly pushed back and separated into the western peninsulas, they called themselves "compatriots," a sign of feeling under pressure from the invading Anglo-Saxons. The word in British was *combrogos,* from which Cymru and hence Cymric were derived. Cymru is the modern name for what the English now call Wales (land of foreigners) but which, in Welsh, means "land of compatriots." The same term, Cymru (pronounced Cum-ree), was given to Cumbria, which was annexed to England in the late eleventh century and where the Celtic language died out in the fourteenth century. As Dumnonia vanished in the westward sweep of the English, the kingdom of Cornwall emerged. This was called Kernow in Cornish, but the English called it Kern—*wealh*—Cornwall.

Welsh Language. Cymraeg. At the time of the last census, only 18.9 percent of the population of Wales (503,549) spoke Welsh. However, the census does not extend to Welsh people living in England, and some Welsh-speaking communities actually straddle the border—the current border being arbitrarily fixed at the time of the acts annexing Wales. There is also a large Welsh-speaking immigrant population in England. Similarly, there is Y Wladfa, the Welsh-speaking colony set up in the 1860s in Patagonia, Argentina. Welsh-speaking communities can also be found in

North America. The survival of Welsh, in spite of the Acts of 1535 and 1542, whose stated aim was to "utterly extirp" the language and its culture, is a remarkable tribute to the tenacity of the Welsh to retain their language and culture.

By 1961 some 656,000 people spoke the language in Wales. Within a year Cymdeithas yr Iaith Gymraeg had started a campaign of civil disobedience to win government recognition and status for the language in Wales. A royal commission on the language was set up and recommended that Welsh should have equal validity with English. A Welsh Language Act in 1968 fell marginally short of this recommendation. However, Welsh is now by far the best-supported Celtic language in terms of English government recognition and support.

Welsh literature dates from the sixth century, although surviving manuscripts are from a later period. Certainly by the eighth century it was a flourishing literary language. Apart from fragmentary remains, the oldest manuscript book wholly in Welsh is the *Black Book of Carmarthen,* from the twelfth century. *The Book of Aneirin,* ca. 1250, contains work that can be positively claimed to date to the sixth century. *The Book of Taliesin,* ca. A.D. 1275, contains 58 poems but not more than a dozen or so can be dated (textually or linguistically) to the sixth century at the time when Taliesin is said to have flourished. *The White Book of Rhydderch,* ca. 1325, and *The Red Book of Hergest,* ca. 1400, make up the early literary records. Obviously, much has been destroyed. Of the Laws of Hywel Dda, for example, we have only the "Computus Fragment" (now in Cambridge University Library), while the complete laws are found in earliest record in a manuscript of A.D. 1200.

Wren. [W] A bird of augury among the Britons.

Wridstan. A ninth century monk at the monastery of Landévennec in Brittany. His *Life of Winwaloe,* the sixth century abbot, known as Guénolé in Brittany and as Gunwalloe in Cornwall, gives details about the struggle between the British Celts and Anglo-Saxons, confirming the line taken by Gildas and Nennius.

Y

Ynys Wair. [W] Lundy Island in the Bristol Channel. It is the island of Gwair, an alternative name for Gwydion, son of Don.

Ysbaddaden Benkawr. [W] See **Yspaddaden Pencawr.**

Ysgithyrwn. [W] "The Chief Boar" from whom Culhwch has to bring a tusk so that Yspaddaden might shave.

Yspaddaden Pencawr. [W] "Chief Giant," whose daughter is Olwen. In the story of "Culhwch and Olwen," the stepmother of Culhwch ap Cilydd ordains that he will never win a wife until he wins the love of Olwen. Culhwch sets out to the court of his cousin, Arthur, and requests that Arthur help him in his quest to find and win Olwen. For a year Arthur's messengers scour the country until news of her whereabouts is obtained. Then Cei, Bedwyr, Cynddelig, Cyfarwydd, Gwrhyr Gwalstawd Ieithoedd, Gwalchmei, and Menw set out with Culhwch to the great fortress of the giant. On the way they meet a shepherd, Custennin, and stay with him. With his wife's connivance, Olwen comes to meet them. But she cannot leave without her father's permission.

So Culhwch and companions enter the fortress, slaying the watchdogs and gatemen. In the presence of Yspaddaden they declare their quest. Servants have to lever the giant's eyelids up with supports so that he might look on Culhwch. In many ways he is similar to the Fomorii, Balor of the Evil Eye, who also has to have his eyelid levered up. But a glance of Balor's eye withers men. This is not the case with Yspaddaden. Balor, too, does not want his daughter Ethlinn to have a relationship with a man, for it has been prophesied that he will be slain by his grandchild. The grandchild, in Balor's case, was Lugh Lámhfada. Yspaddaden, however, promises to give his answer to Culhwch if he and his companions come back on the following day, but as they leave he throws a poisoned spear at them. Bedwyr catches it and throws it back, catching him in the knee. A similar exchange takes places on each of the next three days. The giant is finally wounded in the chest. Then Culhwch returns the spear into the giant's eye. It is only then that Yspaddaden agrees to give Olwen to Culhwch on condition that he perform 13 difficult tasks. Further, there are 26 subsidiary tasks to be undertaken to accomplish the original 13. With the help of Arthur and his warriors, supernatural personages, and allies ranging from ants to magical powers, Culhwch performs the tasks, Yspaddaden is slain, and Olwen becomes his wife.

Select Bibliography

The following works have been chosen to give readers a broad base for further reading on the subject of Celtic mythology. It does not pretend to be in any way comprehensive. The primary sources of Welsh mythology, the *Mabinogi,* are the *White Book of Rhydderch* (ca. A.D. 1300–1325) and the *Red Book of Hergest* (ca. A.D. 1375–1425). These are in Llyfrgell Genedlaethol Cymru (National Library of Wales). The principal sources for the Irish myths are the *Leabhar na hUidhre* (Book of the Dun Cow), dating from the eleventh century, and the *Leabhar Laignech* (Book of Leinster), a twelfth century compilation, both of which are in the Royal Irish Academy.

Ancient Laws of Ireland. 6 vols. Dublin (1865–1879).

Anderson, M. O. *Kings and Kingship in Early Scotland.* Edinburgh: Scottish Academic Press (1980).

Arnold, Matthew. *On The Study of Celtic Literature.* Smith, Elder & Co. (1864).

Ashe, Geoffrey. *Mythology of the British Isles.* London: Methuen (1990).

Bartrum, P. C. *Early Welsh Genealogical Tracts.* Cardiff: University of Wales Press (1966).

Best, R. I. *Bibliography of Irish Philology and Literature.* Dublin (1913).

Brekilien, Yann. *La mythologie celtique.* Paris: Editions Jean Picollec (1981).

Bromwich, Rachel. *Trioedd Ynys Prydein: The Welsh Triads.* Cardiff: University of Wales Press (1961).

Brunaux, J. L. *The Celtic Gauls: Gods, Rites and Sanctuaries.* London: Seaby (1978).

Byrne, Francis John. *Irish Kings and High Kings.* London: B. T. Batsford (1973).

Caldecott, Moyra. *Taliesin and Afagddu.* Frome: Brans Head (1983).

———. *Women in Celtic Myth.* London: Arrow Books (1988).

Campbell, Lord Archibald, ed. *Waifs and Strays of Celtic Tradition.* 3 vols. London (n.d.).

Campbell, John G. *The Fions: Account of the Fenians in Scottish Tradition.* London (1981).

Chadwick, H. M. *The Heroic Age.* Cambridge: Cambridge University Press (1967).

——, and N. K. Chadwick. *The Growth of Literature.* 3 vols. Cambridge: Cambridge University Press (1932–1940).

Chadwick, Nora K. *The Celts.* London: Penguin Books (1970).

——. *The Druids.* Cardiff: University of Wales Press (1966).

Coghlan, Ronan. *A Pocket Dictionary of Irish Myths and Legends.* Belfast: Appletree Press (1985).

Condren, Mary. *The Serpent and the Goddess: Women, Religion and Power in Celtic Ireland.* San Francisco: Harper and Row (1989).

Cross, T. P., and C. H. Slover. *Ancient Irish Tales.* London: Harrap (1937).

Curtin, Jeremiah. *Myths and Folk Tales of Ireland.* New York: Dover (1975).

de Jubainville, H. d'Arbois. *Cours de Littérature celtique.* 12 vols. Paris (1883–1902).

——. *Essai d'un de la Littérature épique de l'Irlande.* Paris (1883).

——. *Le cycle mythologique irlandais et la mythologie celtique.* Paris (1884). Translation, *The Irish Mythological Cycle.* Hodges and Figgis (1903).

Dillon, Myles. *The Cycles of the Kings.* Oxford: Oxford University Press (1946).

——. *Early Irish Literature.* Chicago: University of Chicago Press (1948).

——, ed. *Irish Sagas.* Cork: Mercier Press (1968).

——, and Chadwick, Nora K. *The Celtic Realms.* London: Weidenfeld and Nicholson (1967).

Ellis, Peter Berresford. *The Celtic Empire: The First Millennium of Celtic History 1000 B.C.–51 A.D. London: Constable (1990).*

——. *Celtic Inheritance.* London: Muller (1985).

——. *The Cornish Language and Its Literature.* London: Routledge & Kegan Paul (1974).

——. *A Dictionary of Irish Mythology.* London: Constable (1987) and Santa Barbara, California: ABC-CLIO (1989).

Ellis, T. P., and John Lloyd. *The Mabinogion.* Oxford: Oxford University Press (1929).

Evans, J. Gwenogfryn. *The White Book, Mabinogion.* Pwllheli (1907). Reprint, *Llyfr Gwyn Rhydderch* (The White Book of Rhydderch). Introduction by Professor R. M. Jones. Cardiff (1973).

———, ed. *Facsimile and Text of the Book of Taliesin.* Llanbedrog (1910).

Filip, Jan. *Celtic Civilization and Its Heritage.* Prague: Publishing House of the Czechoslovakia Academy of Science and ARTIA (1960).

Flower, Robin. *Byron and Ossian.* Oxford: Oxford University Press (1928).

———. *The Irish Tradition.* Oxford: Oxford University Press (1947).

Ford, P. K., ed. and tr. *The Mabinogion and Other Medieval Welsh Tales.* Berkeley: University of California Press (1977).

———, ed. and tr. *The Poetry of Llywarch Hen.* Berkeley: University of California Press (1974).

Gantz, Jeffrey. *Early Irish Myths and Sagas.* London: Penguin (1981).

———. *The Mabinogion.* London: Penguin (1976).

Gose, E. G., Jr. *The World of the Irish Wonder Tale.* Ottawa: University of Toronto Press (1985).

Green, Miranda. *The Gods of the Celts.* Gloucester: Alan Sutton (1986).

———. *Symbol and Image in Celtic Religious Art.* London: Routledge (1989).

Gruffydd, W. J. *Math vab Mathonwy.* Cardiff: University of Wales Press (1928).

———. *Rhiannon.* Cardiff: University of Wales Press (1953).

Guest, Lady Charlotte. *The Mabinogion from Llyfr Coch o Hergest.* London (1838–1849). Everyman edition (1906).

Guyonvarc'h, Christian J. *Textes mythologiques irlandais.* Breizh: Ogam-Celticum (1981).

Gwynn, Edward John, ed. and tr. *The Metrical Dindsenchas.* Dublin: Hodges Figgis (1903–1935).

Henderon, George. *Fled Bricrend* (Bricriu's Feast) London (1899).

———. *Survivals in Belief Among the Celts.* Glasgow: J. Maclehose (1911).

Hubert, Henri. *The Greatness and Decline of the Celts.* London: Kegan Paul, Trench and Trubner (1934). New edition, London: Constable (1987).

————. *The Rise of the Celts.* London: Kegan Paul, Trench and Trubner (1934). New edition, London: Constable (1987).

Humphreys, Emyr. *The Taliesin Tradition.* Black Raven Press (1983).

Hunt, Robert. *Cornish Customs and Superstitions.* Penryn, Cornwall: Tor Mark Press (n.d.).

————. *Cornish Folk-Lore.* Penryn, Cornwall: Tor Mark Press (1988).

————. *Cornish Legends.* Penryn, Cornwall: Tor Mark Press (1990).

Hyde, Douglas. *A Literary History of Ireland.* T. Fisher Unwin (1899).

Irish Text Society. *Publications.* Dublin: Irish Text Society (1899–).

Jackson, Kenneth H. *A Celtic Miscellany.* London: Routledge & Kegan Paul (1951).

————. *The International Popular Tale and Early Welsh Tradition.* Cardiff: University of Wales Press (1961).

————. *Language and History in Early Britain.* Edinburgh: Edinburgh University Press (1953).

Jarman, A. O. H., ed. and tr. *Y Gododdin: Britain's Oldest Heroic Poem.* Dyfed: The Welsh Classics (1988).

————, and G. R. Jarman. *A History of Welsh Literature* (vol. 1). Llandybie, Wales: Christopher Davies (1974).

Jones, Gwyn, and Thomas Jones. *The Mabinogion.* London: Everyman, Dent (1949).

Jones, T. G. *Welsh Folk-Lore and Folk Custom.* London: Methuen (1930).

Joyce, P. W. *Old Celtic Romances.* London: Longman (1879).

Kavangh, Peter. *Irish Mythology* (limited edition of 100). New York (1958–1959).

Kinsella, Thomas. *The Táin.* Oxford: Oxford University Press (1970).

Lacy, Norris J., ed. *The Arthurian Encyclopaedia.* Woodbridge, Suffolk: Boydell (1988).

Laing, Lloyd, and Jennifer Laing. *Celtic Britain and Ireland: The Myth of the Dark Ages.* Dublin: Irish Academic Press (1990).

La Villemarqué, Hersart de. *La légende celtique et la poésie des cloitres en Irlande, en Cambrie et en Bretagne.* Breizh: Editions Slatkine (1984).

Loffler, C. M. *The Voyage to the Otherworld Island in Early Irish Literature.* Salzburg, Germany: Institut für Anglistik und Amerikanistik (1983).

Lofmark, C. *Bards and Heroes.* Llanerch, Wales: Llanerch Enterprises (1898).

Loomis, R. S. *The Grail from Celtic Myth to Christian Symbol.* New York (1963).

———. *Wales and the Arthurian Legend.* Cardiff: University of Wales Press (1956).

———, ed. *Arthurian Literature in the Middle Ages.* Oxford: Oxford University Press (1959).

Loth, Joseph. *Les Mabinogion.* Paris (1913).

Mac Alister, R. A. S. *Lebor Gabala Erenn* (Book of Invasions). 5 vols. Dublin: Irish Text Society (1956).

Mac Cana, Proinsias. *Branwen daughter of Llyr.* Cardiff: University of Wales Press (1958).

———. *Celtic Mythology.* London: Hamlyn (1970).

———. *The Mabinogion.* Cardiff: University of Wales Press (1977).

MacCulloch, John Arnott. *Celtic Mythology.* Boston: Gray and Moore (1918).

———. *The Religion of the Ancient Celts.* Edinburgh (1911). Reprint, London: Constable (1991).

Mackenzie, D. A. *Scottish Folk Lore and Folk Life.* Edinburgh: Blackie & Sons (1935).

Markle, Jean. *La Femme Celte.* Paris: Editions Payots (1972). Translation, *Women of the Celts.* London: Gordon Cremonesi (1975).

Matthews, John. *The Song of Taliesin.* London: Unwin Hyman (1991).

———. *Taliesin: Shamanism and the Bardic Mysteries in Britain and Ireland.* London: The Aquarian Press (1991).

———. *The Celtic Shaman.* Dorset: Element Books Ltd. (1991) and Rockport, Massachusetts: Element Inc. (1992).

Meyer, Kuno. *The Triads of Ireland.* Dublin: Royal Irish Academy (1906).

———. *The Vision of MacConglinne.* London: David Nutt (1892).

———. *The Voyage of Bran Son of Febal.* 2 vols. London: David Nutt (1895).

Murphy, Gerard. *The Ossianic Lore and Romantic Tales of Medieval Ireland.* Dublin: Three Candles Press (1955).

———. *Saga and Myth in Ancient Ireland.* Dublin: Three Candles Press (1955).

Nash, D. W. *Taliesin, or the Bards and Druids of Britain.* London: J. Russell Smith (1858).

Neeson, Eoin *The First Book of Irish Myths and Legends.* Cork: Mercier Press (1965).

──── . *The Second Book of Irish Myths and Legends.* Cork: Mercier Press (1966).

Norris, J. *The Age of Arthur.* London: Weidenfeld & Nicholson (1973).

Nutt, Alfred. *Celtic and Medieval Romance.* London: David Nutt (1899).

──── . *Cúchulainn: The Irish Achilles.* London: David Nutt (1900).

──── . *Ossian and Ossianic Literature.* London: David Nutt (1900).

O'Grady, Standish James. *Early Bardic Literature in Ireland.* London (1879).

Ó hOgáin, Dáithi. *Fionn Mac Cumhail: Images of the Gaelic Hero.* Dublin: Gill & Macmillan (1988).

──── . *The Hero in Irish Folk History.* Dublin: Gill and Macmillan (1985).

──── . *Myth, Legend & Romance: An Encyclopedia of the Irish Folk Tradition.* London: Ryan Publishing (1991).

O'Keefe, J. G., ed. and tr. *Buile Suibne.* London: David Nutt (1913).

O'Rahilly, Cecile, ed. *Táin Bó Cuailgne from the Book of Leinster.* Dublin: Institute for Advanced Studies (1967).

O'Rahilly, T. F. *Early Irish History and Mythology.* Dublin: Institute for Advanced Studies (1976).

Parry, Thomas. Tr. by H. Idris Bell. *A History of Welsh Literature.* Oxford: The Clarendon Press (1955).

Parry-Jones, D. *Welsh Legends and Fairy Law.* London: Batsford (1953).

Patch, H. R. *The Otherworld.* Cambridge, Massachusetts: Harvard University Press (1950).

Pearce, Susan M. *The Kingdom of Dumnonia: Studies in History and Tradition in South Western Britain* A.D. 350–1150. Padstow, Cornwall: Lodenek Press (1978).

Pennar, M. *The Black Book of Carmarthen.* Llanerch: Llanerch Enterprises (1989).

Piggot, Stuart. *The Druids.* London: Thames & Hudson (1968).

Powell, T. G. E. *The Celts.* London: Thames & Hudson (1958).

Price, G. *Ireland and the Celtic Connection.* Colin Smythe (1987).

Rees, Alwyn, and Brinley Rees. *Celtic Heritage.* London: Thames & Hudson (1961).

Rhys, John. *Celtic Folk-Lore* (Welsh and Manx). 2 vols. Oxford: Oxford University Press (1901). New edition, Wildwood House (1980).

————, and J. G. Evans *Mabinogion*. Oxford: Oxford University Press (1887).

Roberts, Brinley F. *Y Mabinogion*. Llandysul: Dafydd a Rhiannon Ifans (1980).

Rolleston, T. W. *Myths and Legends of the Celtic Race*. George Harrap (1911). Reprint, London: Constable (1985).

Ross, Anne. *Pagan Celtic Britain*. London: Routledge & Kegan Paul (1967).

Rowland, J. *Early Welsh Saga Poetry*. Cambridge: D. S. Brewer (1990).

Rutherford, Ward. *The Druids and Their Heritage*. London: Gordon Cremonesi (1978).

Sjoestedt, Marie-Louise. Tr. by Myles Dillon. *Gods and Heroes of the Celts*. London: Methuen, (1949).

Skene, William. *Four Ancient Books of Wales*. 2 vols. Edinburgh (1868).

Smyth, Daragh. *A Guide to Irish Mythology*. Dublin: Irish Academic Press (1988).

Spaan, D. B. *The Otherworld in Early Irish Literature*. Ann Arbor: University of Michigan (1969).

Squire, Charles. *Celtic Myth and Legend*. Newcastle (1975). Reprint of *The Mythology of the British Islands* (1905).

Stephens, Meic, ed. *The Oxford Companion to the Literature of Wales*. Oxford: Oxford University Press (1986).

Stokes, Whitley. *The Calendar of Oengus*. Dublin: Hodges Figgis (1880).

Tatlock, J. S. P. *The Legendary History of Britain*. New York: Gordian Press (1979).

Thomas, Charles. *Celtic Britain*. London: Thames & Hudson (1986).

Thompson, Derick. *Brannwen Uerch Lyr* (Branwen Daughter of Lyr). Dublin (1961).

Thompson, Robert L. *Pwyll Pendevic Dyvet* (Pwyll, Lord of Dyfed). Dublin (1957).

Thurneysen, Rudolf. *Sagen aus dem Alten Irland*. Berlin (1901).

Transactions of the Ossianic Society. Dublin (1855–1861).

Trevelyan, M. *Folk-Lore and Folk Stories of Wales.* Eliot Stock (1909).

Van Hamel, A. G. *Aspects of Celtic Mythology.* London: British Academy (1935).

———. *Myth en Historie in Het Oude Ireland.* Amsterdam (1942).

Wentz, W. Y. Evans. *The Fairy Faith in the Celtic Countries.* Oxford: Oxford University Press (1911).

Williams, Sir Ifor. *Pedeir Keinc y Mabinogi* (The Four Branches of the Mabinogi). Cardiff (1930).

Williams, I. Tr. by Rachel Bromwich. *Armes Prydein: The Prophecy of Britain.* Dublin: Institute for Advanced Studies (1982).

———. Tr. by J. E. Caerwyn Williams. *The Poems of Taliesin.* Dublin: Institute for Advanced Studies (1975).